ArtScroll Tanach Series®

A traditional commentary on the Books of the Bible

Rabbi Nosson Scherman/Rabbi Meir Zlotowitz
General Editors

THE FIVE MEGILLOS / A NEW TRANSLATION WITH
OVERVIEWS AND ANNOTATIONS ANTHOLOGIZED FROM
THE CLASSICAL COMMENTATORS

Published by

Mesorah Publications, ltd.

the Book of megillos

Translated and annotated by
Rabbi Meir Zlotowitz

Overviews by
Rabbi Nosson Scherman

FIRST EDITION
First Impression . . . September 1986
Second Impression . . . May 1987
SYNAGOGUE EDITION
First Impression . . . October 1990
Second Impression . . . November 1995
Third Impression . . . August 1996
Fourth Impression . . . January 1998

Published and Distributed by
MESORAH PUBLICATIONS, Ltd.
4401 Second Avenue
Brooklyn, New York 11232

Distributed in Europe by
J. LEHMANN HEBREW BOOKSELLERS
20 Cambridge Terrace
Gateshead, Tyne and Wear
England NE8 1RP

Distributed in Israel by
SIFRIATI / A. GITLER — BOOKS
10 Hashomer Street
Bnei Brak 51361

Distributed in Australia & New Zealand by
GOLDS BOOK & GIFT CO.
36 William Street
Balaclava 3183, Vic., Australia

Distributed in South Africa by
KOLLEL BOOKSHOP
Shop 8A Norwood Hypermarket
Norwood 2196, Johannesburg, South Africa

THE ARTSCROLL MESORAH SERIES ®
"THE BOOK OF MEGILLOS"
© Copyright 1986 by MESORAH PUBLICATIONS, Ltd.
4401 Second Avenue / Brooklyn, N.Y. 11232 / (718) 921-9000

ISBN:
0-89906-225-3 (hard cover)
0-89906-226-1 (paperback)

Typography by CompuScribe at ArtScroll Studios, Ltd.
4401 Second Avenue / Brooklyn, NY 11232 / (718) 921-9000

Printed in the United States of America by Moriah Offset
Bound by Sefercraft, Inc., Brooklyn, NY

This volume is dedicated to the author's mother-in-law מנב"ת

חיה בת ר' ישראל יהודה ע"ה

Mrs. Ida Schulman ע"ה

נפ' ד' חוה"מ פסח תשמ"ז

Intelligent, warm, sensitive, unselfish, caring,
generous — the words give out,
but the memory of this sterling wife,
mother, grandmother and friend
stays always fresh and inspiring.

She was a pioneer educator
when girls' chinuch was new.
Some of her students are leaders in the field
and all cherish her inspiring memory.

She maintained nobility and good cheer
in the face of frightful adversity and suffering —
always seeing the good in others
and thanking God for His infinite goodness.

תנצב"ה

Meir and Rachel Zlotowitz
and Family

Publisher's Preface

It is ten years since the ArtScroll Series was inaugurated with the publication of *Megillas Esther*, followed in quick succession by *Ruth, Eichah, Koheles,* and *Shir Hashirim*. The combination of original commentary and introductory essays coincided with a thirst for authentic Torah knowledge on the parts of English-speaking Jewry, and a growing awareness that the books of the Torah must be understood in accordance with the teachings of the Sages and classic commentators.

With great pleasure, therefore, we present this one-volume edition of the *Five Megillos*. It includes the original ArtScroll translation, along with brief marginal notes culled from the ArtScroll commentary, in order to help the Hebrew comprehend the flow of the narrative and thought. In addition, each *Megillah* is introduced with a brief Overview that explains its philosophical message and the context in which it is read as part of the synagogue service. Those who desire a more comprehensive treatment, or who seek elucidation of individual verses and concepts, are advised to turn to the full-length ArtScroll commentary.

We are grateful to Rabbi Raphael Butler, National Director of NCSY, for perceiving the need for such a one-volume treatment, and for his important insights and suggestions on how best to present it. It is a privilege for Mesorah Publications to be able to make this contribution to NCSY's precedent-setting work for strengthening Jewish life and Torah observance.

May it be said that the beauty and clarity of this book is a tribute to our colleague Reb Shea Brander, whose graphic skills and consummate taste have been a major factor in the success of the ArtScroll Series.

The entire ArtScroll staff has extended itself to make this book worthy of its noble purpose. We are grateful to them and we are hopeful that, with the help of *Hashem Yisborach,* this volume will serve the goals envisioned for it.

Rabbi Meir Zlotowitz/Rabbi Nosson Scherman

Rosh Chodesh Elul 5746
September, 1986

חמש מגילות
the Book of
megillos

אסתר
esther

A Book for the Ages

One of the great Chassidic masters of the last century remarked that because the festival of Purim was proclaimed during a period of Jewish exile, it has special meaning to Jews in a time of diaspora *(S'fas Emes)*. The Book of Esther tells a thrilling, spellbinding story. What a pity that it is so familiar that it no longer thrills us as it should. At the very least, however, let us look at the ancient tale and see how much it speaks to our time, for our Sages saw in it the kind of lessons from which the nation should learn — or which it will be doomed to repeat.

The Twentieth Century has given a new relevance not only to the genocidal intention of Haman, but to his method of pursuing it. No longer can anyone say — as some did a hundred years ago — that modern society could never produce, much less condone, a monster whose announced intention was 'to destroy, to slay, and to exterminate all Jews, young and old, children and women, in a single day ...' *(Esther* 3:13). How naive it now seems that people seriously believed that mass extermination of human beings could never be contemplated by civilized people. Now we know that Haman was the first, but, lamentably, surely not the last. Nor have we recovered from the Holocaust perpetrated by the modern Haman, who came six million souls closer to achieving his goal than did his ancient model.

How striking and ominously familiar were Haman's arguments to gain Ahasuerus' acquiescence. As given briefly in the Book of Esther (3:8-9) and amplified by the Talmudic Sages, Haman's diatribe has been echoed by anti-Semites throughout the ages: Jews are separatists, elitists, racists. They hold themselves apart from all other peoples of the realm. They will not blend into our culture or religion. They are damaging to the unity of the kingdom. Why should the King tolerate their divisive presence — is it worth the price? Would not the world be better served if this nuisance, this friendless nation, were removed from our midst? And, finally, the state will derive an immense economic benefit from the disappearance of this pariah people.

So sophisticated a discourse to justify such a foul end! But it should not surprise anyone. Throughout our history, we have been similarly maligned and our oppressors have indignantly insisted that they were forced to take heroic measures to defend themselves against little Israel. The laws of the Third Reich were carefully phrased in terms that deceived many a naive observer into believing that a tormented nation — call it Persia, Spain, Russia, Germany, or the United Nations — was

merely seeking to protect itself from an internal cancer.

What ignited Haman's anger? There are two answers: the obvious one and the true one. The obvious one was Mordechai's obstinacy. Proud Jew that he was, Mordechai refused to bow to Haman, who, as tradition teaches, brazenly paraded with an image of his idol dangling from his neck. Mordechai insisted that there had to be at least one Jew who would not sacrifice dignity on the altar of expediency; would Haman love Israel any more if even Mordechai's knees scraped the ground in obeisance to a pagan deity? The infuriated Haman sought revenge in the annihilation not only of Mordechai but of his entire people. And the pundits of the time surely reveled in the charge that 'stiff-necked' Mordechai was to blame for Israel's catastrophe.

But, as the Sages teach, that was not the *true* reason for the destruction that threatened Israel. Nine years earlier the Jews had ignored the warnings of Mordechai and his fellow sages not to indulge in forbidden foods and acts at the lavish feast of Ahasuerus. Let Jews be loyal to their government — yes; but let them not set aside their Torah to do so. The people would not listen. They argued that Ahasuerus would never understand their abstinence. He would accuse them of disloyalty, of planning secret conspiracies to return to *Eretz Yisrael*. If their loyalties were to Jerusalem rather than Shushan, they would be branded traitors, and the punishment for treason is …

Dare we antagonize a paranoid, insecure monarch like Ahasuerus? Dare we place our nation's survival at risk by antagonizing a king whose caprices are notorious? And when Ahasuerus ordered the execution of his beloved Queen Vashti simply because she refused to disgrace herself publicly to satisfy his whim — did that not prove that we were wise and right not to provoke his mercurial anger?

On the divine scales, however, Mordechai's judgment was right. Jews do not survive by committing spiritual suicide. For if a Jews lacks pride in his Jewishness, by what virtue does he deserve the right to preserve his separate identity?

The nation had precipitated its own downfall by an act of cowardly faithlessness; only by a parallel act of communal courage could it save itself. Mordechai began the process by defying Haman's decree to bow. *His* knee would not bend. *He* would not grovel. Then came Esther's turn.

Unknown to King Ahasuerus or his viceroy Haman, Queen Esther was a Jewess, and Mordechai demanded that she intercede with the King. She hesitated. Logic dictated that she wait for a more opportune moment to plead with Ahasuerus (see 4:9-11). But Mordechai would

not accept her argument. Could it be that she was somewhat complacent because *she* enjoyed the safety of anonymity and the security of the throne? After all, Ahasuerus had not the slightest suspicion that his beloved was a member of the race he had consigned to the pyre of history. Would she have been so 'rational' if *she* had been in as much jeopardy as her brethren?

Mordechai replied harshly to Esther, 'Do not imagine that you will be able to escape in the King's palace any more than the rest of the Jews. For if you persist in keeping silent at a time like this, relief and deliverance will come to the Jews from some other place, while you and your father's house will perish. And who knows whether it was just for such a time as this that you attained the royal position!' (4:13-14).

A new insight into communal responsibility: To help one's fellow Jews is a privilege, not a chore. The nation will always survive somehow, but the one who spurns its entreaties will himself be doomed. And furthermore, no matter how exalted someone's position or lavish his fortune, let him always regard it as but a means to serve the common good. Now Esther knew why she had been raised to the throne — to save her people, and if she failed to do so she might well be condemning *herself* to oblivion, while another path to salvation would surely open for them.

Esther was more than equal to the challenge, and her bravery, dedication, and cunning precipitated a swiftly moving series of events that brought new glory to her people, and that doomed Haman. But even this is not the primary lesson of Purim.

Amazingly, God's Name does not even appear in the *Megillah* — and precisely that is its lesson: God's ways are not always obvious, His miracles are most often not illuminated by lightning nor punctuated by thunder. In the concisely written 167-verse *Megillah,* no seas split, no heavens roar, no dry bones come to life. But in the truest sense the greatest of all miracles is narrated in the Purim story — the miracle of God's constant supervision and control of events.

With the period of Esther and Mordechai, a new emphasis was added to Jewish history. We had to find God's hand not in the splitting sea or heavenly fire, but in everyday events.

The story of the *Megillah* spanned nine years, and only at the very end did the pieces of God's jigsaw puzzle begin coming together. Suddenly widely separate links began to move together to form a chain and widely separated chains joined to become the anchor upon which Jewish survival was secured. And simple logic turned out to be wrong; Mordechai had been right all along.

One set of links: Ahasuerus' feast led to the execution of Vashti, which led to the coronation of Esther. Because Esther was Queen, she was in a position to approach the King to save her people and she could lull Haman into complacency by inviting him to her private banquet.

Another set of links: Bigsan and Teresh plotted to kill Ahasuerus. Because Esther had secured a royal appointment for Mordechai, he was positioned to overhear them and report the scheme to Esther. She told the King of Mordechai's loyalty. It was inscribed in the royal chronicle, there to lay forgotten until the fateful night when God disturbed the King's sleep.

A third set of links: The King promoted Haman and everyone was required to bow to him, but Mordechai refused. Assured of his power and influence — even with the Queen! — Haman built a gallows and sought royal permission to hang Mordechai, just when Ahasuerus learned that it was Mordechai who had once saved his life.

When the appropriate climactic time arrived, the pieces of God's jigsaw puzzle came together and formed the destruction of Haman and most of Amalek, and salvation for the Jews.

The events of those ancient days determine the mode of Purim's annual observance. The *Megillah* is read morning and evening, and all Jews are required to hear it; its lesson is too important to be restricted only to those who attend the synagogue regularly. Even people who are unable to attend should arrange to have the *Megillah* read for them from a ritually valid scroll. And when we hear the reading, let us remember the eternal lesson beneath the rousing story.

The celebration of Purim is unique among Jewish festivals. Purim is celebrated with an excess of food, drink, and frivolity, because we are marking a time when our *physical* lives were threatened, unlike other festivals that commemorate primarily *spiritual* dangers and salvations.

Furthermore, Purim is a holiday of Jewish fellowship as well, because among the tools that forged the miracle were a sense of communal responsibility, a sense of concern for the plight of every Jew. So the requirements of the day include gifts to friends and to the poor. For indeed, we are one and we must take positive steps to remain one.

As *S'fas Emes* taught, Purim is indeed aimed primarily at Jews without their Temple, for it shows them how to live and survive in a hostile environment where survival is in question, and where God's Presence seems to be absent. Thanks to Purim, we feel more secure about survival and we can 'see' God's hand even where He is invisible.

❧ BLESSINGS OVER THE MEGILLAH READING / בִּרְכוֹת הַמְּגִלָּה }❧

Before reading *Megillas Esther* on Purim, the reader recites the following three blessings.
The congregation should answer אָמֵן, *Amen,* only [not בָּרוּךְ הוּא וּבָרוּךְ שְׁמוֹ] after each, and should have
in mind that they wish to fulfill the obligation of reciting the blessings themselves.
Absolutely no conversation is permitted from the beginning of the first blessing until the conclusion of
the final blessing following the *Megillah* reading.

בָּרוּךְ אַתָּה יהוה אֱלֹהֵינוּ מֶלֶךְ הָעוֹלָם, אֲשֶׁר קִדְּשָׁנוּ
בְּמִצְוֹתָיו, וְצִוָּנוּ עַל מִקְרָא מְגִלָּה. (אָמֵן.—Cong.)

בָּרוּךְ אַתָּה יהוה אֱלֹהֵינוּ מֶלֶךְ הָעוֹלָם, שֶׁעָשָׂה נִסִּים
לַאֲבוֹתֵינוּ, בַּיָּמִים הָהֵם, בַּזְּמַן הַזֶּה. (אָמֵן.—Cong.)

בָּרוּךְ אַתָּה יהוה אֱלֹהֵינוּ מֶלֶךְ הָעוֹלָם, שֶׁהֶחֱיָנוּ, וְקִיְּמָנוּ,
וְהִגִּיעָנוּ לַזְּמַן הַזֶּה. (אָמֵן.—Cong.)

Blessed are You, HASHEM, our God, King of the universe, Who has
sanctified us with His commandments and has commanded us
regarding the reading of the Megillah.   (Cong.—Amen.)

Blessed are You, HASHEM, our God, King of the universe, Who has
wrought miracles for our forefathers, in those days at this season.
                                                  (Cong.—Amen.)

Blessed are You, HASHEM, our God, King of the universe, Who has kept
us alive, sustained us, and brought us to this season.
                                                  (Cong.—Amen.)

א וַיְהִ֖י בִּימֵ֣י אֲחַשְׁוֵר֑וֹשׁ ה֣וּא אֲחַשְׁוֵר֗וֹשׁ הַמֹּלֵךְ֙
מֵהֹ֣דּוּ וְעַד־כּ֔וּשׁ שֶׁ֛בַע וְעֶשְׂרִ֥ים וּמֵאָ֖ה מְדִינָֽה:

ב בַּיָּמִ֖ים הָהֵ֑ם כְּשֶׁ֣בֶת | הַמֶּ֗לֶךְ אֲחַשְׁוֵר֔וֹשׁ עַ֚ל כִּסֵּ֣א
מַלְכוּת֔וֹ אֲשֶׁ֖ר בְּשׁוּשַׁ֥ן הַבִּירָֽה: ג בִּשְׁנַ֣ת שָׁל֔וֹשׁ
לְמָלְכ֔וֹ עָשָׂ֥ה מִשְׁתֶּ֖ה לְכָל־שָׂרָ֣יו וַעֲבָדָ֑יו חֵ֣יל |
פָּרַ֣ס וּמָדַ֗י הַֽפַּרְתְּמִ֛ים וְשָׂרֵ֥י הַמְּדִינ֖וֹת לְפָנָֽיו:

ד בְּהַרְאֹת֗וֹ אֶת־עֹ֨שֶׁר֙ כְּב֣וֹד מַלְכוּת֔וֹ וְאֶ֨ת־יְקָ֔ר
תִּפְאֶ֖רֶת גְּדוּלָּת֑וֹ יָמִ֣ים רַבִּ֔ים שְׁמוֹנִ֥ים וּמְאַ֖ת יֽוֹם:

ה וּבִמְל֣וֹאת | הַיָּמִ֣ים הָאֵ֗לֶּה עָשָׂ֣ה הַמֶּ֡לֶךְ לְכָל־הָעָ֣ם
הַנִּמְצְאִים֩ בְּשׁוּשַׁ֨ן הַבִּירָ֜ה לְמִגָּ֧דוֹל וְעַד־קָטָ֛ן
מִשְׁתֶּ֖ה שִׁבְעַ֣ת יָמִ֑ים בַּחֲצַ֕ר גִּנַּ֖ת בִּיתַ֥ן הַמֶּֽלֶךְ:

ו חוּר֩ | כַּרְפַּ֨ס וּתְכֵ֜לֶת אָח֗וּז בְּחַבְלֵי־ב֤וּץ וְאַרְגָּמָן֙
עַל־גְּלִ֣ילֵי כֶ֔סֶף וְעַמּ֣וּדֵי שֵׁ֑שׁ מִטּ֣וֹת | זָהָ֣ב וָכֶ֗סֶף
ז עַ֛ל רִֽצְפַ֥ת בַּֽהַט־וָשֵׁ֖שׁ וְדַ֥ר וְסֹחָ֑רֶת: וְהַשְׁק֗וֹת
בִּכְלֵ֣י זָהָ֔ב וְכֵלִ֖ים מִכֵּלִ֣ים שׁוֹנִ֑ים וְיֵ֥ין מַלְכ֖וּת רָ֑ב

ח כְּיַ֣ד הַמֶּֽלֶךְ: וְהַשְּׁתִיָּ֥ה כַדָּ֖ת אֵ֣ין אֹנֵ֑ס כִּי־כֵ֣ן | יִסַּ֣ד
הַמֶּ֗לֶךְ עַ֚ל כָּל־רַ֣ב בֵּית֔וֹ לַעֲשׂ֖וֹת כִּרְצ֥וֹן אִישׁ־
ט וָאִֽישׁ:   גַּ֚ם וַשְׁתִּ֣י הַמַּלְכָּ֔ה עָשְׂתָ֖ה
מִשְׁתֵּ֣ה נָשִׁ֑ים בֵּ֚ית הַמַּלְכ֔וּת אֲשֶׁ֖ר לַמֶּ֥לֶךְ
י אֲחַשְׁוֵרֽוֹשׁ: בַּיּוֹם֙ הַשְּׁבִיעִ֔י כְּט֥וֹב לֵב־הַמֶּ֖לֶךְ בַּיָּ֑יִן
אָמַ֡ר לִ֠מְהוּמָ֨ן בִּזְּתָ֜א חַרְבוֹנָ֗א בִּגְתָ֤א וַאֲבַגְתָא֙
זֵתַ֣ר וְכַרְכַּ֔ס שִׁבְעַת֙ הַסָּ֣רִיסִ֔ים הַמְשָׁ֣רְתִ֔ים אֶת־
יא פְּנֵ֖י הַמֶּ֣לֶךְ אֲחַשְׁוֵרֽוֹשׁ: לְ֠הָבִ֠יא אֶת־וַשְׁתִּ֨י
הַמַּלְכָּ֜ה לִפְנֵ֣י הַמֶּ֗לֶךְ בְּכֶ֣תֶר מַלְכ֔וּת לְהַרְא֨וֹת
הָֽעַמִּ֤ים וְהַשָּׂרִים֙ אֶת־יָפְיָ֔הּ כִּֽי־טוֹבַ֥ת מַרְאֶ֖ה
יב הִֽיא: וַתְּמָאֵ֞ן הַמַּלְכָּ֣ה וַשְׁתִּ֗י לָב֛וֹא בִּדְבַ֥ר הַמֶּ֖לֶךְ

1/1. THE FEASTS OF AHASUERUS

— successor to Cyrus toward the end of the 70 years of the Babylonian exile [4th Century B.C.E.].

3. *In the third year:* 3395 from Creation.

According to his (erroneous) calculation, the seventieth year of the Jews' exile had passed, thus belying the prophets who had foretold the exile's end after seventy years, and Ahasuerus rejoiced in this frustration of Jewish hope; he had completed the building of his magnificent throne; he was finally secure in his reign; he took Vashti as his queen. Thus the causes for such a lavish feast *(Midrash)*.

6. The letter נ has the numerical value of 8. In the *Megillah* the נ of the word חור, *white garments,* is enlarged to imply that on that climactic day Ahasuerus adorned himself with the eight garments of the High Priest. In punishment for this, he suffered the multiple evils of the resulting episode with Vashti, her death, his embarrassment, and his subsequent depression *(Alkabetz)*.

9. VASHTI REFUSES THE KING'S SUMMONS

Vashti was the daughter of Belshazzar, and granddaughter of Nebuchadnezzar.

11. *Wearing the royal crown.* She was to wear *only* the royal crown, i.e., she was to be unclothed *(Midrash)*.

Vashti refused, not because of modesty, but because God caused leprosy to break out on her, paving the way for her downfall *(Midrash)*.

¹**A**nd it came to pass in the days of Ahasuerus — the Ahasuerus who reigned from Hodu to Cush over a hundred and twenty-seven provinces — ² that in those days, when King Ahasuerus sat on his royal throne which was in Shushan the Capitol, ³ in the third year of his reign, he made a feast for all his officials and his servants; the army of Persia and Media, the nobles and officials of the provinces being present; ⁴ when he displayed the riches of his glorious kingdom and the splendor of his excellent majesty for many days — a hundred and eighty days. ⁵ And when these days were fulfilled, the King made a week-long feast for all the people who were present in Shushan the Capitol, great and small alike, in the court of the garden of the King's palace. ⁶ There were hangings of white, fine cotton, and blue wool, held with cords of fine linen and purple wool, upon silver rods and marble pillars; the couches of gold and silver were on a pavement of green and white, and shell and onyx marble. ⁷ The drinks were served in golden goblets — no two goblets alike — and royal wine in abundance, according to the bounty of the King. ⁸ And the drinking was according to the law, without coercion, for so the King had ordered all the officers of his house that they should do according to every man's pleasure.

⁹ Vashti the Queen also made a feast for the women in the royal house of King Ahasuerus. ¹⁰ On the seventh day, when the heart of the King was merry with wine, he ordered Mehuman, Bizzetha, Charbona, Bigtha and Abagtha, Zethar, and Carcas, the seven chamberlains who attended King Ahasuerus, ¹¹ to bring Vashti the Queen before the King wearing the royal crown, to show off to the people and the officials her beauty; for she was beautiful to look upon. ¹² But Queen Vashti refused to come at the King's commandment

אֲשֶׁר בְּיַד הַסָּרִיסִים וַיִּקְצֹף הַמֶּלֶךְ מְאֹד וַחֲמָתוֹ
יג בָּעֲרָה בוֹ: וַיֹּאמֶר הַמֶּלֶךְ לַחֲכָמִים
יֹדְעֵי הָעִתִּים כִּי־כֵן דְּבַר הַמֶּלֶךְ לִפְנֵי כָּל־יֹדְעֵי
יד דָת וָדִין: וְהַקָּרֹב אֵלָיו כַּרְשְׁנָא שֵׁתָר אַדְמָתָא
תַרְשִׁישׁ מֶרֶס מַרְסְנָא מְמוּכָן שִׁבְעַת שָׂרֵי ׀ פָּרַס
וּמָדַי רֹאֵי פְּנֵי הַמֶּלֶךְ הַיֹּשְׁבִים רִאשֹׁנָה בַּמַּלְכוּת:
טו כְּדָת מַה־לַּעֲשׂוֹת בַּמַּלְכָּה וַשְׁתִּי עַל ׀ אֲשֶׁר לֹא־
עָשְׂתָה אֶת־מַאֲמַר הַמֶּלֶךְ אֲחַשְׁוֵרוֹשׁ בְּיַד
הַסָּרִיסִים: וַיֹּאמֶר °מוֹמֻכָן לִפְנֵי   טז °מְמוּכָן ק'
הַמֶּלֶךְ וְהַשָּׂרִים לֹא עַל־הַמֶּלֶךְ לְבַדּוֹ עָוְתָה
וַשְׁתִּי הַמַּלְכָּה כִּי עַל־כָּל־הַשָּׂרִים וְעַל־כָּל־
הָעַמִּים אֲשֶׁר בְּכָל־מְדִינוֹת הַמֶּלֶךְ אֲחַשְׁוֵרוֹשׁ:
יז כִּי־יֵצֵא דְבַר־הַמַּלְכָּה עַל־כָּל־הַנָּשִׁים לְהַבְזוֹת
בַּעְלֵיהֶן בְּעֵינֵיהֶן בְּאָמְרָם הַמֶּלֶךְ אֲחַשְׁוֵרוֹשׁ
אָמַר לְהָבִיא אֶת־וַשְׁתִּי הַמַּלְכָּה לְפָנָיו וְלֹא־
יח בָאָה: וְהַיּוֹם הַזֶּה תֹּאמַרְנָה ׀ שָׂרוֹת פָּרַס־וּמָדַי
אֲשֶׁר שָׁמְעוּ אֶת־דְּבַר הַמַּלְכָּה לְכֹל שָׂרֵי הַמֶּלֶךְ
יט וּכְדַי בִּזָּיוֹן וָקָצֶף: אִם־עַל־הַמֶּלֶךְ טוֹב יֵצֵא דְבַר־
מַלְכוּת מִלְּפָנָיו וְיִכָּתֵב בְּדָתֵי פָרַס־וּמָדַי וְלֹא
יַעֲבוֹר אֲשֶׁר לֹא־תָבוֹא וַשְׁתִּי לִפְנֵי הַמֶּלֶךְ
אֲחַשְׁוֵרוֹשׁ וּמַלְכוּתָהּ יִתֵּן הַמֶּלֶךְ לִרְעוּתָהּ
כ הַטּוֹבָה מִמֶּנָּה: וְנִשְׁמַע פִּתְגָם הַמֶּלֶךְ אֲשֶׁר־
יַעֲשֶׂה בְּכָל־מַלְכוּתוֹ כִּי רַבָּה הִיא וְכָל־הַנָּשִׁים
כא יִתְּנוּ יְקָר לְבַעְלֵיהֶן לְמִגָּדוֹל וְעַד־קָטָן: וַיִּיטַב
הַדָּבָר בְּעֵינֵי הַמֶּלֶךְ וְהַשָּׂרִים וַיַּעַשׂ הַמֶּלֶךְ כִּדְבַר
כב מְמוּכָן: וַיִּשְׁלַח סְפָרִים אֶל־כָּל־מְדִינוֹת הַמֶּלֶךְ

conveyed by the chamberlains; the King therefore became very incensed and his anger burned in him.

13. THE KING SEEKS ADVICE

¹³ Then the King conferred with the experts who knew the times (for such was the King's procedure [to turn] to all who knew law and judgment. ¹⁴ Those closest to him were Carshena, Shesar, Admasa, Tarshish, Meres, Marsena and Memuchan, the seven officers of Persia and Media, who had access to the King, and who sat first in the kingdom—) ¹⁵ as to what should be done, legally, to Queen Vashti for not obeying the bidding of the King Ahasuerus conveyed by the chamberlains.

16. MEMUCHAN'S SUGGESTION

'Memuchan is Haman. Why was he called Memuchan? Because he was destined [מוּכָן] for destruction' (Talmud).

¹⁶ Memuchan declared before the King and the officials: 'It is not only the King whom Vashti the Queen has wronged, but also all the officials and all the people in all the provinces of King Ahasuerus. ¹⁷ For this deed of the Queen will come to the attention of all women, making their husbands contemptible in their eyes, by saying: "King Ahasuerus commanded Vashti the Queen to be brought before him but she did not come!" ¹⁸ And this day the princesses of Persia and Media who have heard of the Queen's deed will cite it to all the King's officials, and there will be much contempt and wrath. ¹⁹ If it pleases the King, let there go forth a royal edict from him, and let it be written into the laws of the Persians and the Medes, that it be not revoked, that Vashti never again appear before King Ahasuerus; and let the King confer her royal estate upon another who is better than she. ²⁰ Then, when the King's decree which he shall proclaim shall be resounded throughout all his kingdom — great though it be — all the wives will show respect to their husbands, great and small alike.' ²¹ This proposal pleased the King and the officials, and the King did according to the word of Memuchan; ²² and he sent letters into all the King's provinces,

21. VASHTI IS DEPOSED

This proposal pleased the King. 'He gave the order and they brought in her head on a platter' (Midrash).

אֶל־מְדִינָ֤ה וּמְדִינָה֙ כִּכְתָבָ֔הּ וְאֶל־עַ֥ם וָעָ֖ם

כִּלְשׁוֹנ֑וֹ לִֽהְי֤וֹת כָּל־אִישׁ֙ שֹׂרֵ֣ר בְּבֵית֔וֹ וּמְדַבֵּ֖ר

כִּלְשׁ֥וֹן עַמּֽוֹ:   אַחַר֙ הַדְּבָרִ֣ים הָאֵ֔לֶּה א

כְּשֹׁךְ֙ חֲמַ֣ת הַמֶּ֣לֶךְ אֲחַשְׁוֵר֑וֹשׁ זָכַ֣ר אֶת־וַשְׁתִּ֔י

וְאֵ֥ת אֲשֶׁר־עָשָׂ֖תָה וְאֵ֥ת אֲשֶׁר־נִגְזַ֥ר עָלֶֽיהָ:

וַיֹּאמְר֥וּ נַעֲרֵֽי־הַמֶּ֖לֶךְ מְשָׁרְתָ֑יו יְבַקְשׁ֥וּ לַמֶּ֖לֶךְ ב

נְעָר֥וֹת בְּתוּל֖וֹת טוֹב֥וֹת מַרְאֶֽה: וְיַפְקֵ֨ד הַמֶּ֜לֶךְ ג

פְּקִידִים֮ בְּכָל־מְדִינ֣וֹת מַלְכוּתוֹ֒ וְיִקְבְּצ֣וּ אֶת־כָּל־

נַעֲרָֽה־בְ֠תוּלָה טוֹבַ֨ת מַרְאֶ֜ה אֶל־שׁוּשַׁ֤ן הַבִּירָה֙

אֶל־בֵּ֣ית הַנָּשִׁ֔ים אֶל־יַ֥ד הֵגֶ֛א סְרִ֥יס הַמֶּ֖לֶךְ שֹׁמֵ֣ר

הַנָּשִׁ֑ים וְנָת֖וֹן תַּמְרֻקֵיהֶֽן: וְהַֽנַּעֲרָ֗ה אֲשֶׁ֤ר תִּיטַב֙ ד

בְּעֵינֵ֣י הַמֶּ֔לֶךְ תִּמְלֹ֖ךְ תַּ֣חַת וַשְׁתִּ֑י וַיִּיטַ֧ב הַדָּבָ֛ר

בְּעֵינֵ֥י הַמֶּ֖לֶךְ וַיַּ֥עַשׂ כֵּֽן: אִ֣ישׁ יְהוּדִ֔י ה

הָיָ֖ה בְּשׁוּשַׁ֣ן הַבִּירָ֑ה וּשְׁמ֣וֹ מָרְדֳּכַ֗י בֶּ֣ן יָאִ֧יר בֶּן־

שִׁמְעִ֛י בֶּן־קִ֖ישׁ אִ֥ישׁ יְמִינִֽי: אֲשֶׁ֤ר הָגְלָה֙ ו

מִירֽוּשָׁלַ֔יִם עִם־הַגֹּלָה֙ אֲשֶׁ֣ר הָגְלְתָ֔ה עִ֖ם יְכָנְיָ֣ה

מֶֽלֶךְ־יְהוּדָ֑ה אֲשֶׁ֣ר הֶגְלָ֔ה נְבֽוּכַדְנֶאצַּ֖ר מֶ֥לֶךְ בָּבֶֽל:

וַיְהִ֨י אֹמֵ֜ן אֶת־הֲדַסָּ֗ה הִ֤יא אֶסְתֵּר֙ בַּת־דֹּד֔וֹ כִּ֣י אֵ֥ין ז

לָ֖הּ אָ֣ב וָאֵ֑ם וְהַנַּעֲרָ֤ה יְפַת־תֹּ֙אַר֙ וְטוֹבַ֣ת מַרְאֶ֔ה

וּבְמ֤וֹת אָבִ֙יהָ֙ וְאִמָּ֔הּ לְקָחָ֧הּ מָרְדֳּכַ֛י ל֖וֹ לְבַ֑ת: וַיְהִ֗י ח

בְּהִשָּׁמַ֤ע דְּבַר־הַמֶּ֙לֶךְ֙ וְדָת֔וֹ וּֽבְהִקָּבֵ֞ץ נְעָר֥וֹת

רַבּ֛וֹת אֶל־שׁוּשַׁ֥ן הַבִּירָ֖ה אֶל־יַ֣ד הֵגָ֑י וַתִּלָּקַ֤ח

אֶסְתֵּר֙ אֶל־בֵּ֣ית הַמֶּ֔לֶךְ אֶל־יַ֥ד הֵגַ֖י שֹׁמֵ֥ר הַנָּשִֽׁים:

וַתִּיטַ֨ב הַנַּעֲרָ֣ה בְעֵינָיו֮ וַתִּשָּׂ֣א חֶ֣סֶד לְפָנָיו֒ וַ֠יְבַהֵל ט

אֶת־תַּמְרוּקֶ֜יהָ וְאֶת־מָנוֹתֶ֗הָ לָתֵ֤ת לָהּ֙ וְאֵת֙ שֶׁ֣בַע

הַנְּעָר֣וֹת הָרְאֻי֔וֹת לָֽתֶת־לָ֖הּ מִבֵּ֣ית הַמֶּ֑לֶךְ וַיְשַׁנֶּ֧הָ

to each province in its own script, and to each people in its own language, to the effect that every man should rule in his own home, and speak the language of his own people.

2/1. AHASUERUS SEEKS A NEW QUEEN

He remembered the order he had given her to appear unclothed before him and how she had refused, and how he had been wroth with her and had put her to death *(Midrash)*.

¹After these things, when the wrath of King Ahasuerus subsided, he remembered Vashti, and what she had done, and what had been decreed against her. ² Then the King's pages said: 'Let there be sought for the King beautiful young maidens; ³ and let the King appoint commissioners in all the provinces of his kingdom, that they may gather together every beautiful young maiden to Shushan the Capitol to the harem, under the charge of Hege the King's chamberlain, custodian of the women; and let their cosmetics be given them. ⁴ Then, let the girl who pleases the King be queen instead of Vashti.' This advice pleased the King, and he followed it.

5. MORDECHAI AND ESTHER

This verse is among the four verses recited aloud in the synagogue by the congregation during the public reading of the *Megillah*.

7. The names Hadassah and Esther are both descriptive of her virtues. Hadassah is derived from the Hebrew word הֲדַס — the sweet-smelling 'myrtle'; Esther from אִסְתַּהַר — 'as beautiful as the moon' (Talmud).

8. ESTHER IS BROUGHT TO THE HAREM

⁵ There was a Jewish man in Shushan the Capitol whose name was Mordechai, son of Yair, son of Shim'i, son of Kish, a Benjaminite, ⁶ who had been exiled from Jerusalem along with the exiles who had been exiled with Jechoniah, King of Judah, whom Nebuchadnezzar, King of Babylon, had exiled. ⁷ And he had reared Hadassah, that is, Esther, his uncle's daughter; since she had neither father nor mother. The girl was finely featured and beautiful, and when her father and mother had died, Mordechai adopted her as his daughter. ⁸ So it came to pass, when the King's bidding and decree were published, and when many young girls were being brought together to Shushan the Capitol, under the charge of Hegai, that Esther was taken into the palace, under the charge of Hegai, guardian of the women. ⁹ The girl pleased him, and she obtained his kindness; he hurriedly prepared her cosmetics and her allowance of delicacies to present her, along with the seven special maids from the palace; and he transferred her

י וְאֶת־נַעֲרוֹתֶיהָ לְטוֹב בֵּית הַנָּשִׁים: לֹא־הִגִּידָה
אֶסְתֵּר אֶת־עַמָּהּ וְאֶת־מוֹלַדְתָּהּ כִּי מָרְדֳּכַי צִוָּה
עָלֶיהָ אֲשֶׁר לֹא־תַגִּיד: וּבְכָל־יוֹם וָיוֹם מָרְדֳּכַי
יא מִתְהַלֵּךְ לִפְנֵי חֲצַר בֵּית־הַנָּשִׁים לָדַעַת אֶת־
שְׁלוֹם אֶסְתֵּר וּמַה־יֵּעָשֶׂה בָּהּ: וּבְהַגִּיעַ תֹּר נַעֲרָה
יב וְנַעֲרָה לָבוֹא | אֶל־הַמֶּלֶךְ אֲחַשְׁוֵרוֹשׁ מִקֵּץ הֱיוֹת
לָהּ כְּדָת הַנָּשִׁים שְׁנֵים עָשָׂר חֹדֶשׁ כִּי כֵּן יִמְלְאוּ
יְמֵי מְרוּקֵיהֶן שִׁשָּׁה חֳדָשִׁים בְּשֶׁמֶן הַמֹּר וְשִׁשָּׁה
יג חֳדָשִׁים בַּבְּשָׂמִים וּבְתַמְרוּקֵי הַנָּשִׁים: וּבָזֶה
הַנַּעֲרָה בָּאָה אֶל־הַמֶּלֶךְ אֵת כָּל־אֲשֶׁר תֹּאמַר
יִנָּתֵן לָהּ לָבוֹא עִמָּהּ מִבֵּית הַנָּשִׁים עַד־בֵּית
יד הַמֶּלֶךְ: בָּעֶרֶב | הִיא בָאָה וּבַבֹּקֶר הִיא שָׁבָה אֶל־
בֵּית הַנָּשִׁים שֵׁנִי אֶל־יַד שַׁעֲשְׁגַז סְרִיס הַמֶּלֶךְ
שֹׁמֵר הַפִּילַגְשִׁים לֹא־תָבוֹא עוֹד אֶל־הַמֶּלֶךְ כִּי
אִם־חָפֵץ בָּהּ הַמֶּלֶךְ וְנִקְרְאָה בְשֵׁם: וּבְהַגִּיעַ תֹּר־
טו אֶסְתֵּר בַּת־אֲבִיחַיִל | דֹּד מָרְדֳּכַי אֲשֶׁר לָקַח־לוֹ
לְבַת לָבוֹא אֶל־הַמֶּלֶךְ לֹא בִקְשָׁה דָּבָר כִּי אִם
אֶת־אֲשֶׁר יֹאמַר הֵגַי סְרִיס־הַמֶּלֶךְ שֹׁמֵר הַנָּשִׁים
טז וַתְּהִי אֶסְתֵּר נֹשֵׂאת חֵן בְּעֵינֵי כָּל־רֹאֶיהָ: וַתִּלָּקַח
אֶסְתֵּר אֶל־הַמֶּלֶךְ אֲחַשְׁוֵרוֹשׁ אֶל־בֵּית מַלְכוּתוֹ
בַּחֹדֶשׁ הָעֲשִׂירִי הוּא־חֹדֶשׁ טֵבֵת בִּשְׁנַת־שֶׁבַע
יז לְמַלְכוּתוֹ: וַיֶּאֱהַב הַמֶּלֶךְ אֶת־אֶסְתֵּר מִכָּל־
הַנָּשִׁים וַתִּשָּׂא־חֵן וָחֶסֶד לְפָנָיו מִכָּל־הַבְּתוּלוֹת
וַיָּשֶׂם כֶּתֶר־מַלְכוּת בְּרֹאשָׁהּ וַיַּמְלִיכֶהָ תַּחַת
יח וַשְׁתִּי: וַיַּעַשׂ הַמֶּלֶךְ מִשְׁתֶּה גָדוֹל לְכָל־שָׂרָיו
וַעֲבָדָיו אֵת מִשְׁתֵּה אֶסְתֵּר וַהֲנָחָה לַמְּדִינוֹת

and her maidens to the best quarters in the harem. [10] Esther had not told of her people or her kindred, for Mordechai had instructed her not to tell. [11] Every day Mordechai used to walk about in front of the court of the harem to find out about Esther's well-being and what would become of her.

[12] Now when each girl's turn arrived to come to King Ahasuerus, after having been treated according to the manner prescribed for women for twelve months (for so was the prescribed length of their anointing accomplished: six months with oil of myrrh, and six months with perfumes and feminine cosmetics) — [13] when then the girl thus came to the King, she was given whatever she desired to accompany her from the harem to the palace. [14] In the evening she would come, and the next morning she would return to the second harem in the custody of Shaashgaz, the King's chamberlain, guardian of the concubines. She would never again go to the King unless the King desired her, and she were summoned by name.

14. Having consorted with the King, it would not be proper for any of these girls to marry other men. They were required to return to the harem and remain there for the rest of their lives as concubines, to await the possibility of being crowned Queen if the King found no one better.

[15] Now when the turn came for Esther, daughter of Avichail the uncle of Mordechai (who had adopted her as his own daughter), to come to the King, she requested nothing beyond what Hegai the King's chamberlain, guardian of the women, had advised. Esther would captivate all who saw her. [16] Esther was taken to King Ahasuerus into his palace in the tenth month, which is the month of Teves, in the seventh year of his reign. [17] The King loved Esther more than all the women, and she won more of his grace and favor than all the other girls; so that he set the royal crown upon her head, and made her Queen in place of Vashti. [18] Then the King made a great banquet for all his officers and his servants — it was Esther's Banquet — and he proclaimed an amnesty for the provinces,

17. ESTHER IS CHOSEN QUEEN

יט עָשָׂה וַיִּתֵּן מַשְׂאֵת כְּיַ֣ד הַמֶּ֑לֶךְ: וּבְהִקָּבֵ֥ץ בְּתוּל֖וֹת

כ שֵׁנִ֑ית וּמָרְדֳּכַ֖י יֹשֵׁ֥ב בְּשַֽׁעַר־הַמֶּֽלֶךְ: אֵ֣ין אֶסְתֵּ֗ר
מַגֶּ֤דֶת מֽוֹלַדְתָּהּ֙ וְאֶת־עַמָּ֔הּ כַּאֲשֶׁ֛ר צִוָּ֥ה עָלֶ֖יהָ
מָרְדֳּכָ֑י וְאֶת־מַאֲמַ֤ר מָרְדֳּכַי֙ אֶסְתֵּ֣ר עֹשָׂ֔ה כַּאֲשֶׁ֛ר

כא הָיְתָ֥ה בְאָמְנָ֖ה אִתּֽוֹ: בַּיָּמִ֣ים
הָהֵ֔ם וּמָרְדֳּכַ֖י יוֹשֵׁ֣ב בְּשַֽׁעַר־הַמֶּ֑לֶךְ קָצַף֩ בִּגְתָ֨ן
וָתֶ֜רֶשׁ שְׁנֵֽי־סָרִיסֵ֤י הַמֶּ֙לֶךְ֙ מִשֹּׁמְרֵ֣י הַסַּ֔ף וַיְבַקְשׁוּ֙

כב לִשְׁלֹ֣חַ יָ֔ד בַּמֶּ֖לֶךְ אֲחַשְׁוֵרֽשׁ: וַיִּוָּדַ֣ע הַדָּבָ֗ר
לְמָרְדֳּכַי֙ וַיַּגֵּ֣ד לְאֶסְתֵּ֣ר הַמַּלְכָּ֑ה וַתֹּ֧אמֶר אֶסְתֵּ֛ר

כג לַמֶּ֖לֶךְ בְּשֵׁ֥ם מָרְדֳּכָֽי: וַיְבֻקַּ֤שׁ הַדָּבָר֙ וַיִּמָּצֵ֔א וַיִּתָּל֥וּ
שְׁנֵיהֶ֖ם עַל־עֵ֑ץ וַיִּכָּתֵ֗ב בְּסֵ֛פֶר דִּבְרֵ֥י הַיָּמִ֖ים לִפְנֵ֥י

ג הַמֶּֽלֶךְ: א אַחַ֣ר׀ הַדְּבָרִ֣ים
הָאֵ֗לֶּה גִּדַּל֩ הַמֶּ֨לֶךְ אֲחַשְׁוֵר֜וֹשׁ אֶת־הָמָ֧ן בֶּֽן־
הַמְּדָ֛תָא הָאֲגָגִ֖י וַֽיְנַשְּׂאֵ֑הוּ וַיָּ֙שֶׂם֙ אֶת־כִּסְא֔וֹ מֵעַ֕ל

ב כָּל־הַשָּׂרִ֖ים אֲשֶׁ֥ר אִתּֽוֹ: וְכָל־עַבְדֵ֨י הַמֶּ֜לֶךְ אֲשֶׁר־
בְּשַׁ֣עַר הַמֶּ֗לֶךְ כֹּרְעִ֤ים וּמִֽשְׁתַּחֲוִים֙ לְהָמָ֔ן כִּי־
כֵ֖ן צִוָּה־ל֣וֹ הַמֶּ֑לֶךְ וּמָ֨רְדֳּכַ֔י לֹ֥א יִכְרַ֖ע וְלֹ֥א

ג יִֽשְׁתַּחֲוֶֽה: וַיֹּ֨אמְר֜וּ עַבְדֵ֥י הַמֶּ֛לֶךְ אֲשֶׁר־בְּשַׁ֣עַר
הַמֶּ֖לֶךְ לְמָרְדֳּכָ֑י מַדּ֙וּעַ֙ אַתָּ֣ה עוֹבֵ֔ר אֵ֖ת מִצְוַ֥ת

ד הַמֶּֽלֶךְ: וַיְהִ֗י °בְּאָמְרָ֤ם אֵלָיו֙ י֣וֹם וָי֔וֹם וְלֹ֥א שָׁמַ֖ע °כְּאָמְרָ֖ם ק
אֲלֵיהֶ֑ם וַיַּגִּ֣ידוּ לְהָמָ֗ן לִרְאוֹת֙ הֲיַֽעַמְדוּ֙ דִּבְרֵ֣י

ה מָרְדֳּכַ֔י כִּֽי־הִגִּ֥יד לָהֶ֖ם אֲשֶׁר־ה֥וּא יְהוּדִֽי: וַיַּ֣רְא
הָמָ֔ן כִּי־אֵ֣ין מָרְדֳּכַ֔י כֹּרֵ֥עַ וּמִֽשְׁתַּחֲוֶ֖ה ל֑וֹ וַיִּמָּלֵ֥א

ו הָמָ֖ן חֵמָֽה: וַיִּ֣בֶז בְּעֵינָ֗יו לִשְׁלֹ֤חַ יָד֙ בְּמָרְדֳּכַ֣י לְבַדּ֔וֹ
כִּֽי־הִגִּ֥ידוּ ל֖וֹ אֶת־עַ֣ם מָרְדֳּכָ֑י וַיְבַקֵּ֣שׁ הָמָ֗ן
לְהַשְׁמִ֧יד אֶת־כָּל־הַיְּהוּדִ֛ים אֲשֶׁ֥ר בְּכָל־מַלְכ֖וּת

19. THE SECOND GATHERING

At Esther's advice, the King appointed Mordechai to sit at the gate and judge the people. Ahasuerus then took counsel of Mordechai as to how he could extract from Esther the secret of her origin. Mordechai suggested that the King once again organize a gathering of beautiful young maidens from throughout the kingdom. Esther, fearing that she would be replaced as Queen, would certainly divulge her secret. Mordechai made this suggestion because he wanted to ascertain whether Esther's coronation was truly the will of Heaven. If the King could find no one superior to Esther, Mordechai would be assured that her reign was part of God's plan (Me'am Loez).

21. MORDECHAI FOILS A PLOT AGAINST THE KING.

Being a member of the Sanhedrin, Mordechai knew seventy languages. Bigsan and Teresh spoke in their native Tarsian tongue in Mordechai's presence, not expecting him to understand them (Talmud).

3/1. HAMAN IS ADVANCED

Haman was a descendant of Agag, King of Amalek [I Samuel 15:9].

2. To make it manifest that the homage due him was of an idolatrous character, Haman had the image of an idol fastened to his clothes, so that whoever bowed down before him worshiped an idol at the same time. Therefore Mordechai would not bow down or prostrate himself (Midrash).

6. HAMAN PLANS THE DESTRUCTION OF ALL THE JEWS

The reaction of Haman to a personal affront is typical of the most rabid anti-Semites throughout the ages.

and gave gifts worthy of the King.

[19] And when the maidens were gathered together the second time, and Mordechai sat at the King's gate, [20] (Esther still told nothing of her kindred or her people as Mordechai had instructed her; for Esther continued to obey Mordechai, just as when she was raised by him.)

[21] In those days, while Mordechai was sitting at the King's gate, Bigsan and Teresh, two of the King's chamberlains of the guardians of the threshold, became angry and planned to assassinate King Ahasuerus. [22] The plot became known to Mordechai, who told it to Queen Esther, and Esther informed the King in Mordechai's name. [23] The matter was investigated and corroborated, and they were both hanged on a gallows. It was recorded in the book of chronicles in the King's presence.

[1] After these things King Ahasuerus promoted Haman, the son of Hammedasa the Agagite, and advanced him; he set his seat above all the officers who were with him. [2] All the King's servants at the King's gate would bow down and prostrate themselves before Haman, for this is what the King had commanded concerning him. But Mordechai would not bow down nor prostrate himself. [3] So the King's servants at the King's gate said to Mordechai, 'Why do you disobey the King's command?' [4] Finally, when they said this to him day after day and he did not heed them, they told Haman, to see whether Mordechai's words would avail; for he had told them that he was a Jew. [5] When Haman, himself, saw that Mordechai did not bow down and prostrate himself before him, then Haman was filled with rage. [6] However it seemed contemptible to him to lay hands on Mordechai alone, for they had made known to him the people of Mordechai. So Haman sought to destroy all the Jews who were throughout the entire king-

ז אֲחַשְׁוֵרוֹשׁ עִם מָרְדֳּכָי: בַּחֹדֶשׁ הָרִאשׁוֹן הוּא־
חֹדֶשׁ נִיסָן בִּשְׁנַת שְׁתֵּים עֶשְׂרֵה לַמֶּלֶךְ
אֲחַשְׁוֵרוֹשׁ הִפִּיל פּוּר הוּא הַגּוֹרָל לִפְנֵי הָמָן
מִיּוֹם | לְיוֹם וּמֵחֹדֶשׁ לְחֹדֶשׁ שְׁנֵים־עָשָׂר הוּא־
חֹדֶשׁ אֲדָר: וַיֹּאמֶר הָמָן
ח לַמֶּלֶךְ אֲחַשְׁוֵרוֹשׁ יֶשְׁנוֹ עַם־אֶחָד מְפֻזָּר וּמְפֹרָד
בֵּין הָעַמִּים בְּכֹל מְדִינוֹת מַלְכוּתֶךָ וְדָתֵיהֶם
שֹׁנוֹת מִכָּל־עָם וְאֶת־דָּתֵי הַמֶּלֶךְ אֵינָם עֹשִׂים
ט וְלַמֶּלֶךְ אֵין־שֹׁוֶה לְהַנִּיחָם: אִם־עַל־הַמֶּלֶךְ טוֹב
יִכָּתֵב לְאַבְּדָם וַעֲשֶׂרֶת אֲלָפִים כִּכַּר־כֶּסֶף
אֶשְׁקוֹל עַל־יְדֵי עֹשֵׂי הַמְּלָאכָה לְהָבִיא אֶל־
י גִּנְזֵי הַמֶּלֶךְ: וַיָּסַר הַמֶּלֶךְ אֶת־טַבַּעְתּוֹ מֵעַל יָדוֹ
וַיִּתְּנָהּ לְהָמָן בֶּן־הַמְּדָתָא הָאֲגָגִי צֹרֵר הַיְּהוּדִים:
יא וַיֹּאמֶר הַמֶּלֶךְ לְהָמָן הַכֶּסֶף נָתוּן לָךְ וְהָעָם
יב לַעֲשׂוֹת בּוֹ כַּטּוֹב בְּעֵינֶיךָ: וַיִּקָּרְאוּ סֹפְרֵי הַמֶּלֶךְ
בַּחֹדֶשׁ הָרִאשׁוֹן בִּשְׁלוֹשָׁה עָשָׂר יוֹם בּוֹ וַיִּכָּתֵב
כְּכָל־אֲשֶׁר־צִוָּה הָמָן אֶל אֲחַשְׁדַּרְפְּנֵי־הַמֶּלֶךְ
וְאֶל־הַפַּחוֹת אֲשֶׁר | עַל־מְדִינָה וּמְדִינָה וְאֶל־
שָׂרֵי עַם וָעָם מְדִינָה וּמְדִינָה כִּכְתָבָהּ וְעַם וָעָם
כִּלְשׁוֹנוֹ בְּשֵׁם הַמֶּלֶךְ אֲחַשְׁוֵרֹשׁ נִכְתָּב וְנֶחְתָּם
יג בְּטַבַּעַת הַמֶּלֶךְ: וְנִשְׁלוֹחַ סְפָרִים בְּיַד הָרָצִים
אֶל־כָּל־מְדִינוֹת הַמֶּלֶךְ לְהַשְׁמִיד לַהֲרֹג וּלְאַבֵּד
אֶת־כָּל־הַיְּהוּדִים מִנַּעַר וְעַד־זָקֵן טַף וְנָשִׁים
בְּיוֹם אֶחָד בִּשְׁלוֹשָׁה עָשָׂר לְחֹדֶשׁ שְׁנֵים־עָשָׂר
יד הוּא־חֹדֶשׁ אֲדָר וּשְׁלָלָם לָבוֹז: פַּתְשֶׁגֶן
הַכְּתָב לְהִנָּתֵן דָּת בְּכָל־מְדִינָה וּמְדִינָה גָּלוּי

dom of Ahasuerus — the people of Mordechai. [7] In the first month, which is the month of Nissan, in the twelfth year of King Ahasuerus, *pur* (that is, the lot) was cast in the presence of Haman from day to day, and from month to month, to the twelfth month, which is the month of Adar.

8. HAMAN SLANDERS THE JEWS TO THE KING

Haman said: 'They eat and drink and despise the throne. For if a fly falls into a Jew's cup, he throws out the fly and drinks the wine; but if His Majesty were to merely touch his cup, he would throw it to the ground and not drink from it' (Talmud).

9. The price Haman was ready to pay for the right to exterminate the Jews, 10,000 talents, was 24 million ounces, or 750 tons of silver!

10. THE KING CONSENTS TO THE DESTRUCTION OF THE JEWS

14. The strange haste in publishing a decree that would not be executed for eleven months was because Haman was afraid that the fickle King would have a change of heart. Also, he wanted to prolong the agony of the Jews throughout the kingdom by telling them of the impending massacre so far in advance.

[8] Then Haman said to King Ahasuerus: 'There is a certain people scattered abroad and dispersed among the peoples in all the provinces of your realm. Their laws are different from every other people's. They do not observe even the King's laws; therefore it is not befitting the King to tolerate them. [9] If it pleases the King, let it be recorded that they be destroyed; and I will pay ten thousand silver talents into the hands of those who perform the duties for deposit in the King's treasuries.' [10] So the King took his signet ring from his hand, and gave it to Haman, the son of Hammedasa the Agagite, the enemy of the Jews. [11] Then the King said to Haman: 'The silver is given to you, the people also, to do with as you see fit.' [12] The King's secretaries were summoned on the thirteenth day of the first month, and everything was written exactly as Haman had dictated, to the King's satraps, to the governors of every province, and to the officials of every people; each province in its own script, and to each people in its own language; in King Ahasuerus' name it was written, and it was sealed with the King's signet ring. [13] Letters were sent by courier to all the King's provinces, to destroy, to slay, and to exterminate all Jews, young and old, children and women, in a single day, the thirteenth day of the twelfth month, which is the month of Adar, and to plunder their possessions. [14] The copies of the document were to be promulgated in every province, and be published

טו לְכָל־הָעַמִּים לִהְיוֹת עֲתִדִים לַיּוֹם הַזֶּה: הָרָצִים
יָצְאוּ דְחוּפִים בִּדְבַר הַמֶּלֶךְ וְהַדָּת נִתְּנָה בְּשׁוּשַׁן
הַבִּירָה וְהַמֶּלֶךְ וְהָמָן יָשְׁבוּ לִשְׁתּוֹת וְהָעִיר שׁוּשָׁן
א נָבוֹכָה: וּמָרְדֳּכַי יָדַע אֶת־כָּל־אֲשֶׁר
נַעֲשָׂה וַיִּקְרַע מָרְדֳּכַי אֶת־בְּגָדָיו וַיִּלְבַּשׁ שַׂק
וָאֵפֶר וַיֵּצֵא בְּתוֹךְ הָעִיר וַיִּזְעַק זְעָקָה גְדוֹלָה
ב וּמָרָה: וַיָּבוֹא עַד לִפְנֵי שַׁעַר־הַמֶּלֶךְ כִּי אֵין לָבוֹא
ג אֶל־שַׁעַר הַמֶּלֶךְ בִּלְבוּשׁ שָׂק: וּבְכָל־מְדִינָה
וּמְדִינָה מְקוֹם אֲשֶׁר דְּבַר־הַמֶּלֶךְ וְדָתוֹ מַגִּיעַ אֵבֶל
גָּדוֹל לַיְּהוּדִים וְצוֹם וּבְכִי וּמִסְפֵּד שַׂק וָאֵפֶר יֻצַּע
ד לָרַבִּים: °וַתְּבוֹאֶינָה נַעֲרוֹת אֶסְתֵּר וְסָרִיסֶיהָ °וַתָּבוֹאנָה ק
וַיַּגִּידוּ לָהּ וַתִּתְחַלְחַל הַמַּלְכָּה מְאֹד וַתִּשְׁלַח
בְּגָדִים לְהַלְבִּישׁ אֶת־מָרְדֳּכַי וּלְהָסִיר שַׂקּוֹ מֵעָלָיו
ה וְלֹא קִבֵּל: וַתִּקְרָא אֶסְתֵּר לַהֲתָךְ מִסָּרִיסֵי הַמֶּלֶךְ
אֲשֶׁר הֶעֱמִיד לְפָנֶיהָ וַתְּצַוֵּהוּ עַל־מָרְדֳּכָי לָדַעַת
ו מַה־זֶּה וְעַל־מַה־זֶּה: וַיֵּצֵא הֲתָךְ אֶל־מָרְדֳּכָי אֶל־
ז רְחוֹב הָעִיר אֲשֶׁר לִפְנֵי שַׁעַר־הַמֶּלֶךְ: וַיַּגֶּד־לוֹ
מָרְדֳּכַי אֵת כָּל־אֲשֶׁר קָרָהוּ וְאֵת | פָּרָשַׁת הַכֶּסֶף
אֲשֶׁר אָמַר הָמָן לִשְׁקוֹל עַל־גִּנְזֵי הַמֶּלֶךְ
ח °בִּיהוּדִיִּים לְאַבְּדָם: וְאֶת־פַּתְשֶׁגֶן כְּתָב־הַדָּת °בַּיְּהוּדִים ק
אֲשֶׁר־נִתַּן בְּשׁוּשָׁן לְהַשְׁמִידָם נָתַן לוֹ לְהַרְאוֹת
אֶת־אֶסְתֵּר וּלְהַגִּיד לָהּ וּלְצַוּוֹת עָלֶיהָ לָבוֹא אֶל־
הַמֶּלֶךְ לְהִתְחַנֶּן־לוֹ וּלְבַקֵּשׁ מִלְּפָנָיו עַל־עַמָּהּ:
ט וַיָּבוֹא הֲתָךְ וַיַּגֵּד לְאֶסְתֵּר אֵת דִּבְרֵי מָרְדֳּכָי:
י-יא וַתֹּאמֶר אֶסְתֵּר לַהֲתָךְ וַתְּצַוֵּהוּ אֶל־מָרְדֳּכָי: כָּל־
עַבְדֵי הַמֶּלֶךְ וְעַם מְדִינוֹת הַמֶּלֶךְ יֹדְעִים אֲשֶׁר

to all peoples, that they should be ready for that day. ¹⁵ The couriers went forth hurriedly by order of the King, and the edict was distributed in Shushan the Capitol. The King and Haman sat down to drink, but the city of Shushan was bewildered.

4/1. MORDECHAI AND THE JEWS MOURN

¹ **M**ordechai learned of all that had been done; and Mordechai tore his clothes and put on sackcloth with ashes. He went out into the midst of the city, and cried loudly and bitterly. ² He came until the front of the King's gate for it was forbidden to enter the King's gate, clothed with sackcloth. ³ (In every province, wherever the King's command and his decree extended, there was great mourning among the Jews, with fasting, and weeping, and wailing; most of them lying in sackcloth and ashes.)

4. Esther had not yet revealed her origins, but her interest in Mordechai — who had always inquired about her welfare — was well known throughout the palace.

⁴ And Esther's maids and chamberlains came and told her about it, and the Queen was greatly distressed; she sent garments to clothe Mordechai so that he might take off his sackcloth, but he would not accept them.

5. Hasach was a great man, Esther's confidant, one who could keep secrets, and whom no one would suspect or dare to question about his mission. In the Talmud he is identified with Daniel.

⁵ Then Esther summoned Hasach, one of the King's chamberlains whom he had appointed to attend her, and ordered him to go to Mordechai, to learn what this was about and why. ⁶ So Hasach went out to Mordechai unto the city square, which was in front of the King's gate, ⁷ and Mordechai told him of all that had happened to him, and all about the sum of money that Haman had promised to pay to the royal treasuries for the annihilation of the Jews. ⁸ He also gave him a copy of the text of the decree which was distributed in Shushan for their destruction — so that he might show it to Esther and inform her, bidding her to go to the King, to appeal to him, and to plead with him for her people.

8. MORDECHAI ASKS ESTHER TO INTERCEDE

10. ESTHER'S RECALCITRANT RESPONSE

⁹ Hasach came and told Esther what Mordechai had said. ¹⁰ Then Esther told Hasach to return to Mordechai with this message: ¹¹ 'All the King's servants and the people of the King's provinces are well

כָּל־אִישׁ וְאִשָּׁה אֲשֶׁר יָבוֹא אֶל־הַמֶּלֶךְ אֶל־
הֶחָצֵר הַפְּנִימִית אֲשֶׁר לֹא־יִקָּרֵא אַחַת דָּתוֹ
לְהָמִית לְבַד מֵאֲשֶׁר יוֹשִׁיט־לוֹ הַמֶּלֶךְ אֶת־
שַׁרְבִיט הַזָּהָב וְחָיָה וַאֲנִי לֹא נִקְרֵאתִי לָבוֹא אֶל־

יב הַמֶּלֶךְ זֶה שְׁלוֹשִׁים יוֹם: וַיַּגִּידוּ לְמָרְדֳּכָי אֵת

יג דִּבְרֵי אֶסְתֵּר: וַיֹּאמֶר מָרְדֳּכַי לְהָשִׁיב אֶל־אֶסְתֵּר
אַל־תְּדַמִּי בְנַפְשֵׁךְ לְהִמָּלֵט בֵּית־הַמֶּלֶךְ מִכָּל־

יד הַיְּהוּדִים: כִּי אִם־הַחֲרֵשׁ תַּחֲרִישִׁי בָּעֵת הַזֹּאת
רֶוַח וְהַצָּלָה יַעֲמוֹד לַיְּהוּדִים מִמָּקוֹם אַחֵר וְאַתְּ
וּבֵית־אָבִיךְ תֹּאבֵדוּ וּמִי יוֹדֵעַ אִם־לְעֵת כָּזֹאת

טו הִגַּעַתְּ לַמַּלְכוּת: וַתֹּאמֶר אֶסְתֵּר לְהָשִׁיב אֶל־

טז מָרְדֳּכָי: לֵךְ כְּנוֹס אֶת־כָּל־הַיְּהוּדִים הַנִּמְצְאִים
בְּשׁוּשָׁן וְצוּמוּ עָלַי וְאַל־תֹּאכְלוּ וְאַל־תִּשְׁתּוּ
שְׁלֹשֶׁת יָמִים לַיְלָה וָיוֹם גַּם־אֲנִי וְנַעֲרֹתַי אָצוּם
כֵּן וּבְכֵן אָבוֹא אֶל־הַמֶּלֶךְ אֲשֶׁר לֹא־כַדָּת וְכַאֲשֶׁר

יז אָבַדְתִּי אָבָדְתִּי: וַיַּעֲבֹר מָרְדֳּכָי וַיַּעַשׂ כְּכֹל אֲשֶׁר

א צִוְּתָה עָלָיו אֶסְתֵּר: וַיְהִי | בַּיּוֹם הַשְּׁלִישִׁי וַתִּלְבַּשׁ
אֶסְתֵּר מַלְכוּת וַתַּעֲמֹד בַּחֲצַר בֵּית־הַמֶּלֶךְ
הַפְּנִימִית נֹכַח בֵּית הַמֶּלֶךְ וְהַמֶּלֶךְ יוֹשֵׁב עַל־כִּסֵּא

ב מַלְכוּתוֹ בְּבֵית הַמַּלְכוּת נֹכַח פֶּתַח הַבָּיִת: וַיְהִי
כִרְאוֹת הַמֶּלֶךְ אֶת־אֶסְתֵּר הַמַּלְכָּה עֹמֶדֶת בֶּחָצֵר
נָשְׂאָה חֵן בְּעֵינָיו וַיּוֹשֶׁט הַמֶּלֶךְ לְאֶסְתֵּר אֶת־
שַׁרְבִיט הַזָּהָב אֲשֶׁר בְּיָדוֹ וַתִּקְרַב אֶסְתֵּר וַתִּגַּע

ג בְּרֹאשׁ הַשַּׁרְבִיט: וַיֹּאמֶר לָהּ הַמֶּלֶךְ מַה־לָּךְ
אֶסְתֵּר הַמַּלְכָּה וּמַה־בַּקָּשָׁתֵךְ עַד־חֲצִי הַמַּלְכוּת

ד וְיִנָּתֵן לָךְ: וַתֹּאמֶר אֶסְתֵּר אִם־עַל־הַמֶּלֶךְ טוֹב

ה

13. MORDECHAI ENCOURAGES ESTHER

'You may, by some remote twist of fate, manage to save your body. But how will you save your soul?'

15. ESTHER AGREES TO GO UNSUMMONED TO THE KING

16. Esther limited the assembly to the Jews in Shushan because it would have been impossible to assemble Jews living further away on such short notice (Gaon of Vilna).

5/1. ESTHER GOES BEFORE THE KING

The third day — of the fast. It was, according to the Talmud, the first day of Passover.

4. ESTHER LAYS A TRAP FOR HAMAN

The first Hebrew letters of the words יָבא הַמֶּלֶךְ וְהָמָן הַיּוֹם form the Holy Name of God. This is one of the several places throughout the Megillah where God's Name is indirectly hinted (Kad HaKemach).

aware that if anyone, man or woman, approaches the King in the inner court without being summoned, there is but one law for him: that he be put to death; except for the person to whom the King shall extend the gold scepter so that he may live. Now I have not been summoned to come to the King for the past thirty days.'

12 They related Esther's words to Mordechai. 13 Then Mordechai said to reply to Esther: 'Do not imagine that you will be able to escape in the King's palace any more than the rest of the Jews. 14 For if you persist in keeping silent at a time like this, relief and deliverance will come to the Jews from some other place, while you and your father's house will perish. And who knows whether it was just for such a time as this that you attained the royal position!'

15 Then Esther sent this return answer to Mordechai: 16 'Go, assemble all the Jews to be found in Shushan, and fast for me. Do not eat or drink for three days, night or day; I, with my maids, will fast also. Then I will go in to the King though it's unlawful. And if I perish, I perish.' 17 Mordechai then left and did exactly as Esther had commanded him.

1 Now it came to pass on the third day, Esther donned royalty and stood in the inner court of the King's palace facing the King's house while the King was sitting on his throne in the throne room facing the chamber's entrance. 2 When the King noticed Queen Esther standing in the court, she won his favor. The King extended to Esther the gold scepter that was in his hand, and Esther approached and touched the tip of the scepter.

3 The King said to her: 'What is your petition, Queen Esther? Even if it be half the kingdom, it shall be granted you.' 4 Esther said: 'If it please the King,

יָבוֹא הַמֶּלֶךְ וְהָמָן הַיּוֹם אֶל־הַמִּשְׁתֶּה אֲשֶׁר־
עָשִׂיתִי לוֹ: וַיֹּאמֶר הַמֶּלֶךְ מַהֲרוּ אֶת־הָמָן ה
לַעֲשׂוֹת אֶת־דְּבַר אֶסְתֵּר וַיָּבֹא הַמֶּלֶךְ וְהָמָן אֶל־
הַמִּשְׁתֶּה אֲשֶׁר־עָשְׂתָה אֶסְתֵּר: וַיֹּאמֶר הַמֶּלֶךְ ו
לְאֶסְתֵּר בְּמִשְׁתֵּה הַיַּיִן מַה־שְּׁאֵלָתֵךְ וְיִנָּתֵן לָךְ
וּמַה־בַּקָּשָׁתֵךְ עַד־חֲצִי הַמַּלְכוּת וְתֵעָשׂ: וַתַּעַן ז
אֶסְתֵּר וַתֹּאמַר שְׁאֵלָתִי וּבַקָּשָׁתִי: אִם־מָצָאתִי חֵן ח
בְּעֵינֵי הַמֶּלֶךְ וְאִם־עַל־הַמֶּלֶךְ טוֹב לָתֵת אֶת־
שְׁאֵלָתִי וְלַעֲשׂוֹת אֶת־בַּקָּשָׁתִי יָבוֹא הַמֶּלֶךְ וְהָמָן
אֶל־הַמִּשְׁתֶּה אֲשֶׁר אֶעֱשֶׂה לָהֶם וּמָחָר אֶעֱשֶׂה
כִּדְבַר הַמֶּלֶךְ: וַיֵּצֵא הָמָן בַּיּוֹם הַהוּא שָׂמֵחַ וְטוֹב ט
לֵב וְכִרְאוֹת הָמָן אֶת־מָרְדֳּכַי בְּשַׁעַר הַמֶּלֶךְ וְלֹא־
קָם וְלֹא־זָע מִמֶּנּוּ וַיִּמָּלֵא הָמָן עַל־מָרְדֳּכַי חֵמָה:
וַיִּתְאַפַּק הָמָן וַיָּבוֹא אֶל־בֵּיתוֹ וַיִּשְׁלַח וַיָּבֵא אֶת־ י
אֹהֲבָיו וְאֶת־זֶרֶשׁ אִשְׁתּוֹ: וַיְסַפֵּר לָהֶם הָמָן אֶת־ יא
כְּבוֹד עָשְׁרוֹ וְרֹב בָּנָיו וְאֵת כָּל־אֲשֶׁר גִּדְּלוֹ הַמֶּלֶךְ
וְאֵת אֲשֶׁר נִשְּׂאוֹ עַל־הַשָּׂרִים וְעַבְדֵי הַמֶּלֶךְ:
וַיֹּאמֶר הָמָן אַף לֹא־הֵבִיאָה אֶסְתֵּר הַמַּלְכָּה יב
עִם־הַמֶּלֶךְ אֶל־הַמִּשְׁתֶּה אֲשֶׁר־עָשָׂתָה כִּי אִם־
אוֹתִי וְגַם־לְמָחָר אֲנִי קָרוּא־לָהּ עִם־הַמֶּלֶךְ:
וְכָל־זֶה אֵינֶנּוּ שֹׁוֶה לִי בְּכָל־עֵת אֲשֶׁר אֲנִי יג
רֹאֶה אֶת־מָרְדֳּכַי הַיְּהוּדִי יוֹשֵׁב בְּשַׁעַר הַמֶּלֶךְ:
וַתֹּאמֶר לוֹ זֶרֶשׁ אִשְׁתּוֹ וְכָל־אֹהֲבָיו יַעֲשׂוּ־ יד
עֵץ גָּבֹהַּ חֲמִשִּׁים אַמָּה וּבַבֹּקֶר | אֱמֹר לַמֶּלֶךְ
וְיִתְלוּ אֶת־מָרְדֳּכַי עָלָיו וּבֹא עִם־הַמֶּלֶךְ אֶל־
הַמִּשְׁתֶּה שָׂמֵחַ וַיִּיטַב הַדָּבָר לִפְנֵי הָמָן וַיַּעַשׂ

let the King and Haman come today to the banquet that I have prepared for him.' ⁵ Then the King commanded: 'Tell Haman to hurry and fulfill Esther's wish.' So the King and Haman came to the banquet that Esther had prepared.

6. THE FIRST BANQUET

⁶ The King said to Esther during the wine feast: 'What is your request? It shall be granted you. And what is your petition? Even if it be half the kingdom, it shall be fulfilled.' ⁷ So Esther answered and said: 'My request and my petition: ⁸ If I have won the King's favor, and if it pleases the King to grant my request and to perform my petition — let the King and Haman come to the banquet that I shall prepare for them, and tomorrow I will do the King's bidding.'

8. Esther's ruse worked. When Haman arrived at Esther's first banquet, he was apprehensive of Esther's reason for inviting him. He suspected a connection between the new edict concerning the Jews and his invitation. Only now, having left the first party at which he was overwhelmed with flattery, was he joyous and confident. He was unprepared, therefore, for the consequences of Esther's next banquet (Alkabetz).

9. HAMAN IS INFURIATED BY MORDECHAI

⁹ That day Haman went out joyful and exuberant. But when Haman noticed Mordechai in the King's gate and that he neither stood up nor stirred before him, Haman was infuriated with Mordechai. ¹⁰ Nevertheless Haman restrained himself and went home. He sent for his friends and his wife, Zeresh, ¹¹ and Haman recounted to them the glory of his wealth and his large number of sons, and every instance where the King had promoted him and advanced him above the officials and royal servants. ¹² Haman said: 'Moreover, Queen Esther invited no one but myself to accompany the King to the banquet that she had prepared, and tomorrow, too, I am invited by her along with the King. ¹³ Yet all this means nothing to me so long as I see that Jew Mordechai sitting at the King's gate.' ¹⁴ Then his wife, Zeresh, and all his friends said to him: 'Let a gallows be made, fifty cubits high; and tomorrow morning speak to the King and have them hang Mordechai on it. Then, in good spirits, accompany the King to the banquet.' This suggestion pleased Haman, and he had the gallows erected

13. Notice that Haman did not mention to his wife and children that he was angry because of Mordechai's refusal to bow down to him; he thought it beneath his dignity to admit that such a minor slight could ruffle him so. Rather he claimed that he was angry because 'the Jew Mordechai was sitting at the King's gate' and he was totally unworthy of such a high honor (Me'am Loez).

א בַּלַּיְלָה הַהוּא נָדְדָה שְׁנַת הַמֶּלֶךְ וַיֹּאמֶר לְהָבִיא אֶת־סֵפֶר הַזִּכְרֹנוֹת דִּבְרֵי

ב הַיָּמִים וַיִּהְיוּ נִקְרָאִים לִפְנֵי הַמֶּלֶךְ: וַיִּמָּצֵא כָתוּב אֲשֶׁר הִגִּיד מָרְדֳּכַי עַל־בִּגְתָנָא וָתֶרֶשׁ שְׁנֵי סָרִיסֵי הַמֶּלֶךְ מִשֹּׁמְרֵי הַסַּף אֲשֶׁר בִּקְשׁוּ לִשְׁלֹחַ יָד

ג בַּמֶּלֶךְ אֲחַשְׁוֵרוֹשׁ: וַיֹּאמֶר הַמֶּלֶךְ מַה־נַּעֲשָׂה יְקָר וּגְדוּלָּה לְמָרְדֳּכַי עַל־זֶה וַיֹּאמְרוּ נַעֲרֵי הַמֶּלֶךְ

ד מְשָׁרְתָיו לֹא־נַעֲשָׂה עִמּוֹ דָּבָר: וַיֹּאמֶר הַמֶּלֶךְ מִי בֶחָצֵר וְהָמָן בָּא לַחֲצַר בֵּית־הַמֶּלֶךְ הַחִיצוֹנָה לֵאמֹר לַמֶּלֶךְ לִתְלוֹת אֶת־מָרְדֳּכַי עַל־הָעֵץ

ה אֲשֶׁר־הֵכִין לוֹ: וַיֹּאמְרוּ נַעֲרֵי הַמֶּלֶךְ אֵלָיו הִנֵּה

ו הָמָן עֹמֵד בֶּחָצֵר וַיֹּאמֶר הַמֶּלֶךְ יָבוֹא: וַיָּבוֹא הָמָן וַיֹּאמֶר לוֹ הַמֶּלֶךְ מַה־לַעֲשׂוֹת בָּאִישׁ אֲשֶׁר הַמֶּלֶךְ חָפֵץ בִּיקָרוֹ וַיֹּאמֶר הָמָן בְּלִבּוֹ לְמִי יַחְפֹּץ הַמֶּלֶךְ

ז לַעֲשׂוֹת יְקָר יוֹתֵר מִמֶּנִּי: וַיֹּאמֶר הָמָן אֶל־הַמֶּלֶךְ

ח אִישׁ אֲשֶׁר הַמֶּלֶךְ חָפֵץ בִּיקָרוֹ: יָבִיאוּ לְבוּשׁ מַלְכוּת אֲשֶׁר לָבַשׁ־בּוֹ הַמֶּלֶךְ וְסוּס אֲשֶׁר רָכַב עָלָיו הַמֶּלֶךְ וַאֲשֶׁר נִתַּן כֶּתֶר מַלְכוּת בְּרֹאשׁוֹ:

ט וְנָתוֹן הַלְּבוּשׁ וְהַסּוּס עַל־יַד־אִישׁ מִשָּׂרֵי הַמֶּלֶךְ הַפַּרְתְּמִים וְהִלְבִּשׁוּ אֶת־הָאִישׁ אֲשֶׁר הַמֶּלֶךְ חָפֵץ בִּיקָרוֹ וְהִרְכִּיבֻהוּ עַל־הַסּוּס בִּרְחוֹב הָעִיר וְקָרְאוּ לְפָנָיו כָּכָה יֵעָשֶׂה לָאִישׁ אֲשֶׁר הַמֶּלֶךְ

י חָפֵץ בִּיקָרוֹ: וַיֹּאמֶר הַמֶּלֶךְ לְהָמָן מַהֵר קַח אֶת־הַלְּבוּשׁ וְאֶת־הַסּוּס כַּאֲשֶׁר דִּבַּרְתָּ וַעֲשֵׂה־כֵן לְמָרְדֳּכַי הַיְהוּדִי הַיּוֹשֵׁב בְּשַׁעַר הַמֶּלֶךְ אַל־תַּפֵּל

יא דָּבָר מִכֹּל אֲשֶׁר דִּבַּרְתָּ: וַיִּקַּח הָמָן אֶת־הַלְּבוּשׁ

6/1. MORDECHAI IS FINALLY REWARDED

¹That night sleep eluded the King so he ordered that the record book, the annals, be brought and be read before the King. ² There it was found recorded that Mordechai had denounced Bigsana and Teresh, two of the King's chamberlains of the guardians of the threshold, who had plotted to lay hands on King Ahasuerus. ³ 'What honor or dignity has been conferred on Mordechai for this?' asked the King. 'Nothing has been done for him,' replied the King's pages. ⁴ The King said: 'Who is in the court?' (Now Haman had just come into the outer court of the palace to speak to the King about hanging Mordechai on the gallows he had prepared for him.) ⁵ So the King's servants answered him: 'It is Haman standing in the court.' And the King said: 'Let him enter.' ⁶ When Haman came in the King said unto him: 'What should be done for the man whom the King especially wants to honor?' (Now Haman reasoned to himself: 'Whom would the King especially want to honor besides me?') ⁷ So Haman said to the King: 'For the man whom the King especially wants to honor, ⁸ have them bring a royal robe that the King has worn and a horse that the King has ridden, one with a royal crown on his head. ⁹ Then let the robe and horse be entrusted to one of the King's most noble officers, and let them attire the man whom the King especially wants to honor, and parade him on horseback through the city square proclaiming before him: "This is what is done for the man whom the King especially wants to honor." '

10. HAMAN'S HUMILIATION ¹⁰ Then the King said to Haman: 'Hurry, then, get the robe and the horse as you have said and do all this for Mordechai the Jew, who sits at the King's gate. Do not omit a single detail that you have suggested!' ¹¹ So Haman took the robe

וְאֶת־הַסּוּס וַיַּלְבֵּשׁ אֶת־מׇרְדְּכַי וַיַּרְכִּיבֵהוּ בִּרְחוֹב
הָעִיר וַיִּקְרָא לְפָנָיו כָּכָה יֵעָשֶׂה לָאִישׁ אֲשֶׁר
הַמֶּלֶךְ חָפֵץ בִּיקָרוֹ: וַיָּשׇׁב מׇרְדְּכַי אֶל־שַׁעַר יב
הַמֶּלֶךְ וְהָמָן נִדְחַף אֶל־בֵּיתוֹ אָבֵל וַחֲפוּי רֹאשׁ:
וַיְסַפֵּר הָמָן לְזֶרֶשׁ אִשְׁתּוֹ וּלְכׇל־אֹהֲבָיו אֵת כׇּל־ יג
אֲשֶׁר קָרָהוּ וַיֹּאמְרוּ לוֹ חֲכָמָיו וְזֶרֶשׁ אִשְׁתּוֹ אִם
מִזֶּרַע הַיְּהוּדִים מׇרְדְּכַי אֲשֶׁר הַחִלּוֹתָ לִנְפֹּל
לְפָנָיו לֹא־תוּכַל לוֹ כִּי־נָפוֹל תִּפּוֹל לְפָנָיו: עוֹדָם יד
מְדַבְּרִים עִמּוֹ וְסָרִיסֵי הַמֶּלֶךְ הִגִּיעוּ וַיַּבְהִלוּ
לְהָבִיא אֶת־הָמָן אֶל־הַמִּשְׁתֶּה אֲשֶׁר־עָשְׂתָה
אֶסְתֵּר: וַיָּבֹא הַמֶּלֶךְ וְהָמָן לִשְׁתּוֹת עִם־אֶסְתֵּר א
הַמַּלְכָּה: וַיֹּאמֶר הַמֶּלֶךְ לְאֶסְתֵּר גַּם בַּיּוֹם הַשֵּׁנִי ב
בְּמִשְׁתֵּה הַיַּיִן מַה־שְּׁאֵלָתֵךְ אֶסְתֵּר הַמַּלְכָּה
וְתִנָּתֵן לָךְ וּמַה־בַּקָּשָׁתֵךְ עַד־חֲצִי הַמַּלְכוּת
וְתֵעָשׂ: וַתַּעַן אֶסְתֵּר הַמַּלְכָּה וַתֹּאמַר אִם־ ג
מָצָאתִי חֵן בְּעֵינֶיךָ הַמֶּלֶךְ וְאִם־עַל־הַמֶּלֶךְ טוֹב
תִּנָּתֶן־לִי נַפְשִׁי בִּשְׁאֵלָתִי וְעַמִּי בְּבַקָּשָׁתִי: כִּי ד
נִמְכַּרְנוּ אֲנִי וְעַמִּי לְהַשְׁמִיד לַהֲרוֹג וּלְאַבֵּד וְאִלּוּ
לַעֲבָדִים וְלִשְׁפָחוֹת נִמְכַּרְנוּ הֶחֱרַשְׁתִּי כִּי אֵין
הַצָּר שֹׁוֶה בְּנֵזֶק הַמֶּלֶךְ: וַיֹּאמֶר ה
הַמֶּלֶךְ אֲחַשְׁוֵרוֹשׁ וַיֹּאמֶר לְאֶסְתֵּר הַמַּלְכָּה מִי
הוּא זֶה וְאֵי־זֶה הוּא אֲשֶׁר־מְלָאוֹ לִבּוֹ לַעֲשׂוֹת
כֵּן: וַתֹּאמֶר אֶסְתֵּר אִישׁ צַר וְאוֹיֵב הָמָן הָרָע ו
הַזֶּה וְהָמָן נִבְעַת מִלִּפְנֵי הַמֶּלֶךְ וְהַמַּלְכָּה:
וְהַמֶּלֶךְ קָם בַּחֲמָתוֹ מִמִּשְׁתֵּה הַיַּיִן אֶל־גִּנַּת ז
הַבִּיתָן וְהָמָן עָמַד לְבַקֵּשׁ עַל־נַפְשׁוֹ מֵאֶסְתֵּר

ז

and the horse and attired Mordechai, and led him through the city square proclaiming before him: 'This is what is done for the man whom the King especially wants to honor.'

¹² Mordechai returned to the King's gate; but Haman hurried home, despondent and with his head covered. ¹³ Haman told his wife, Zeresh, and all his friends everything that had happened to him, and his advisors and his wife, Zeresh, said to him: 'If Mordechai, before whom you have begun to fall, is of Jewish descent, you will not prevail against him, but will undoubtedly fall before him.' ¹⁴ While they were still talking with him, the King's chamberlains arrived, and they hurried to bring Haman to the banquet which Esther had arranged.

13. HAMAN'S DOOM IS FORECAST

7/1. THE SECOND BANQUET: ESTHER PRESENTS HER REQUEST

It was one of God's miracles that, as disturbed as Ahasuerus was, he came to the feast, was cheered by the wine, and regained his good cheer to the extent that he was prepared to fulfill Esther's every wish.

3. The first הַמֶּלֶךְ, *King,* is taken to refer to God, the second to Ahasuerus. 'Esther cast her eyes heavenward and said: "If I have found favor in Your sight, O Supreme King, and if it pleases thee, O King Ahasuerus, let my life be given me, and let my people be rescued out of the hands of the enemy"' *(Targum).*

6. HAMAN IS ACCUSED

7. The King went out to 'cool off' from his anger, part of God's master plan to give Haman the opportunity to incriminate himself even further in the King's absence.

¹ So the King and Haman came to feast with Queen Esther. ²The King asked Esther again on the second day at the wine feast: 'What is your request, Queen Esther? — it shall be granted you. And what is your petition? — Even if it be up to half the kingdom, it shall be fulfilled.' ³ So Queen Esther answered and said: 'If I have won Your Majesty's favor and if it pleases the King, let my life be granted to me as my request and my people as my petition. ⁴ For we have been sold, I and my people, to be destroyed, slain, and annihilated. Had we been sold as slaves and servant-girls, I would have kept quiet, for the adversary is not worthy of the King's damage.'

⁵ Thereupon, King Ahasuerus exclaimed and said to Queen Esther: 'Who is it? Where is the one who dared to do this?' ⁶ And Esther said: 'An adversary and an enemy! This wicked Haman!' Haman trembled in terror before the King and Queen. ⁷ The King rose in a rage from the wine feast and went into the palace garden while Haman remained to beg Queen Esther for his life,

הַמַּלְכָּה כִּי רָאָה כִּי־כָלְתָה אֵלָיו הָרָעָה מֵאֵת

ח הַמֶּלֶךְ: וְהַמֶּלֶךְ שָׁב מִגִּנַּת הַבִּיתָן אֶל־בֵּית |
מִשְׁתֵּה הַיַּיִן וְהָמָן נֹפֵל עַל־הַמִּטָּה אֲשֶׁר אֶסְתֵּר
עָלֶיהָ וַיֹּאמֶר הַמֶּלֶךְ הֲגַם לִכְבּוֹשׁ אֶת־הַמַּלְכָּה
עִמִּי בַּבָּיִת הַדָּבָר יָצָא מִפִּי הַמֶּלֶךְ וּפְנֵי הָמָן

ט חָפוּ: וַיֹּאמֶר חַרְבוֹנָה אֶחָד מִן־הַסָּרִיסִים לִפְנֵי
הַמֶּלֶךְ גַּם הִנֵּה־הָעֵץ אֲשֶׁר־עָשָׂה הָמָן לְמָרְדֳּכַי
אֲשֶׁר דִּבֶּר־טוֹב עַל־הַמֶּלֶךְ עֹמֵד בְּבֵית הָמָן
גָּבֹהַּ חֲמִשִּׁים אַמָּה וַיֹּאמֶר הַמֶּלֶךְ תְּלֻהוּ עָלָיו:

י וַיִּתְלוּ אֶת־הָמָן עַל־הָעֵץ אֲשֶׁר־הֵכִין לְמָרְדֳּכָי

א וַחֲמַת הַמֶּלֶךְ שָׁכָכָה: בַּיּוֹם

ח

הַהוּא נָתַן הַמֶּלֶךְ אֲחַשְׁוֵרוֹשׁ לְאֶסְתֵּר הַמַּלְכָּה
אֶת־בֵּית הָמָן צֹרֵר °הַיְּהוּדִים וּמָרְדֳּכַי בָּא לִפְנֵי   °הַיְּהוּדִים ק

ב הַמֶּלֶךְ כִּי־הִגִּידָה אֶסְתֵּר מָה הוּא־לָהּ: וַיָּסַר
הַמֶּלֶךְ אֶת־טַבַּעְתּוֹ אֲשֶׁר הֶעֱבִיר מֵהָמָן וַיִּתְּנָהּ
לְמָרְדֳּכָי וַתָּשֶׂם אֶסְתֵּר אֶת־מָרְדֳּכַי עַל־בֵּית

ג הָמָן: וַתּוֹסֶף אֶסְתֵּר וַתְּדַבֵּר לִפְנֵי
הַמֶּלֶךְ וַתִּפֹּל לִפְנֵי רַגְלָיו וַתֵּבְךְּ וַתִּתְחַנֶּן־לוֹ
לְהַעֲבִיר אֶת־רָעַת הָמָן הָאֲגָגִי וְאֵת מַחֲשַׁבְתּוֹ

ד אֲשֶׁר חָשַׁב עַל־הַיְּהוּדִים: וַיּוֹשֶׁט הַמֶּלֶךְ לְאֶסְתֵּר
אֵת שַׁרְבִט הַזָּהָב וַתָּקָם אֶסְתֵּר וַתַּעֲמֹד
לִפְנֵי הַמֶּלֶךְ: וַתֹּאמֶר אִם־עַל־הַמֶּלֶךְ טוֹב וְאִם־

ה מָצָאתִי חֵן לְפָנָיו וְכָשֵׁר הַדָּבָר לִפְנֵי הַמֶּלֶךְ
וְטוֹבָה אֲנִי בְּעֵינָיו יִכָּתֵב לְהָשִׁיב אֶת־הַסְּפָרִים
מַחֲשֶׁבֶת הָמָן בֶּן־הַמְּדָתָא הָאֲגָגִי אֲשֶׁר כָּתַב
לְאַבֵּד אֶת־הַיְּהוּדִים אֲשֶׁר בְּכָל־מְדִינוֹת הַמֶּלֶךְ:

for he saw that the King's evil determination against him was final. [8] When the King returned from the palace garden to the banquet room, Haman was prostrated on the couch upon which Esther was; so the King exclaimed: 'Would he actually assault the Queen while I'm in the house?' As soon as the King uttered this, they covered Haman's face. [9] Then Charbonah, one of the chamberlains in attendance of the King, said: 'Furthermore, the fifty-cubit-high gallows which Haman made for Mordechai — who spoke good for the King — is standing in Haman's house.' And the King said: 'Hang him on it.' [10] So they hanged Haman on the gallows which he had prepared for Mordechai, and the King's anger abated.

9. HAMAN IS EXECUTED

Our Sages ordained that one should always say חַרְבוֹנָה זָכוּר לַטוֹב — 'Charbonah of blessed memory,' because it was Charbonah's swift advice that prevented Haman from possibly talking — or bribing — his way back into the King's good graces.

8/1. MORDECHAI IS APPOINTED PRIME MINISTER

[1] That very day, King Ahasuerus gave the estate of Haman, the enemy of the Jews, to Queen Esther. Mordechai presented himself to the King (for Esther had revealed his relationship to her). [2] The King slipped off his signet ring, which he had removed from Haman, and gave it to Mordechai; and Esther put Mordechai in charge of Haman's estate.

3. ESTHER BEGS THE KING TO AVERT HAMAN'S DECREE

[3] Esther yet again spoke to the King, collapsed at his feet, and cried and begged him to avert the evil intention of Haman the Agagite, and his scheme which he had plotted against the Jews. [4] The King extended the gold scepter to Esther, and Esther arose and stood before the King. [5] She said: 'If it pleases the King, and if I have won his favor, and the proposal seems proper in the King's opinion, and I be pleasing to him, let a decree be written to countermand those dispatches devised by Haman, the son of Hammedasa the Agagite, which he wrote ordering the destruction of the Jews who are in all the King's provinces.

ו כִּי אֵיכָכָה אוּכַל וְרָאִיתִי בֶּרָעָה אֲשֶׁר־יִמְצָא
אֶת־עַמִּי וְאֵיכָכָה אוּכַל וְרָאִיתִי בְּאָבְדַן
מוֹלַדְתִּי: ז וַיֹּאמֶר הַמֶּלֶךְ אֲחַשְׁוֵרֹשׁ
לְאֶסְתֵּר הַמַּלְכָּה וּלְמָרְדֳּכַי הַיְּהוּדִי הִנֵּה בֵית־
הָמָן נָתַתִּי לְאֶסְתֵּר וְאֹתוֹ תָּלוּ עַל־הָעֵץ עַל
אֲשֶׁר־שָׁלַח יָדוֹ °בַּיְּהוּדִים: ח וְאַתֶּם כִּתְבוּ עַל־ °בַּיְּהוּדִיים ק
הַיְּהוּדִים כַּטּוֹב בְּעֵינֵיכֶם בְּשֵׁם הַמֶּלֶךְ וְחִתְמוּ
בְּטַבַּעַת הַמֶּלֶךְ כִּי־כְתָב אֲשֶׁר־נִכְתָּב בְּשֵׁם־הַמֶּלֶךְ
ט וְנַחְתּוֹם בְּטַבַּעַת הַמֶּלֶךְ אֵין לְהָשִׁיב: וַיִּקָּרְאוּ
סֹפְרֵי־הַמֶּלֶךְ בָּעֵת־הַהִיא בַּחֹדֶשׁ הַשְּׁלִישִׁי
הוּא־חֹדֶשׁ סִיוָן בִּשְׁלוֹשָׁה וְעֶשְׂרִים בּוֹ וַיִּכָּתֵב
כְּכָל־אֲשֶׁר־צִוָּה מָרְדֳּכַי אֶל־הַיְּהוּדִים וְאֶל
הָאֲחַשְׁדַּרְפְּנִים וְהַפַּחוֹת וְשָׂרֵי הַמְּדִינוֹת אֲשֶׁר |
מֵהֹדּוּ וְעַד־כּוּשׁ שֶׁבַע וְעֶשְׂרִים וּמֵאָה מְדִינָה
מְדִינָה וּמְדִינָה כִּכְתָבָהּ וְעַם וָעָם כִּלְשֹׁנוֹ וְאֶל־
הַיְּהוּדִים כִּכְתָבָם וְכִלְשׁוֹנָם: י וַיִּכְתֹּב בְּשֵׁם הַמֶּלֶךְ
אֲחַשְׁוֵרֹשׁ וַיַּחְתֹּם בְּטַבַּעַת הַמֶּלֶךְ וַיִּשְׁלַח סְפָרִים
בְּיַד הָרָצִים בַּסּוּסִים רֹכְבֵי הָרֶכֶשׁ הָאֲחַשְׁתְּרָנִים
בְּנֵי הָרַמָּכִים: יא אֲשֶׁר נָתַן הַמֶּלֶךְ לַיְּהוּדִים | אֲשֶׁר |
בְּכָל־עִיר וָעִיר לְהִקָּהֵל וְלַעֲמֹד עַל־נַפְשָׁם
לְהַשְׁמִיד וְלַהֲרֹג וּלְאַבֵּד אֶת־כָּל־חֵיל עַם
וּמְדִינָה הַצָּרִים אֹתָם טַף וְנָשִׁים וּשְׁלָלָם לָבוֹז:
יב בְּיוֹם אֶחָד בְּכָל־מְדִינוֹת הַמֶּלֶךְ אֲחַשְׁוֵרֹשׁ
בִּשְׁלוֹשָׁה עָשָׂר לְחֹדֶשׁ שְׁנֵים־עָשָׂר הוּא־חֹדֶשׁ
יג אֲדָר: פַּתְשֶׁגֶן הַכְּתָב לְהִנָּתֵן דָּת בְּכָל־מְדִינָה
וּמְדִינָה גָּלוּי לְכָל־הָעַמִּים וְלִהְיוֹת °הַיְּהוּדִים °הַיְּהוּדִיים ק

⁶ For how can I bear to witness the disaster which will befall my people! How can I bear to witness the destruction of my relatives!'

7. PERMISSION IS GRANTED TO OVERRIDE THE DECREE

⁷ Then King Ahasuerus said to Queen Esther and Mordechai the Jew: 'Behold, I have given Haman's estate to Esther, and he has been hanged on the gallows because he plotted against the Jews. ⁸ You may write concerning the Jews whatever you desire, in the King's name, and seal it with the royal signet, for an edict which is written in the King's name and sealed with the royal signet may not be revoked.' ⁹ So the King's secretaries were summoned at that time, on the twenty-third day of the third month, that is, the month of Sivan, and it was written exactly as Mordechai had dictated to the Jews and to the satraps, the governors and officials of the provinces from Hodu to Cush, a hundred and twenty-seven provinces, to each province in its own script, and each people in its own language, and to the Jews in their own script and language. ¹⁰ He wrote in the name of the King Ahasuerus and sealed it with the King's signet. He sent letters by couriers on horseback, riders of swift mules bred of mares, ¹¹ to the effect that the King had permitted the Jews of every single city to organize and defend themselves; to destroy, slay, and exterminate every armed force of any people or province that threaten them, along with their children and women, and to plunder their possessions, ¹² on a single day in all the provinces of King Ahasuerus, namely, upon the thirteenth day of the twelfth month, that is, the month of Adar. ¹³ The contents of the document were to be promulgated in every province, and be published to all peoples so that the Jews should be ready on that day to avenge themselves

8. The Holy One, Blessed is He, now performed an unprecedented miracle. Was there ever in history such a miracle that Israel should wreak vengeance on the other nations and do with their enemies as they pleased? *(Midrash).*

11. Only by organizing and unifying themselves in begging for God's assistance could the Jews be victorious despite being seriously outnumbered.

°עֲתוּדִים֩ לַיּ֨וֹם הַזֶּ֜ה לְהִנָּקֵ֤ם מֵאֹֽיְבֵיהֶ֔ם: הָרָצִ֞ים °עֲתִידִים ק' יד

רֹכְבֵ֤י הָרֶ֙כֶשׁ֙ הָֽאֲחַשְׁתְּרָנִ֔ים יָֽצְא֥וּ מְבֹֽהָלִ֖ים

וּדְחוּפִ֑ים בִּדְבַ֣ר הַמֶּ֑לֶךְ וְהַדָּ֥ת נִתְּנָ֖ה בְּשׁוּשַׁ֥ן

הַבִּירָֽה: וּמָרְדֳּכַ֞י יָצָ֣א טו

מִלִּפְנֵ֣י הַמֶּ֗לֶךְ בִּלְב֤וּשׁ מַלְכוּת֙ תְּכֵ֣לֶת וָח֔וּר

וַֽעֲטֶ֤רֶת זָהָב֙ גְּדוֹלָ֔ה וְתַכְרִ֥יךְ בּ֖וּץ וְאַרְגָּמָ֑ן וְהָעִ֣יר

שׁוּשָׁ֔ן צָֽהֲלָ֖ה וְשָׂמֵֽחָה: לַיְּהוּדִ֕ים הָֽיְתָ֖ה אוֹרָ֣ה טז

וְשִׂמְחָ֑ה וְשָׂשֹׂ֖ן וִיקָֽר: וּבְכָל־מְדִינָ֣ה וּמְדִינָ֗ה יז

וּבְכָל־עִ֣יר וָעִ֡יר מְקוֹם֩ אֲשֶׁ֨ר דְּבַר־הַמֶּ֤לֶךְ וְדָתוֹ֙

מַגִּ֔יעַ שִׂמְחָ֤ה וְשָׂשׂוֹן֙ לַיְּהוּדִ֔ים מִשְׁתֶּ֖ה וְי֣וֹם ט֑וֹב

וְרַבִּ֞ים מֵֽעַמֵּ֤י הָאָ֙רֶץ֙ מִתְיַֽהֲדִ֔ים כִּֽי־נָפַ֥ל פַּֽחַד־

הַיְּהוּדִ֖ים עֲלֵיהֶֽם: וּבִשְׁנֵים֩ עָשָׂ֨ר חֹ֜דֶשׁ הוּא־חֹ֣דֶשׁ ט א

אֲדָ֗ר בִּשְׁלוֹשָׁ֨ה עָשָׂ֥ר יוֹם֙ בּ֔וֹ אֲשֶׁ֨ר הִגִּ֧יעַ דְּבַר־

הַמֶּ֛לֶךְ וְדָת֖וֹ לְהֵֽעָשׂ֑וֹת בַּיּ֗וֹם אֲשֶׁ֨ר שִׂבְּר֜וּ אֹֽיְבֵ֤י

הַיְּהוּדִים֙ לִשְׁל֣וֹט בָּהֶ֔ם וְנַֽהֲפ֣וֹךְ ה֔וּא אֲשֶׁ֨ר יִשְׁלְט֧וּ

הַיְּהוּדִ֛ים הֵ֖מָּה בְּשֹֽׂנְאֵיהֶֽם: נִקְהֲל֣וּ הַיְּהוּדִ֗ים ב

בְּעָֽרֵיהֶ֗ם בְּכָל־מְדִינוֹת֙ הַמֶּ֣לֶךְ אֲחַשְׁוֵר֔וֹשׁ לִשְׁלֹ֣חַ

יָ֔ד בִּמְבַקְשֵׁ֖י רָֽעָתָ֑ם וְאִישׁ֙ לֹֽא־עָמַ֣ד לִפְנֵיהֶ֔ם כִּֽי־

נָפַ֥ל פַּחְדָּ֖ם עַל־כָּל־הָֽעַמִּֽים: וְכָל־שָׂרֵ֣י הַמְּדִינ֡וֹת ג

וְהָֽאֲחַשְׁדַּרְפְּנִ֣ים וְהַפַּחוֹת֩ וְעֹשֵׂ֨י הַמְּלָאכָ֜ה אֲשֶׁ֣ר

לַמֶּ֗לֶךְ מְנַשְּׂאִ֖ים אֶת־הַיְּהוּדִ֑ים כִּֽי־נָפַ֥ל פַּֽחַד־

מָרְדֳּכַ֖י עֲלֵיהֶֽם: כִּֽי־גָד֤וֹל מָרְדֳּכַי֙ בְּבֵ֣ית הַמֶּ֔לֶךְ ד

וְשָׁמְע֖וֹ הוֹלֵ֣ךְ בְּכָל־הַמְּדִינ֑וֹת כִּֽי־הָאִ֥ישׁ מָרְדֳּכַ֖י

הוֹלֵ֥ךְ וְגָדֽוֹל: וַיַּכּ֤וּ הַיְּהוּדִים֙ בְּכָל־אֹ֣יְבֵיהֶ֔ם מַכַּת־ ה

חֶ֥רֶב וְהֶ֖רֶג וְאַבְדָּ֑ן וַיַּֽעֲשׂ֥וּ בְשֹֽׂנְאֵיהֶ֖ם כִּרְצוֹנָֽם:

וּבְשׁוּשַׁ֣ן הַבִּירָ֗ה הָֽרְג֤וּ הַיְּהוּדִים֙ וְאַבֵּ֔ד חֲמֵ֥שׁ ו

on their enemies. ¹⁴ The couriers, riders of swift mules, went forth in urgent haste by order of the King, and the edict was distributed in Shushan the Capitol.

15-16. These are among the four verses recited aloud in the synagogue by the congregation during the public reading of the Megillah.

16. Rav Yehudah said: אוֹרָה, *light,* refers to Torah; שִׂמְחָה, *gladness,* refers to holiday; שָׂשֹׂן, *joy,* refers to circumcision; and יְקָר, *honor,* refers to תְּפִילִין, *tefillin* [i.e., they were finally able to resume the study of Torah and the performance of *mitzvos* without hindrance] *(Talmud).*

[Some commentators say that the amusing Purim custom of masquerading in outlandish costumes is derived from this verse. Just as non-Jews 'masqueraded' as proselytes in order to curry favor, so we masquerade merrily to commemorate the miracle.]

9/1. THE TURNABOUT: THE JEWS AVENGE THEMSELVES

¹⁵ Mordechai left the King's presence clad in royal apparel of blue and white with a large gold crown and a robe of fine linen and purple; then the city of Shushan was cheerful and glad. ¹⁶ The Jews had light and gladness, and joy and honor. ¹⁷ Likewise, in every province, and in every city, wherever the King's command and his decree reached, the Jews had gladness and joy, a feast and a holiday. Moreover, many from among the people of the land professed themselves Jews, for the fear of the Jews had fallen upon them.

¹ And so, on the thirteenth day of the twelfth month, which is the month of Adar, when the King's command and edict were about to be enforced — on the very day that the enemies of the Jews expected to gain the upper hand over them — and it was turned about: The Jews gained the upper hand over their adversaries; ² the Jews organized themselves in their cities throughout all the provinces of King Ahasuerus, to attack those who sought their hurt; and no one stood in their way, for fear of them had fallen upon all the peoples. ³ Moreover, all the provincial officials, satraps, and governors and those that conduct the King's affairs, deferred to the Jews because the fear of Mordechai had fallen upon them. ⁴ For Mordechai was now preeminent in the royal palace and his fame was spreading throughout all the provinces, for the man Mordechai grew increasingly greater. ⁵ And the Jews struck at all their enemies with the sword, slaughtering and annihilating; they treated their enemies as they pleased. ⁶ In Shushan the Capitol, the Jews slew and annihilated five

וְאֶת|	ז מֵא֥וֹת אִֽישׁ:
וְאֶת|	פַּרְשַׁנְדָּ֖תָא
וְאֶת|	דַּֽלְפ֑וֹן
וְאֶת|	ח אַסְפָּֽתָא:
וְאֶת|	פּוֹרָ֖תָא
וְאֶת|	אֲדַלְיָ֑א
וְאֶת|	ט אֲרִידָֽתָא:
וְאֶת|	פַּרְמַ֖שְׁתָּא
וְאֶת|	אֲרִיסַ֑י
וְאֶת|	אֲרִדַ֖י
עֲשֶׂ֜רֶת	י וַיְזָֽתָא:

בְּנֵ֨י הָמָ֧ן בֶּֽן־הַמְּדָ֛תָא צֹרֵ֥ר הַיְּהוּדִ֖ים הָרָ֑גוּ וּבַ֨בִּזָּ֔ה

יא לֹ֥א שָֽׁלְח֖וּ אֶת־יָדָֽם: בַּיּ֣וֹם הַה֗וּא בָּ֣א מִסְפַּ֞ר

הַֽהֲרוּגִ֛ים בְּשׁוּשַׁ֥ן הַבִּירָ֖ה לִפְנֵ֥י הַמֶּֽלֶךְ: יב וַיֹּ֨אמֶר

הַמֶּ֜לֶךְ לְאֶסְתֵּ֣ר הַמַּלְכָּ֗ה בְּשׁוּשַׁ֣ן הַבִּירָ֡ה הָרְג֩וּ

הַיְּהוּדִ֨ים וְאַבֵּ֜ד חֲמֵ֧שׁ מֵא֣וֹת אִ֗ישׁ וְאֵת֙ עֲשֶׂ֣רֶת

בְּנֵֽי־הָמָ֔ן בִּשְׁאָ֛ר מְדִינ֥וֹת הַמֶּ֖לֶךְ מֶ֣ה עָשׂ֑וּ וּמַה־

שְּׁאֵֽלָתֵךְ֙ וְיִנָּ֣תֵֽן לָ֔ךְ וּמַה־בַּקָּשָׁתֵ֥ךְ ע֖וֹד וְתֵעָֽשׂ:

יג וַתֹּ֤אמֶר אֶסְתֵּר֙ אִם־עַל־הַמֶּ֣לֶךְ ט֔וֹב יִנָּתֵ֣ן גַּם־

מָחָ֗ר לַיְּהוּדִים֙ אֲשֶׁ֣ר בְּשׁוּשָׁ֔ן לַעֲשׂ֖וֹת כְּדָ֣ת הַיּ֑וֹם

וְאֵ֛ת עֲשֶׂ֥רֶת בְּנֵֽי־הָמָ֖ן יִתְל֥וּ עַל־הָעֵֽץ: יד וַיֹּ֤אמֶר

הַמֶּ֨לֶךְ֙ לְהֵֽעָשׂ֣וֹת כֵּ֔ן וַתִּנָּתֵ֥ן דָּ֖ת בְּשׁוּשָׁ֑ן וְאֵ֛ת

עֲשֶׂ֥רֶת בְּנֵֽי־הָמָ֖ן תָּלֽוּ: טו וַיִּקָּהֲל֞וּ °הַיְּהוּדִיים֙ אֲשֶׁר־ | °הַיְּהוּדִ֖ים ק' טו

בְּשׁוּשָׁ֗ן גַּ֠ם בְּי֣וֹם אַרְבָּעָ֤ה עָשָׂר֙ לְחֹ֣דֶשׁ אֲדָ֔ר

וַיַּֽהַרְג֣וּ בְשׁוּשָׁ֔ן שְׁלֹ֥שׁ מֵא֖וֹת אִ֑ישׁ וּבַ֨בִּזָּ֔ה לֹ֥א

טז שָֽׁלְח֖וּ אֶת־יָדָֽם: וּשְׁאָ֣ר הַיְּהוּדִ֗ים אֲשֶׁר֙ בִּמְדִינ֣וֹת

7. The ten sons of Haman and the word עֲשֶׂרֶת, *ten*, which follows, should be said [by the one reading the *Megillah* on Purim] in one breath … to indicate that they all died together *(Talmud).*

9. The letter Vav [ו] of *Vayzasa* is enlarged in the *Megillah* like a long pole to indicate that they were all strung [one underneath the other] on one long pole *(Talmud).*

10. It was obviously most difficult for poor Jews to restrain themselves from taking spoils. In reward for their restraint, it was established that, throughout all generations, the poor — without exception and investigation as to need — will be the recipients of מַתָּנוֹת לָאֶבְיוֹנִים, *gifts to the poor,* on Purim *(Rebbe of Ger).*

13. THE JEWS IN SHUSHAN ARE GRANTED A SECOND DAY

hundred men.   ⁷ including

Parshandasa   and

Dalphon   and

Aspasa   ⁸ and

Porasa   and

Adalia   and

Aridasa   ⁹ and

Parmashta   and

Arisai   and

Aridai   and

Vayzasa   ¹⁰ the ten

sons of Haman, son of Hammedasa, the Jews' enemy; but they did not lay their hand on the spoils.

¹¹ That same day the number of those killed in Shushan the Capitol was reported to the King. ¹² The King said onto Queen Esther: 'In Shushan the Capitol the Jews have slain and annihilated five hundred men as well as the ten sons of Haman; what must they have done in the rest of the King's provinces! What is your request now? It shall be granted you. What is your petition further? It shall be fulfilled.' ¹³ Esther replied: 'If it pleases His Majesty, allow the Jews who are in Shushan to act tomorrow as they did today, and let Haman's ten sons be hanged on the gallows.' ¹⁴ The King ordered that this be done. A decree was distributed in Shushan, and they hanged Haman's tens sons. ¹⁵ The Jews that were in Shushan assembled again on the fourteenth day of the month of Adar, and slew three hundred men in Shushan; but they did not lay their hand on the spoils.

¹⁶ The rest of the Jews throughout the King's provinces organized and defended themselves

הַמֶּ֖לֶךְ נִקְהֲל֑וּ | וְעָמֹ֤ד עַל־נַפְשָׁם֙ וְנ֔וֹחַ מֵאֹ֣יְבֵיהֶ֔ם
וְהָרֹ֔וֹג בְּשֹׂ֣נְאֵיהֶ֔ם חֲמִשָּׁ֥ה וְשִׁבְעִ֖ים אָ֑לֶף וּבַ֨בִּזָּ֔ה

יז לֹ֥א שָׁלְח֖וּ אֶת־יָדָ֑ם: בְּיוֹם־שְׁלוֹשָׁ֤ה עָשָׂר֙ לְחֹ֣דֶשׁ
אֲדָ֔ר וְנ֕וֹחַ בְּאַרְבָּעָ֥ה עָשָׂ֖ר בּ֑וֹ וְעָשֹׂ֣ה אֹת֔וֹ י֖וֹם
מִשְׁתֶּ֥ה וְשִׂמְחָֽה: °וְהַיְּהוּדִ֤ים אֲשֶׁר־בְּשׁוּשָׁ֔ן   °וְהַיְּהוּדִ֖ים ק' יח

נִקְהֲל֗וּ בִּשְׁלוֹשָׁ֤ה עָשָׂר֙ בּ֔וֹ וּבְאַרְבָּעָ֥ה עָשָׂ֖ר בּ֑וֹ
וְנ֕וֹחַ בַּחֲמִשָּׁ֥ה עָשָׂ֖ר בּ֑וֹ וְעָשֹׂ֣ה אֹת֔וֹ י֖וֹם מִשְׁתֶּ֥ה

יט וְשִׂמְחָֽה: עַל־כֵּ֞ן הַיְּהוּדִ֣ים °הַפְּרוֹזִים֮ הַיֹּשְׁבִים֒   °הַפְּרָזִ֖ים ק' יט
בְּעָרֵ֣י הַפְּרָז֗וֹת עֹשִׂ֞ים אֵ֣ת י֤וֹם אַרְבָּעָ֤ה עָשָׂר֙
לְחֹ֣דֶשׁ אֲדָ֔ר שִׂמְחָ֥ה וּמִשְׁתֶּ֖ה וְי֣וֹם ט֑וֹב וּמִשְׁלֹ֥חַ

כ מָנ֖וֹת אִ֣ישׁ לְרֵעֵֽהוּ: וַיִּכְתֹּ֣ב מׇרְדֳּכַ֔י אֶת־הַדְּבָרִ֖ים
הָאֵ֑לֶּה וַיִּשְׁלַ֣ח סְפָרִ֗ים אֶל־כׇּל־הַיְּהוּדִים֙ אֲשֶׁר֙
בְּכׇל־מְדִינוֹת֙ הַמֶּ֣לֶךְ אֲחַשְׁוֵר֔וֹשׁ הַקְּרוֹבִ֖ים

כא וְהָרְחוֹקִֽים: לְקַיֵּם֙ עֲלֵיהֶ֔ם לִהְי֣וֹת עֹשִׂ֗ים אֵ֠ת י֣וֹם
אַרְבָּעָ֤ה עָשָׂר֙ לְחֹ֣דֶשׁ אֲדָ֔ר וְאֵ֛ת יוֹם־חֲמִשָּׁ֥ה

כב עָשָׂ֖ר בּ֑וֹ בְּכׇל־שָׁנָ֥ה וְשָׁנָֽה: כַּיָּמִ֗ים אֲשֶׁר־נָ֨חוּ בָהֶ֤ם
הַיְּהוּדִים֙ מֵאֹ֣יְבֵיהֶ֔ם וְהַחֹ֗דֶשׁ אֲשֶׁר֩ נֶהְפַּ֨ךְ לָהֶ֤ם
מִיָּגוֹן֙ לְשִׂמְחָ֔ה וּמֵאֵ֖בֶל לְי֣וֹם ט֑וֹב לַעֲשֹׂ֣ות אוֹתָ֗ם
יְמֵ֤י מִשְׁתֶּה֙ וְשִׂמְחָ֔ה וּמִשְׁלֹ֤חַ מָנוֹת֙ אִ֣ישׁ לְרֵעֵ֔הוּ

כג וּמַתָּנ֖וֹת לָֽאֶבְיוֹנִֽים: וְקִבֵּל֙ הַיְּהוּדִ֔ים אֵ֛ת אֲשֶׁר־
הֵחֵ֖לּוּ לַעֲשֹׂ֑ות וְאֵ֛ת אֲשֶׁר־כָּתַ֥ב מׇרְדֳּכַ֖י אֲלֵיהֶֽם:

כד כִּי֩ הָמָ֨ן בֶּֽן־הַמְּדָ֜תָא הָֽאֲגָגִ֗י צֹרֵר֙ כׇּל־הַיְּהוּדִ֔ים
חָשַׁ֥ב עַל־הַיְּהוּדִ֖ים לְאַבְּדָ֑ם וְהִפִּ֥ל פּוּר֙ ה֣וּא

כה הַגּוֹרָ֔ל לְהֻמָּ֖ם וּֽלְאַבְּדָֽם: וּבְבֹאָהּ֮ לִפְנֵ֣י הַמֶּ֒לֶךְ֒
אָמַ֣ר עִם־הַסֵּ֔פֶר יָשׁ֞וּב מַחֲשַׁבְתּ֧וֹ הָרָעָ֛ה אֲשֶׁר־
חָשַׁ֥ב עַל־הַיְּהוּדִ֖ים עַל־רֹאשׁ֑וֹ וְתָל֥וּ אֹת֛וֹ וְאֶת־

gaining relief from their foes, slaying seventy-five thousand of their enemies — but they did not lay their hand on the spoils. 17 That was the thirteenth day of the month of Adar; and they gained relief on the fourteenth day, making it a day of feasting and gladness. 18 But the Jews that were in Shushan assembled on both the thirteenth and fourteenth, and they gained relief on the fifteenth, making it a day of feasting and gladness. 19 That is why Jewish villagers who live in unwalled towns celebrate the fourteenth day of the month of Adar as an occasion of gladness and feasting, for holiday-making and for sending delicacies to one another.

19. The law of 'Shushan Purim' — celebrating Purim on the fifteenth day of Adar in walled cities in commemoration of the victory in Shushan — is not specifically stated in the Megillah. It is implied in verses 19 and 21 and so established by the Rabbis.

20 Mordechai recorded these events and sent letters to all the Jews throughout the provinces of King Ahasuerus, near and far, 21 charging them that they should observe annually the fourteenth and fifteenth days of Adar, 22 as the days on which the Jews gained relief from their enemies, and the month which had been transformed for them from one of sorrow to gladness, and from mourning to festivity. They were to observe them as days of feasting and gladness, and for sending delicacies to one another, and gifts to the poor. 23 The Jews undertook to continue the practice they had begun, just as Mordechai had prescribed to them.

20. MORDECHAI RECORDS THESE EVENTS AND LEGISLATES ANNUAL COMMEMORATION

He wrote this Megillah exactly as it appears in its present text.

22. *Sending delicacies to one another* — at least two *delicacies*, i.e., ready-to-eat foods [מָנוֹת being plural] to one person. *And gifts to the poor* — this means two gifts to two people [one gift to each of the two, the minimum number of the plural word אֶבְיוֹנִים, *poor*, being two] *(Talmud)*.

24 For Haman, the son of Hammedasa the Agagite, enemy of all the Jews, had plotted to destroy the Jews and had cast a *pur* (that is, the lot) to terrify and destroy them; 25 but when she appeared before the King, he commanded by means of letters that the wicked scheme, which [Haman] had devised against the Jews, should recoil on his own head; and they hanged him and

אסתר ט:כו-י:ג

כו בָּנָיו עַל־הָעֵץ: עַל־כֵּן קָרְאוּ לַיָּמִים הָאֵלֶּה פוּרִים
עַל־שֵׁם הַפּוּר עַל־כֵּן עַל־כָּל־דִּבְרֵי הָאִגֶּרֶת הַזֹּאת

כז וּמָה־רָאוּ עַל־כָּכָה וּמָה הִגִּיעַ אֲלֵיהֶם: קִיְּמוּ
וְקִבְּל הַיְּהוּדִים ׀ עֲלֵיהֶם ׀ וְעַל־זַרְעָם וְעַל כָּל־
הַנִּלְוִים עֲלֵיהֶם וְלֹא יַעֲבוֹר לִהְיוֹת עֹשִׂים אֶת־
שְׁנֵי הַיָּמִים הָאֵלֶּה כִּכְתָבָם וְכִזְמַנָּם בְּכָל־שָׁנָה

כח וְשָׁנָה: וְהַיָּמִים הָאֵלֶּה נִזְכָּרִים וְנַעֲשִׂים בְּכָל־דּוֹר
וָדוֹר מִשְׁפָּחָה וּמִשְׁפָּחָה מְדִינָה וּמְדִינָה וְעִיר
וָעִיר וִימֵי הַפּוּרִים הָאֵלֶּה לֹא יַעַבְרוּ מִתּוֹךְ

כט הַיְּהוּדִים וְזִכְרָם לֹא־יָסוּף מִזַּרְעָם: וַתִּכְתֹּב
אֶסְתֵּר הַמַּלְכָּה בַת־אֲבִיחַיִל וּמָרְדֳּכַי הַיְּהוּדִי
אֶת־כָּל־תֹּקֶף לְקַיֵּם אֵת אִגֶּרֶת הַפֻּרִים הַזֹּאת

ל הַשֵּׁנִית: וַיִּשְׁלַח סְפָרִים אֶל־כָּל־הַיְּהוּדִים אֶל־
שֶׁבַע וְעֶשְׂרִים וּמֵאָה מְדִינָה מַלְכוּת אֲחַשְׁוֵרוֹשׁ

לא דִּבְרֵי שָׁלוֹם וֶאֱמֶת: לְקַיֵּם אֶת־יְמֵי הַפֻּרִים הָאֵלֶּה
בִּזְמַנֵּיהֶם כַּאֲשֶׁר קִיַּם עֲלֵיהֶם מָרְדֳּכַי הַיְּהוּדִי
וְאֶסְתֵּר הַמַּלְכָּה וְכַאֲשֶׁר קִיְּמוּ עַל־נַפְשָׁם

לב וְעַל־זַרְעָם דִּבְרֵי הַצּוֹמוֹת וְזַעֲקָתָם: וּמַאֲמַר
אֶסְתֵּר קִיַּם דִּבְרֵי הַפֻּרִים הָאֵלֶּה וְנִכְתָּב
בַּסֵּפֶר: וַיָּשֶׂם הַמֶּלֶךְ °אֲחַשְׁרֹשׁ ׀ מַס י א

°אֲחַשְׁוֵרוֹשׁ ק׳

ב עַל־הָאָרֶץ וְאִיֵּי הַיָּם: וְכָל־מַעֲשֵׂה תָקְפּוֹ וּגְבוּרָתוֹ
וּפָרָשַׁת גְּדֻלַּת מָרְדֳּכַי אֲשֶׁר גִּדְּלוֹ הַמֶּלֶךְ הֲלוֹא־
הֵם כְּתוּבִים עַל־סֵפֶר דִּבְרֵי הַיָּמִים לְמַלְכֵי מָדַי

ג וּפָרָס: כִּי ׀ מָרְדֳּכַי הַיְּהוּדִי מִשְׁנֶה לַמֶּלֶךְ
אֲחַשְׁוֵרוֹשׁ וְגָדוֹל לַיְּהוּדִים וְרָצוּי לְרֹב אֶחָיו
דֹּרֵשׁ טוֹב לְעַמּוֹ וְדֹבֵר שָׁלוֹם לְכָל־זַרְעוֹ:

27. Confirmed and undertook —
i.e., they confirmed what they had
undertaken long before at Sinai
(Talmud).

28. 'Even if all the festivals should
be annulled, Purim will never be
annulled' (Midrash).

29. וַתִּכְתֹּב — Wrote. The letter ת in
this word is enlarged to indicate
that just as the ת is the last letter of
the alphabet, so is the story of
Esther the end of all the miracles to
be included in the Bible (Talmud).

10/1. EPILOGUE

With the salvation of the Jews,
affairs of state returned to normal.
Under Mordechai, the empire grew
stronger.

3. With the mention of שָׁלוֹם,
welfare [literally peace], and a
picture of the stature and security
of the Jews under Mordechai, the
Megillah closes.

The last verse is among the four
verses recited aloud by the
congregation during the reading of
the Megillah in the synagogue.
Among the reasons offered for this
widespread custom are: to
popularize the miracle
[פִּירְסוּמֵי נִיסָא]; these verses express
the essence of the miracle; and to
keep the children alert and prevent
them from dozing off. The
congregation recites the verses
loudly as an expression of the joy of
the day. The reader then repeats
the verses because each verse must
be read from a halachically valid
Megillah scroll.

his sons on the gallows. ²⁶ That is why they called
these days "Purim" from the word "pur." Therefore,
because of all that was written in this letter, and
because of what they had experienced, and what
has happened to them, ²⁷ the Jews confirmed and
undertook upon themselves, and their posterity,
and upon all who might join them, to observe these
two days, without fail, in the manner prescribed,
and at the proper time each year. ²⁸ Consequently,
these days should be remembered and celebrated
by every single generation, family, province, and
city; and these days of Purim should never cease
among the Jews, nor shall their remembrance
perish from their descendants.

²⁹ Then Queen Esther, daughter of Avichail, and
Mordechai the Jew, wrote with full authority to ratify
this second letter of Purim. ³⁰ Dispatches were sent
to all the Jews, to the hundred and twenty-seven
provinces of the kingdom of Ahasuerus — with
words of peace and truth — ³¹ to establish these
days of Purim on their proper dates just as
Mordechai the Jew and Queen Esther had enjoined
them, and as they had undertook upon themselves
and their posterity the matter of the fasts and their
lamentations. ³² Esther's ordinance validated these
regulations for Purim; and it was recorded in the
book.

¹ King Ahasuerus levied taxes on both the
mainland and the islands. ² All his mighty and
powerful acts, and a full account of the greatness of
Mordechai, whom the King had promoted, are
recorded in the book of chronicles of the Kings of
Media and Persia. ³ For Mordechai the Jew was
viceroy to King Ahasuerus; he was a great man
among the Jews, and popular with the multitude of
his brethren; he sought the good of his people and
was concerned for the welfare of all his posterity.

If a *minyan* is present for the *Megillah* reading, the following blessing is recited after the reading.

בָּרוּךְ אַתָּה יהוה אֱלֹהֵינוּ מֶלֶךְ הָעוֹלָם, הָרָב אֶת רִיבֵנוּ, וְהַדָּן אֶת דִּינֵנוּ, וְהַנּוֹקֵם אֶת נִקְמָתֵנוּ, וְהַמְשַׁלֵּם גְּמוּל לְכָל אֹיְבֵי נַפְשֵׁנוּ, וְהַנִּפְרָע לָנוּ מִצָּרֵנוּ. בָּרוּךְ אַתָּה יהוה, הַנִּפְרָע לְעַמּוֹ יִשְׂרָאֵל מִכָּל צָרֵיהֶם, הָאֵל הַמּוֹשִׁיעַ. (Cong.—אָמֵן.)

The following poetic narrative of the Purim story is recited only after the evening *Megillah* reading.
After the morning reading continue with, שׁוֹשַׁנַּת יַעֲקֹב, below.

אֲשֶׁר הֵנִיא עֲצַת גּוֹיִם, וַיָּפֶר מַחְשְׁבוֹת עֲרוּמִים.
בְּקוּם עָלֵינוּ אָדָם רָשָׁע, נֵצֶר זָדוֹן, מִזֶּרַע עֲמָלֵק.
גָּאָה בְעָשְׁרוֹ, וְכָרָה לוֹ בוֹר, וּגְדֻלָּתוֹ יָקְשָׁה לּוֹ לָכֶד.
דִּמָּה בְנַפְשׁוֹ לִלְכֹּד, וְנִלְכַּד, בִּקֵּשׁ לְהַשְׁמִיד, וְנִשְׁמַד מְהֵרָה.
הָמָן הוֹדִיעַ אֵיבַת אֲבוֹתָיו, וְעוֹרֵר שִׂנְאַת אַחִים לַבָּנִים.
וְלֹא זָכַר רַחֲמֵי שָׁאוּל, כִּי בְחֶמְלָתוֹ עַל אֲגָג נוֹלַד אוֹיֵב.
זָמַם רָשָׁע לְהַכְרִית צַדִּיק, וְנִלְכַּד טָמֵא, בִּידֵי טָהוֹר.
חֶסֶד גָּבַר עַל שִׁגְגַת אָב, וְרָשָׁע הוֹסִיף חֵטְא עַל חֲטָאָיו.
טָמַן בְּלִבּוֹ מַחְשְׁבוֹת עֲרוּמָיו, וַיִּתְמַכֵּר לַעֲשׂוֹת רָעָה.
יָדוֹ שָׁלַח בִּקְדוֹשֵׁי אֵל, כַּסְפּוֹ נָתַן לְהַכְרִית זִכְרָם.
כִּרְאוֹת מָרְדְּכַי, כִּי יָצָא קֶצֶף, וְדָתֵי הָמָן נִתְּנוּ בְשׁוּשָׁן.
לָבַשׁ שַׂק וְקָשַׁר מִסְפֵּד, וְגָזַר צוֹם, וַיֵּשֶׁב עַל הָאֵפֶר.
מִי זֶה יַעֲמֹד לְכַפֵּר שְׁגָגָה, וְלִמְחֹל חַטַּאת עֲוֹן אֲבוֹתֵינוּ.
נֵץ פָּרַח מִלּוּלָב, הֵן הֲדַסָּה עָמְדָה לְעוֹרֵר יְשֵׁנִים.
סָרִיסֶיהָ הִבְהִילוּ לְהָמָן, לְהַשְׁקוֹתוֹ יֵין חֲמַת תַּנִּינִים.
עָמַד בְּעָשְׁרוֹ, וְנָפַל בְּרִשְׁעוֹ, עָשָׂה לּוֹ עֵץ, וְנִתְלָה עָלָיו.
פִּיהֶם פָּתְחוּ, כָּל יוֹשְׁבֵי תֵבֵל, כִּי פוּר הָמָן נֶהְפַּךְ לְפוּרֵנוּ.
צַדִּיק נֶחֱלַץ מִיַּד רָשָׁע, אוֹיֵב נִתַּן תַּחַת נַפְשׁוֹ.
קִיְּמוּ עֲלֵיהֶם, לַעֲשׂוֹת פּוּרִים, וְלִשְׂמֹחַ בְּכָל שָׁנָה וְשָׁנָה.
רָאִיתָ אֶת תְּפִלַּת מָרְדְּכַי וְאֶסְתֵּר, הָמָן וּבָנָיו עַל הָעֵץ תָּלִיתָ.

The following is recited after both *Megillah* readings.

שׁוֹשַׁנַּת יַעֲקֹב צָהֲלָה וְשָׂמֵחָה, בִּרְאוֹתָם יַחַד תְּכֵלֶת מָרְדְּכָי.
תְּשׁוּעָתָם הָיִיתָ לָנֶצַח, וְתִקְוָתָם בְּכָל דּוֹר וָדוֹר.
לְהוֹדִיעַ, שֶׁכָּל קֹוֶיךָ לֹא יֵבֹשׁוּ, וְלֹא יִכָּלְמוּ לָנֶצַח כָּל הַחוֹסִים בָּךְ.
אָרוּר הָמָן, אֲשֶׁר בִּקֵּשׁ לְאַבְּדִי, בָּרוּךְ מָרְדְּכַי הַיְּהוּדִי. אֲרוּרָה זֶרֶשׁ, אֵשֶׁת מַפְחִידִי, בְּרוּכָה אֶסְתֵּר בַּעֲדִי, וְגַם חַרְבוֹנָה זָכוּר לַטּוֹב.

ESTHER

If a Minyan is present for the Megillah reading, the following blessing is recited after the reading.

Blessed are You, Hashem, our God, King of the universe, Who takes up our grievance, judges our claim, avenges our wrong; exacts vengeance for us from our foes, and Who brings just retribution upon all enemies of our soul. Blessed are you Hashem, Who exacts vengeance for His people Israel from all their foes, the God Who brings salvation. (Cong.—Amen.)

The following poetic narrative of the Purim story is recited only after the evening Megillah reading. After the morning reading continue with, 'The Rose of Jacob,' below.

א Who balked the counsel of the nations and annulled the designs of the cunning,
ב When a wicked man stood up against us,
    a wantonly evil branch of Amalek's offspring.
ג Haughty with his wealth he dug himself a grave,
    and his very greatness snared him in a trap.
ד Fancying to trap, he became entrapped;
    attempting to destroy, he was swiftly destroyed.
ה Haman showed his forebears' enmity,
    and aroused the brotherly hate of Esau on the children.
ו He would not remember Saul's compassion,
    that through his pity on Agag the foe was born.
ז The wicked one conspired to cut away the righteous,
    but the impure one was trapped in the pure one's hands.
ח Kindness overcame the father's error, and the wicked one piled sin on sins.
ט In his heart he hid his cunning thoughts, and devoted himself to evildoing.
י He stretched his hand against God's holy ones,
    he spent his silver to destroy their memory.
כ When Mordecai saw the wrath commence,
    and Haman's decrees be issued in Shushan,
ל He put on sackcloth and bound himself in mourning,
    decreed a fast and sat on ashes:
מ 'Who would arise to atone for error, to gain forgiveness for our ancestors' sins?'
נ A blossom bloomed from a lulav branch — behold!
    Hadassah stood up to arouse the sleeping.
ס Her servants hastened Haman, to serve him wine of serpent's poison.
ע He stood tall through his wealth and toppled through his evil —
    he built the gallows on which he was hung.
פ The earth's inhabitants opened their mouths, for Haman's lot became our Purim,
צ The righteous man was saved from the wicked's hand;
    the foe was substituted for him.
ק They undertook to establish Purim, to rejoice in every single year.
ר You noted the prayer of Mordechai and Esther;
    Haman and his sons You hung on the gallows.

The following is recited after both Megillah readings.

ש The Rose of Jacob was cheerful and glad,
    when they jointly saw Mordechai robed in royal blue.
ת You have been their eternal salvation, and their hope throughout generations.
To make known that all who hope in You will not be shamed; nor ever be humiliated, those taking refuge in You. Accursed be Haman who sought to destroy me, blessed be Mordechai the Jew. Accursed be Zeresh the wife of my terrorizer, blessed be Esther [who sacrificed] for me — and Charbonah, too, be remembered for good.

שיר השירים

shir hashirim

A Song of Love

Without question, King Solomon's Song of Songs, *Shir HaShirim*, is one of the most difficult books of Scripture — not because it is so hard to understand but because it is so easy to misunderstand. Not only is it a love song, it is a love song of uncommon passion. No other book seems to be so out of place among the twenty-four books of prophecy and sacred spirit. Even harder to understand is how one of the greatest and holiest of all the Sages of the Talmud, Rabbi Akiva, would say, 'All of the songs [of Scripture] are holy, but *Shir HaShirim* is holy of holies.' How is a 'love song' holy?

This question is perplexing only if *Shir HaShirim* is taken literally, but neither the Sages nor the commentators do so. The Song is an allegory. It is the duet of love between God and Israel. Its verses are so saturated with meaning that nearly every one of the major commentators finds new themes in its beautiful but cryptic words. All agree, however, that the true and simple meaning of *Shir HaShirim* is the allegorical meaning. The literal meaning of the words is so far from their meaning that it is false.

That is why our translation of *Shir HaShirim* is completely different from any other ArtScroll translation. We translate it according to *Rashi's* allegorical interpretation. As he writes in his own introduction:

> Solomon foresaw through רוּחַ הַקֹּדֶשׁ, *the Holy Spirit,* that Israel is destined to suffer a series of exiles and will lament, nostalgically recalling her former status as God's chosen beloved. She will say, *'I shall return to my first husband* [i.e., to God] *for it was better with me then than now'* [Hoshea 2:9]. The children of Israel will recall His beneficence and *'the trespasses which they trespassed'* [Leviticus 26:40]. And they will recall the goodness which He promised for the End of Days.
>
> The prophets frequently likened the relationship between God and Israel to that of a loving husband angered by a straying wife who betrayed him. Solomon composed *Shir HaShirim* in the form of that same allegory. It is a passionate dialogue* between the husband [God] who still loves his exiled wife [Israel], and a 'veritable widow of a living husband' [*II Samuel* 20:3] who longs

---

* For the reader's convenience, the Hebrew text has not been set with the Masoretic divisions [פְּתוּחוֹת וּסְתוּמוֹת], but in conversational form, i.e., with a new paragraph for each change of speaker. Additionally, commas have been inserted into the text, to facilitate the identification of the Hebrew phrases with their allegorical translations.

for her husband and seeks to endear herself to him once more, as she recalls her youthful love for him and admits her guilt.

God, too, is 'afflicted by her afflictions' [Isaiah 63:9], and He recalls the kindness of her youth, her beauty, and her skillful deeds for which He loved her [Israel] so. He proclaimed that He has 'not afflicted her capriciously' [Lamentations 3:33], nor is she cast away permanently. For she is still His 'wife' and He her 'husband,' and He will yet return to her.

During the mid-nineteenth century period of the most vicious Czarist persecutions of Jews, it was common for the leading rabbis to visit St. Petersburg to plead the case of their people with the Czar's ministers. During one of these visits a Russian official asked one of the rabbis how he could account for the many Aggadic tales in the Talmud which were patently 'inconceivable.'

The rabbi answered, 'You know very well that the Czar and his advisors have often planned decrees that would order the expulsion of the Jews. If God had not thwarted your plans, the decree would have been written and placed before the Czar for his signature. He would have dipped his pen into the inkwell and signed. His signature would have made final the greatest Jewish catastrophe in centuries. A poet might write that a drop of ink drowned three million people. All of us would have understood what he meant. But a hundred years later, someone might read it and consider it nonsense. Could a small drop of ink drown people? In truth, the expression is apt and pithy; it is only a lack of knowledge that could lead a reader to dismiss it out of hand. So it is with many parables of our Sages. They were written in the form of far-fetched stories to conceal their meaning from those unqualified to understand. Those same unqualified people laugh at the stories, instead of lamenting their own puny stature. (See also *Maamar al HaAggados* by *Rabbi Moshe Chaim Luzzatto*.)

In general history as well, many figures of speech have an obvious meaning to those familiar with them, but would be incomprehensible to the uninitiated. Everyone knows that a shot cannot be heard more than several hundred yards away. But every American knows that 'a shot heard round the world' began the American Revolution.

We can understand that *Shir HaShirim* is an allegory, but why should Solomon have chosen to use the vehicle of an explicit love song?

It has been said that the Hebrew word for love, אהבה, is related to the Aramaic word הב, *give*. To love is to give. Love in its truest form is selfless; to whatever extent it is self-serving it is not love at all.

The love between man and woman is the prime example of a human

being's capacity for selflessness. That is why *Reishis Chochmah*, the classic medieval book of ethics and fear of God, states that the love between man and woman is the greatest human expression of man's love for God. In that sense, therefore, such human love is truly an allegory, and the truth it attempts to portray is Israel's love for God and His love for Israel.

Shir HaShirim is read on Pesach because the Sages interpret it as the story of Israel after the Exodus, a time of such great spiritual passion, that God said many centuries later: *I remember for your sake the kindness of your youth, the love of your bridal days, how you followed Me in the Wilderness in an unsown land (Jeremiah 2:2).*

It is surely not coincidental that, of all the Sages, it was Rabbi Akiva who transmitted this perception to us. His story is well known. At the age of forty he was an unlearned shepherd who so despised Torah scholars that he would have violently attacked them had he been given the opportunity. Rachel, daughter of one of Israel's wealthiest men, saw a hidden spark in the lowly shepherd. Because she married him she was disinherited, ostracized by her family, and forced to live in the most abject poverty. Her husband began to study Torah and she sent him to learn in the academies of Rabbi Eliezer and Rabbi Yehoshua, the great sages of the time.

Twenty-four years later, *Rabbi* Akiva, teacher of all Israel, returned with twenty-four thousand students. Shabbily dressed, Rachel pressed through the welcoming throngs and threw herself at his feet. Rabbi Akiva's students were aghast, infuriated at the stranger's temerity. As they advanced to remove her, Rabbi Akiva waved them away: 'Leave her, for all of my Torah and all of your Torah belong to her.'

In his own life story Rabbi Akiva had seen what selfless devotion was. Because of it, an embittered shepherd became his generation's greatest man. Who was more qualified than Rabbi Akiva to perceive the holiness of Song of Songs?

The message of *Shir HaShirim* is so lofty, so exalted, so spiritual, so holy that God in His infinite wisdom knew that it could be presented to us only in its present form. Only in this manner could it engender the passionate love for God which is Israel's highest mission.

Has it been misinterpreted by fools and twisted by scoundrels? Most assuredly yes! But: לֹא חָשׁ הקב"ה לְהָאִיר הַחַמָּה מִפְּנֵי עוֹבְדֶיהָ, *God did not refrain from creating the sun because it would have worshipers.*

Let us, therefore, read and understand *Shir HaShirim* with the ecstasy of love between God and Israel, for it is this intimacy that it expresses more than any other Song in Scripture.

א

א שִׁיר הַשִּׁירִים אֲשֶׁר לִשְׁלֹמֹה.

ב יִשָּׁקֵנִי מִנְּשִׁיקוֹת פִּיהוּ, כִּי־טוֹבִים דֹּדֶיךָ מִיָּיִן.

ג לְרֵיחַ שְׁמָנֶיךָ טוֹבִים, שֶׁמֶן תּוּרַק שְׁמֶךָ, עַל־כֵּן עֲלָמוֹת אֲהֵבוּךָ.

ד מָשְׁכֵנִי אַחֲרֶיךָ נָּרוּצָה, הֱבִיאַנִי הַמֶּלֶךְ חֲדָרָיו, נָגִילָה וְנִשְׂמְחָה בָּךְ, נַזְכִּירָה דֹדֶיךָ מִיַּיִן, מֵישָׁרִים אֲהֵבוּךָ.

ה שְׁחוֹרָה אֲנִי וְנָאוָה, בְּנוֹת יְרוּשָׁלָיִם, כְּאָהֳלֵי

ו קֵדָר, כִּירִיעוֹת שְׁלֹמֹה. אַל־תִּרְאוּנִי שֶׁאֲנִי שְׁחַרְחֹרֶת, שֶׁשְּׁזָפַתְנִי הַשָּׁמֶשׁ, בְּנֵי אִמִּי נִחֲרוּ־בִי, שָׂמֻנִי נֹטֵרָה אֶת־הַכְּרָמִים, כַּרְמִי שֶׁלִּי לֹא נָטָרְתִּי.

ז הַגִּידָה לִּי, שֶׁאָהֲבָה נַפְשִׁי, אֵיכָה תִרְעֶה, אֵיכָה תַּרְבִּיץ בַּצָּהֳרָיִם, שַׁלָּמָה אֶהְיֶה כְּעֹטְיָה עַל עֶדְרֵי חֲבֵרֶיךָ.

ח אִם־לֹא תֵדְעִי לָךְ, הַיָּפָה בַּנָּשִׁים, צְאִי־לָךְ בְּעִקְבֵי הַצֹּאן, וּרְעִי אֶת־גְּדִיֹּתַיִךְ עַל מִשְׁכְּנוֹת הָרֹעִים.

ט-י לְסֻסָתִי בְּרִכְבֵי פַרְעֹה דִּמִּיתִיךְ, רַעְיָתִי. נָאווּ

יא לְחָיַיִךְ בַּתֹּרִים, צַוָּארֵךְ בַּחֲרוּזִים. תּוֹרֵי זָהָב נַעֲשֶׂה־לָּךְ, עִם נְקֻדּוֹת הַכָּסֶף.

יב-יג עַד־שֶׁהַמֶּלֶךְ בִּמְסִבּוֹ, נִרְדִּי נָתַן רֵיחוֹ. צְרוֹר

יד הַמֹּר | דּוֹדִי לִי, בֵּין שָׁדַי יָלִין. אֶשְׁכֹּל הַכֹּפֶר | דּוֹדִי לִי, בְּכַרְמֵי עֵין גֶּדִי.

טו הִנָּךְ יָפָה, רַעְיָתִי, הִנָּךְ יָפָה, עֵינַיִךְ יוֹנִים.

טז הִנְּךָ יָפֶה, דוֹדִי, אַף נָעִים, אַף־עַרְשֵׂנוּ רַעֲנָנָה.

1/1. PROLOGUE

God, Him to Whom peace belongs. Throughout this Book the word שְׁלֹמֹה standing by itself refers not to Solomon but to שֶׁהַשָּׁלוֹם שֶׁלּוֹ, *Him to Whom peace belongs* [שלמה = שֶׁלּוֹ שָׁלוֹם]; i.e., God, the Source of all peace *(Talmud).*

2-4. ISRAEL IN EXILE TO GOD

5-6. ISRAEL TO THE NATIONS

Jerusalem will one day become the metropolis of all countries and will draw people to her in streams to honor her. Thus the nations of the world are figuratively referred to as 'daughters' of the great metropolis Jerusalem *(Midrash; Rashi).*

7. ISRAEL TO GOD

Israel, allegorized here as a sheep beloved by its shepherd, addresses God directly as a woman addressing her husband, and remonstrates with Him that the exile is too difficult for her and too unbecoming to Him.

8-11. GOD RESPONDS TO ISRAEL

In these verses God continues recounting His beneficence to the Jews while, at the same time, implying their ingratitude.

12-15. ISRAEL ABOUT GOD

16-2:1. ISRAEL TO GOD

¹ The song that excels all songs dedicated to God, the King to Whom peace belongs.

² Communicate Your innermost wisdom to me again in loving closeness, for Your friendship is dearer than all earthly delights. ³ Like the scent of goodly oils is the spreading fame of Your great deeds; Your very name is Flowing Oil, therefore have nations loved You.

⁴ Upon perceiving a mere hint that You wished to draw me, we rushed with perfect faith after You into the wilderness. The King brought me into His cloud-pillared chamber; whatever our travail we shall always be glad and rejoice in Your Torah. We recall Your love more than earthly delights, unrestrainedly do they love You.

⁵ Though I am black with sin, I am comely with virtue, O nations who are destined to ascend to Jerusalem; though sullied as the tents of Kedar, I will be immaculate as the draperies of Him to Whom peace belongs. ⁶ Do not view me with contempt despite my swarthiness, for it is but the sun which has glared upon me. The alien children of my mother were incensed with me and made me a keeper of the vineyards of idols, but the vineyard of my own true God I did not keep.

⁷ Tell me, You Whom my soul loves: Where will You graze Your flock? Where will You rest them under the fiercest sun of harshest Exile? Why shall I be like one veiled in mourning among the flocks of Your fellow shepherds?

⁸ If you know not where to graze, O fairest of nations, follow the footsteps of the sheep — your forefathers who traced a straight, unswerving path after My Torah. Then you can graze your tender kids even among the dwellings of foreign shepherds.

⁹ With My mighty steeds who battled Pharaoh's riders I revealed that you are My beloved. ¹⁰ Your cheeks are lovely with rows of gems, your neck with necklaces — My gifts to you from the splitting sea, ¹¹ by inducing Pharaoh to engage in pursuit, to add circlets of gold to your spangles of silver.

¹² While the King was yet at Sinai my malodorous deed gave forth its scent as my Golden Calf defiled the covenant. ¹³ But my Beloved responded with a bundle of myrrh — the fragrant atonement of erecting a Tabernacle where His Presence would dwell amid the Holy Ark's staves. ¹⁴ Like a cluster of henna in Ein Gedi vineyards has my Beloved multiplied his forgiveness to me.

¹⁵ He said, 'I forgive you, My friend, for you are lovely in deed and lovely in resolve. The righteous among you are loyal as a dove.'

¹⁶ It is You Who are lovely, my Beloved, so pleasant that You pardoned my sin enabling our Temple to make me

קָרוֹת בָּתֵּינוּ אֲרָזִים, °רַחִיטֵנוּ בְּרוֹתִים. °רַהִיטֵנוּ ק'

ב

א אֲנִי חֲבַצֶּלֶת הַשָּׁרוֹן, שׁוֹשַׁנַּת הָעֲמָקִים.

ב כְּשׁוֹשַׁנָּה בֵּין הַחוֹחִים, כֵּן רַעְיָתִי בֵּין הַבָּנוֹת.

ג כְּתַפּוּחַ בַּעֲצֵי הַיַּעַר, כֵּן דּוֹדִי בֵּין הַבָּנִים, בְּצִלּוֹ

ד חִמַּדְתִּי וְיָשַׁבְתִּי, וּפִרְיוֹ מָתוֹק לְחִכִּי. הֱבִיאַנִי אֶל-

ה בֵּית הַיַּיִן, וְדִגְלוֹ עָלַי אַהֲבָה. סַמְּכוּנִי בָּאֲשִׁישׁוֹת,

ו רַפְּדוּנִי בַּתַּפּוּחִים, כִּי-חוֹלַת אַהֲבָה אָנִי. שְׂמֹאלוֹ

ז תַּחַת לְרֹאשִׁי, וִימִינוֹ תְּחַבְּקֵנִי. הִשְׁבַּעְתִּי אֶתְכֶם,
בְּנוֹת יְרוּשָׁלַםִ, בִּצְבָאוֹת אוֹ בְּאַיְלוֹת הַשָּׂדֶה, אִם-
תָּעִירוּ| וְאִם-תְּעוֹרְרוּ אֶת-הָאַהֲבָה עַד שֶׁתֶּחְפָּץ.

ח קוֹל דּוֹדִי הִנֵּה-זֶה בָּא, מְדַלֵּג עַל-הֶהָרִים,

ט מְקַפֵּץ עַל-הַגְּבָעוֹת. דּוֹמֶה דוֹדִי לִצְבִי, אוֹ לְעֹפֶר
הָאַיָּלִים, הִנֵּה-זֶה עוֹמֵד אַחַר כָּתְלֵנוּ, מַשְׁגִּיחַ מִן-
הַחַלֹּנוֹת, מֵצִיץ מִן-הַחֲרַכִּים.

י עָנָה דוֹדִי וְאָמַר לִי, קוּמִי לָךְ, רַעְיָתִי, יָפָתִי,

יא וּלְכִי-לָךְ. כִּי-הִנֵּה הַסְּתָו עָבָר, הַגֶּשֶׁם חָלַף הָלַךְ

יב לוֹ. הַנִּצָּנִים נִרְאוּ בָאָרֶץ, עֵת הַזָּמִיר הִגִּיעַ, וְקוֹל

יג הַתּוֹר נִשְׁמַע בְּאַרְצֵנוּ. הַתְּאֵנָה חָנְטָה פַגֶּיהָ,
וְהַגְּפָנִים| סְמָדַר נָתְנוּ רֵיחַ, קוּמִי °לְכִי, רַעְיָתִי, °לָךְ ק'
יָפָתִי, וּלְכִי-לָךְ.

יד יוֹנָתִי, בְּחַגְוֵי הַסֶּלַע, בְּסֵתֶר הַמַּדְרֵגָה, הַרְאִינִי
אֶת-מַרְאַיִךְ, הַשְׁמִיעִנִי אֶת-קוֹלֵךְ, כִּי קוֹלֵךְ עָרֵב,

טו וּמַרְאֵיךְ נָאוֶה. אֶחֱזוּ-לָנוּ שׁוּעָלִים, שֻׁעָלִים
קְטַנִּים, מְחַבְּלִים כְּרָמִים, וּכְרָמֵינוּ סְמָדַר.

טז-יז דּוֹדִי לִי, וַאֲנִי לוֹ, הָרֹעֶה בַּשּׁוֹשַׁנִּים. עַד שֶׁיָּפוּחַ

2/ The chapter division of Scripture is of non-Jewish origin, introduced by Christian Bible printers. We follow these divisions for convenience of identification only. Accordingly verse 2:1 does not begin a new thought, but is a continuation of the previous verses.

2. GOD TO ISRAEL

3-6. ISRAEL REMINISCES ...

5. Proper love for God is to be constantly enraptured by Him like a love-sick individual whose mind is never free from the passion that fills his heart at all times *(Rambam).*

7. ... TURNS TO THE NATIONS ...

8-17. ... THEN REMINISCES FURTHER
The Community of Israel reminisces how God, rushing to deliver her from Egyptian bondage, called upon her to bestir her to carry out His precepts and become worthy of deliverance.

11-13. These verses paint a beautiful picture describing the propitiousness of the season of Redemption. They conjure up an image of the worst being over — Delivery at hand.

13. The *K'siv* [Masoretic written form] of the word לָךְ, spelled לכי in this verse, has a superfluous י, *yud,* the numerical equivalent of ten. This suggests that the intent of the verse is: 'Arise to receive the *Ten* Commandments, My love, My fair one' *(Rashi).*

ever fresh. [17] The beams of our House are cedar, our panels are cypress.

[1] I am but a rose of Sharon, even an ever-fresh rose of the valleys. [2] Like the rose maintaining its beauty among the thorns, so is My faithful beloved among the nations. [3] Like the fruitful, fragrant apple tree among the barren trees of the forest, so is my Beloved among the gods. In His shade I delighted and there I sat, and the fruit of His Torah was sweet to my palate. [4] He brought me to the chamber of Torah delights and clustered my encampments about Him in love. [5] I say to Him, 'Sustain me in exile with dainty cakes, spread fragrant apples about me to comfort my dispersion — for, bereft of Your Presence, I am sick with love.' [6] With memories of His loving support in the desert, of His left hand under my head, of His right hand enveloping me. [7] I adjure you, O nations who are destined to ascend to Jerusalem — for if you violate your oath you will become as defenseless as gazelles or hinds of the field — if you dare provoke God to hate me or disturb His love for me while He still desires it.

[8] The voice of my Beloved! Behold it came suddenly to redeem me, as if leaping over mountains, skipping over hills. [9] In His swiftness to redeem me, my Beloved is like a gazelle or a young hart. I thought I would be forever alone, but behold! He was standing behind our wall, observing through the windows, peering through the lattices.

[10] When He redeemed me from Egypt, my Beloved called out and said to me, 'Arise My love, My fair one, and go forth. [11] For the winter of bondage has passed, the deluge of suffering is over and gone. [12] The righteous blossoms are seen in the land, the time of your song has arrived, and the voice of your guide is heard in the land. [13] The fig tree has formed its first small figs, ready for ascent to the Temple. The vines are in blossom, their fragrance declaring they are ready for libation. Arise, My love, My fair one, and go forth!'

[14] At the sea, He said to me, 'O My dove, trapped at the sea as if in the clefts of the rock, the concealment of the terrace. Show Me your prayerful gaze, let Me hear your supplicating voice, for your voice is sweet and your countenance comely.' [15] Then He told the sea, 'Seize for us the Egyptian foxes, even the small foxes who spoiled Israel's vineyards while our vineyards had just begun to blossom.'

[16] My Beloved is mine, He fills all my needs and I seek from Him and none other. He grazes me in roselike bounty. [17] Until my sin blows His friendship away and

הַיּוֹם, וְנָסוּ הַצְּלָלִים,
סֹב דְּמֵה-לְךָ, דוֹדִי, לִצְבִי אוֹ לְעֹפֶר הָאַיָּלִים,
עַל-הָרֵי בָתֶר.

ג א עַל-מִשְׁכָּבִי בַּלֵּילוֹת בִּקַּשְׁתִּי אֵת שֶׁאָהֲבָה ב נַפְשִׁי, בִּקַּשְׁתִּיו וְלֹא מְצָאתִיו. אָקוּמָה נָּא וַאֲסוֹבְבָה בָעִיר, בַּשְּׁוָקִים וּבָרְחֹבוֹת, אֲבַקְשָׁה אֵת שֶׁאָהֲבָה נַפְשִׁי, בִּקַּשְׁתִּיו וְלֹא מְצָאתִיו. ג מְצָאוּנִי הַשֹּׁמְרִים הַסֹּבְבִים בָּעִיר, אֵת שֶׁאָהֲבָה ד נַפְשִׁי רְאִיתֶם. כִּמְעַט שֶׁעָבַרְתִּי מֵהֶם, עַד שֶׁמָּצָאתִי אֵת שֶׁאָהֲבָה נַפְשִׁי, אֲחַזְתִּיו וְלֹא אַרְפֶּנּוּ, עַד-שֶׁהֲבֵיאתִיו אֶל-בֵּית אִמִּי, וְאֶל-חֶדֶר ה הוֹרָתִי. הִשְׁבַּעְתִּי אֶתְכֶם, בְּנוֹת יְרוּשָׁלַם, בִּצְבָאוֹת אוֹ בְּאַיְלוֹת הַשָּׂדֶה, אִם-תָּעִירוּ | וְאִם-תְּעוֹרְרוּ אֶת-הָאַהֲבָה עַד שֶׁתֶּחְפָּץ.

ו מִי זֹאת עֹלָה מִן-הַמִּדְבָּר, כְּתִימְרוֹת עָשָׁן, מְקֻטֶּרֶת מֹר וּלְבוֹנָה, מִכֹּל אַבְקַת רוֹכֵל. הִנֵּה ז מִטָּתוֹ שֶׁלִּשְׁלֹמֹה, שִׁשִּׁים גִּבֹּרִים סָבִיב לָהּ, ח מִגִּבֹּרֵי יִשְׂרָאֵל. כֻּלָּם אֲחֻזֵי חֶרֶב, מְלֻמְּדֵי מִלְחָמָה, אִישׁ חַרְבּוֹ עַל-יְרֵכוֹ, מִפַּחַד בַּלֵּילוֹת. ט אַפִּרְיוֹן עָשָׂה לוֹ הַמֶּלֶךְ שְׁלֹמֹה מֵעֲצֵי הַלְּבָנוֹן. י עַמּוּדָיו עָשָׂה כֶסֶף, רְפִידָתוֹ זָהָב, מֶרְכָּבוֹ אַרְגָּמָן, יא תּוֹכוֹ רָצוּף אַהֲבָה מִבְּנוֹת יְרוּשָׁלָם | צְאֶינָה וּרְאֶינָה, בְּנוֹת צִיּוֹן, בַּמֶּלֶךְ שְׁלֹמֹה, בָּעֲטָרָה שֶׁעִטְּרָה-לּוֹ אִמּוֹ, בְּיוֹם חֲתֻנָּתוֹ, וּבְיוֹם שִׂמְחַת לִבּוֹ.

ד א הִנָּךְ יָפָה, רַעְיָתִי, הִנָּךְ יָפָה, עֵינַיִךְ יוֹנִים,

sears me like the midday sun and His protection departs, my sin caused Him to turn away.

I say to him, 'My Beloved, You became like a gazelle or a young hart on the distant mountains.'

3/ ISRAEL TO THE NATIONS.
In context with the previous verse, *Rashi* explains *'night'* as referring to the torment of Israel's thirty-eight year sojourn in the desert in spiritual darkness when they were under the 'Ban' [incurred because of the sin of the Spies who turned the people against the land. During this period, the *Midrash* (2:11) explains, God did not speak with Moses (see *Deut.* 2:14-17). This verse metaphorically describes Israel's quest for God, *'Whom my soul loves,'* during these years of silence].

[1] As I lay on my bed in the night of my desert travail, I sought Him Whom my soul loves. I sought Him but I found Him not, for He maintained His aloofness. [2] I resolved to arise then, and roam through the city, in the streets and squares; that I would seek through Moses, Him Whom my soul loved. I sought Him, but I found Him not. [3] They found me, Moses and Aaron, the watchmen patrolling the city. 'You have seen Him Whom my soul loves — what has He said?' [4] Scarcely had I departed from them when, in the days of Joshua, I found Him Whom my soul loves. I grasped Him, determined that my deeds would never again cause me to lose hold of Him, until I brought His Presence to the Tabernacle of my mother and to the chamber of the one who conceived me. [5] I adjure you, O nations who are destined to ascend to Jerusalem — for if you violate your oath you will become as defenseless as gazelles or hinds of the field — if you dare provoke God to hate me or disturb His love for me while He still desires it.

6-11. These verses follow Israel's adjuration to the nations of the world, as if to say, 'Do not attempt to disturb God's love for us. It was *we* who followed Him into the desert; it was *us* whom He engulfed in His cloud; *we* accepted His Torah; *we* built the Tabernacle as He commanded; *we* crowned Him as our God. He will, therefore, surely resume His love for us, and we adjure you not to attempt to interfere with our love' *(Metzudas David).*

[6] You nations have asked, 'Who is this ascending from the desert, its way secured and smoothed by palmlike pillars of smoke, burning fragrant myrrh and frankincense, of all the perfumer's powders?' [7] Behold the resting place of Him to Whom peace belongs, with sixty myriads of Israel's mighty encircling it. [8] All of them gripping the sword of tradition, skilled in the battle of Torah, each with his sword ready at his side, lest he succumb in the nights of exile. [9] A Tabernacle for His presence has the King to Whom peace belongs made of the wood of Lebanon. [10] Its pillars He made of silver, His resting place was gold, its suspended curtain was purplewool, its midst was decked with implements bespeaking love by the daughters of Jerusalem. [11] Go forth and gaze, O daughters distinguished by loyalty to God, upon the King to Whom peace belongs adorned with the crown His nation made for Him, on the day His Law was given and He became one with Israel, and on the day His heart was gladdened by His Tabernacle's consecration.

4/1-16. GOD TO ISRAEL
Dovelike constancy. Your quality and actions are like the dove which is loyal to its mate; and which, when it is to be slaughtered, does not fidget, but [willingly] stretches forth its neck. So have you bent your shoulders to endure My yoke and My awe *(Rashi).*

[1] Behold, you are lovely, My friend, behold you are lovely, your very appearance radiates dovelike

מִבַּעַד לְצַמָּתֵךְ, שַׂעְרֵךְ כְּעֵדֶר הָעִזִּים, שֶׁגָּלְשׁוּ

ב מֵהַר גִּלְעָד. שִׁנַּיִךְ כְּעֵדֶר הַקְּצוּבוֹת שֶׁעָלוּ מִן־
הָרַחְצָה, שֶׁכֻּלָּם מַתְאִימוֹת, וְשַׁכֻּלָה אֵין בָּהֶם.

ג כְּחוּט הַשָּׁנִי שִׂפְתוֹתַיִךְ, וּמִדְבָּרֵךְ נָאוֶה, כְּפֶלַח

ד הָרִמּוֹן רַקָּתֵךְ, מִבַּעַד לְצַמָּתֵךְ. כְּמִגְדַּל דָּוִיד
צַוָּארֵךְ, בָּנוּי לְתַלְפִּיּוֹת, אֶלֶף הַמָּגֵן תָּלוּי עָלָיו,

ה כֹּל שִׁלְטֵי הַגִּבֹּרִים. שְׁנֵי שָׁדַיִךְ כִּשְׁנֵי עֳפָרִים,
תְּאוֹמֵי צְבִיָּה, הָרֹעִים בַּשּׁוֹשַׁנִּים.

ו עַד שֶׁיָּפוּחַ הַיּוֹם, וְנָסוּ הַצְּלָלִים, אֵלֶךְ לִי אֶל־

ז הַר הַמּוֹר, וְאֶל־גִּבְעַת הַלְּבוֹנָה. כֻּלָּךְ יָפָה,
רַעְיָתִי, וּמוּם אֵין בָּךְ.

ח אִתִּי מִלְּבָנוֹן, כַּלָּה, אִתִּי מִלְּבָנוֹן תָּבוֹאִי,
תָּשׁוּרִי | מֵרֹאשׁ אֲמָנָה, מֵרֹאשׁ שְׂנִיר וְחֶרְמוֹן,
מִמְּעֹנוֹת אֲרָיוֹת, מֵהַרְרֵי נְמֵרִים.

ט לִבַּבְתִּנִי, אֲחֹתִי כַלָּה, לִבַּבְתִּנִי °בְּאֶחָד   °בְּאַחַת ק
מֵעֵינַיִךְ, בְּאַחַד עֲנָק מִצַּוְּרֹנָיִךְ. מַה־יָּפוּ דֹדַיִךְ,

י אֲחֹתִי כַלָּה, מַה־טֹּבוּ דֹדַיִךְ מִיַּיִן, וְרֵיחַ שְׁמָנַיִךְ
מִכָּל־בְּשָׂמִים.

יא נֹפֶת תִּטֹּפְנָה שִׂפְתוֹתַיִךְ, כַּלָּה, דְּבַשׁ וְחָלָב

יב תַּחַת לְשׁוֹנֵךְ, וְרֵיחַ שַׂלְמֹתַיִךְ כְּרֵיחַ לְבָנוֹן. גַּן |

יג נָעוּל אֲחֹתִי כַלָּה, גַּל נָעוּל, מַעְיָן חָתוּם. שְׁלָחַיִךְ
פַּרְדֵּס רִמּוֹנִים, עִם פְּרִי מְגָדִים, כְּפָרִים עִם־

יד נְרָדִים. נֵרְדְּ | וְכַרְכֹּם, קָנֶה וְקִנָּמוֹן, עִם כָּל־עֲצֵי
לְבוֹנָה, מֹר וַאֲהָלוֹת, עִם כָּל־רָאשֵׁי בְשָׂמִים.

טו מַעְיַן גַּנִּים, בְּאֵר מַיִם חַיִּים, וְנֹזְלִים מִן־לְבָנוֹן.

constancy. The most common sons within your encampments are as dearly beloved as the children of Jacob in the goatlike procession descending the slopes of Mount Gilead. ² Accountable in deed are your fiercest warriors like a well-numbered flock come up from the washing, all of them unblemished with no miscarriage of action in them.

³ Like the scarlet thread, guarantor of Rachav's safety, is the sincerity of your lips, and your word is unfeigned. As many as a pomegranate's seeds are the merits of your unworthiest within your modest veil. ⁴ As stately as the Tower of David is the site of your Sanhedrin built as a model to emulate, with a thousand shields of Torah armor hung upon it, all the disciple-filled quivers of the mighty. ⁵ Moses and Aaron, your two sustainers, are like two fawns, twins of the gazelle, who graze their sheep in roselike bounty.

⁶ Until My sunny benevolence was withdrawn from Shiloh and the protective shadows were dispersed by your sin. I will go to Mount Moriah and the hill of frankincense — ⁷ where you will be completely fair, My beloved, and no blemish will be in you.

⁸ With Me will you be exiled from the Temple, O bride, with Me from the Temple until you return; then to contemplate the fruits of your faith from its earliest beginnings from your first arrival at the summits of Snir and of Hermon, the lands of mighty Sichon and Og, as impregnable as dens of lions, and as mountains of leopards.

⁹ You captured My heart, My sister, O bride; you captured My heart with but one of your virtues, with but one of the precepts that adorn you like beads of a necklace resplendent. ¹⁰ How fair was your love in so many settings, My sister, O bride; so superior is your love to wine and your spreading fame to all perfumes.

¹¹ The sweetness of Torah drops from your lips, like honey and milk it lies under your tongue; your very garments are scented with precepts like the scent of Lebanon. ¹² As chaste as a garden locked, My sister, O bride; a spring locked up, a fountain sealed. ¹³ Your least gifted ones are a pomegranate orchard with luscious fruit; henna with nard; ¹⁴ nard and saffron, calamus and cinnamon, with all trees of frankincense, myrrh and aloes with all the chief spices; ¹⁵ purified in a garden spring, a well of waters alive and flowing clean from Lebanon.

---

4. An erect posture in a woman is beautiful, and the simile to *Tower of David* refers to מְצֻדַת צִיוֹן, the Stronghold of Zion, a beautiful, stately tower and fortification. So is you 'neck' — i.e. the לִשְׁכַּת הַגָּזִית, the Chamber of Hewn Stone [the seat of the Sanhedrin] which was the spiritual stronghold of Israel (Rashi).

9. Precepts of the Torah are allegorized as beads (see *Proverbs* 1:9).

11. *Kol Bo* cites 'honey and milk under your tongue' as a reason for the custom of eating dairy foods and honey on Shavuos, the holiday commemorating the giving of the Torah, which is symbolized by honey and milk.

עוּרִי צָפוֹן, וּבוֹאִי תֵימָן, הָפִיחִי גַנִּי, יִזְּלוּ בְשָׂמָיו,
יָבֹא דוֹדִי לְגַנּוֹ, וְיֹאכַל פְּרִי מְגָדָיו.

ה

א בָּאתִי לְגַנִּי, אֲחֹתִי כַלָּה, אָרִיתִי מוֹרִי עִם־בְּשָׂמִי, אָכַלְתִּי יַעְרִי עִם־דִּבְשִׁי, שָׁתִיתִי יֵינִי עִם־חֲלָבִי, אִכְלוּ רֵעִים, שְׁתוּ וְשִׁכְרוּ דּוֹדִים.

ב אֲנִי יְשֵׁנָה וְלִבִּי עֵר, קוֹל | דּוֹדִי דוֹפֵק, פִּתְחִי־לִי, אֲחֹתִי, רַעְיָתִי, יוֹנָתִי, תַמָּתִי, שֶׁרֹאשִׁי נִמְלָא־טָל, קְוֻצּוֹתַי רְסִיסֵי לָיְלָה.

ג פָּשַׁטְתִּי אֶת־כֻּתָּנְתִּי, אֵיכָכָה אֶלְבָּשֶׁנָּה, רָחַצְתִּי אֶת רַגְלַי, אֵיכָכָה אֲטַנְּפֵם.

ד דּוֹדִי שָׁלַח יָדוֹ מִן־הַחוֹר, וּמֵעַי הָמוּ עָלָיו.

ה קַמְתִּי אֲנִי לִפְתֹּחַ לְדוֹדִי, וְיָדַי נָטְפוּ־מוֹר,

ו וְאֶצְבְּעֹתַי מוֹר עֹבֵר, עַל כַּפּוֹת הַמַּנְעוּל. פָּתַחְתִּי אֲנִי לְדוֹדִי, וְדוֹדִי חָמַק עָבָר, נַפְשִׁי יָצְאָה בְדַבְּרוֹ, בִּקַּשְׁתִּיהוּ וְלֹא מְצָאתִיהוּ, קְרָאתִיו וְלֹא עָנָנִי.

ז מְצָאֻנִי הַשֹּׁמְרִים הַסֹּבְבִים בָּעִיר, הִכּוּנִי פְצָעוּנִי, נָשְׂאוּ אֶת־רְדִידִי מֵעָלַי שֹׁמְרֵי הַחֹמוֹת.

ח הִשְׁבַּעְתִּי אֶתְכֶם, בְּנוֹת יְרוּשָׁלָ‍ִם, אִם־תִּמְצְאוּ אֶת־דּוֹדִי, מַה־תַּגִּידוּ לוֹ שֶׁחוֹלַת אַהֲבָה אָנִי.

ט מַה־דּוֹדֵךְ מִדּוֹד, הַיָּפָה בַּנָּשִׁים, מַה־דּוֹדֵךְ מִדּוֹד, שֶׁכָּכָה הִשְׁבַּעְתָּנוּ.

יא דּוֹדִי צַח וְאָדוֹם, דָּגוּל מֵרְבָבָה. רֹאשׁוֹ כֶּתֶם פָּז, קְוֻצּוֹתָיו תַּלְתַּלִּים, שְׁחֹרוֹת כָּעוֹרֵב.

יב עֵינָיו כְּיוֹנִים עַל־אֲפִיקֵי מָיִם, רֹחֲצוֹת בֶּחָלָב,

ISRAEL RESPONDS

5/1. GOD REPLIES

2-7. ISRAEL REMINISCES REGRETFULLY

My Beloved knocks! [throughout all my slumbering.] God caused His *Shechinah* to dwell upon the prophets, issuing daily warnings through them [see *Jeremiah* 7:25]. Now Israel remorsefully recalls how, secure in the peaceful period of the First Temple, she neglected the call of the prophets to return to the service of God, as if she slumbered and slept; but God nevertheless was wakeful to guard her and grant her goodness *(Rashi)*.

8. ISRAEL TO THE NATIONS

9. THE NATIONS ASK ISRAEL

'Why are you so loyal to a God who has forsaken you? Let us become one nation, and together serve our god!' *(Metzudas David)*.

10-16. ISRAEL RESPONDS

16. *This is my Beloved* — and it is for all these virtues that 'I am sick for His love' *(Rashi)*.

¹⁶ Awake from the north and come from the south! Like the winds let My exiles return to My garden, let their fragrant goodness flow in Jerusalem.

Let but my Beloved come to His garden and enjoy His precious people.

¹ To your Tabernacle Dedication, My sister, O bride, I came as if to My garden. I gathered My myrrh with My spice from your princely incense; I accepted your unbidden as well as your bidden offerings to Me; I drank your libations pure as milk. Eat, My beloved priests! Drink and become God-intoxicated, O friends!

² I let my devotion slumber, but the God of my heart was awake! A sound! My Beloved knocks!

He said, 'Open your heart to Me, My sister, My love, My dove, My perfection; admit Me and My head is filled with dewlike memories of Abraham; spurn Me and I bear collections of punishing rains in exile-nights.'

³ And I responded, 'I have doffed my robe of devotion; how can I don it? I have washed my feet that trod Your path; how can I soil them?'

⁴ In anger at my recalcitrance, my Beloved sent forth His Hand from the portal in wrath, and my intestines churned with longing for Him. ⁵ I arose to open for my Beloved and my hands dripped myrrh of repentant devotion to Torah and God, and my fingers flowing with myrrh to remove the traces of my foolish rebuke from the handles of the lock. ⁶ I opened for my Beloved; but, alas, my Beloved had turned His back on my plea and was gone. My soul departed at His decree! I sought His closeness but could not find it; I beseeched Him but He would not answer.

⁷ They found me, the enemy watchmen patrolling the city; they struck me, they bloodied me wreaking God's revenge on me. They stripped my mantle of holiness from me, the angelic watchmen of the wall.

⁸ I adjure you, O nations who are destined to ascend to Jerusalem, when you see my Beloved on the future Day of Judgment, won't you tell Him that I bore all travails for love of Him?

⁹ With what does your beloved God excel all others that you suffer for His Name, O fairest of nations? With what does your beloved God excel all others that you dare to adjure us?

¹⁰ My Beloved is pure and purifies sin, and ruddy with vengeance to punish betrayers, surrounded with myriad angels. ¹¹ His opening words were finest gold, His crowns hold mounds of statutes written in raven-black flame.

¹² Like the gaze of doves toward their cotes, His eyes are fixed on the waters of Torah, bathing all things in

יג יֹשְׁבוֹת עַל־מִלֵּאת. לְחָיָו כַּעֲרוּגַת הַבֹּשֶׂם,
מִגְדְּלוֹת מֶרְקָחִים, שִׂפְתוֹתָיו שׁוֹשַׁנִּים, נֹטְפוֹת
מוֹר עֹבֵר. יד יָדָיו גְּלִילֵי זָהָב, מְמֻלָּאִים בַּתַּרְשִׁישׁ,
טו מֵעָיו עֶשֶׁת שֵׁן, מְעֻלֶּפֶת סַפִּירִים. שׁוֹקָיו עַמּוּדֵי
שֵׁשׁ, מְיֻסָּדִים עַל־אַדְנֵי־פָז, מַרְאֵהוּ כַּלְּבָנוֹן,
בָּחוּר כָּאֲרָזִים. טז חִכּוֹ מַמְתַקִּים, וְכֻלּוֹ מַחֲמַדִּים,
זֶה דוֹדִי וְזֶה רֵעִי, בְּנוֹת יְרוּשָׁלָ͏ִם.

ו א אָנָה הָלַךְ דּוֹדֵךְ, הַיָּפָה בַּנָּשִׁים, אָנָה פָּנָה
דוֹדֵךְ, וּנְבַקְשֶׁנּוּ עִמָּךְ.
ב דּוֹדִי יָרַד לְגַנּוֹ, לַעֲרוּגוֹת הַבֹּשֶׂם, לִרְעוֹת בַּגַּנִּים
ג וְלִלְקֹט שׁוֹשַׁנִּים. אֲנִי לְדוֹדִי, וְדוֹדִי לִי, הָרוֹעֶה
בַּשּׁוֹשַׁנִּים.
ד יָפָה אַתְּ רַעְיָתִי כְּתִרְצָה, נָאוָה כִּירוּשָׁלָ͏ִם,
אֲיֻמָּה כַּנִּדְגָּלוֹת. ה הָסֵבִּי עֵינַיִךְ מִנֶּגְדִּי, שֶׁהֵם
הִרְהִיבֻנִי, שַׂעְרֵךְ כְּעֵדֶר הָעִזִּים, שֶׁגָּלְשׁוּ מִן־
הַגִּלְעָד. ו שִׁנַּיִךְ כְּעֵדֶר הָרְחֵלִים, שֶׁעָלוּ מִן־
הָרַחְצָה, שֶׁכֻּלָּם מַתְאִימוֹת, וְשַׁכֻּלָה אֵין בָּהֶם.
ז-ח כְּפֶלַח הָרִמּוֹן רַקָּתֵךְ, מִבַּעַד לְצַמָּתֵךְ. שִׁשִּׁים
הֵמָּה מְלָכוֹת, וּשְׁמֹנִים פִּילַגְשִׁים, וַעֲלָמוֹת אֵין
מִסְפָּר.
ט אַחַת הִיא יוֹנָתִי תַמָּתִי, אַחַת הִיא לְאִמָּהּ,
בָּרָה הִיא לְיוֹלַדְתָּהּ, רָאוּהָ בָנוֹת וַיְאַשְּׁרוּהָ,
מְלָכוֹת וּפִילַגְשִׁים, וַיְהַלְלוּהָ. י מִי־זֹאת הַנִּשְׁקָפָה
כְּמוֹ־שָׁחַר, יָפָה כַלְּבָנָה, בָּרָה כַּחַמָּה, אֲיֻמָּה
כַּנִּדְגָּלוֹת.

clarity, established upon creation's fullness. ¹³ Like a bed of spices are His words at Sinai, like towers of perfume. His comforting words from the Tabernacle are roses dripping flowing myrrh. ¹⁴ The Tablets, His handiwork, are desirable above even rolls of gold; they are studded with commandments precious as gems, the Torah's innards are sparkling as ivory intricately overlaid with precious stone. ¹⁵ The Torah's columns are marble set in contexts of finest gold, its contemplation flowers like Lebanon, it is sturdy as cedars. ¹⁶ The words of His palate are sweet and He is all delight.

16. *This is my Beloved* — and it is for all these virtues that 'I am sick for His love' *(Rashi).*

This is my Beloved and this is my Friend, O nations who are destined to ascend to Jerusalem.

6/1. THE NATIONS, DERISIVELY, TO ISRAEL

Why has your Beloved left you alone, widowed? *(Rashi).*

2-3. ISRAEL RESPONDS

3. I, alone, am My Beloved's. You are not His, and you will not assist us in constructing of our new Temple [see *Ezra* 4:3] *(Rashi).*

4-11. GOD TO ISRAEL

5. Another interpretaion: 'Turn your pleading eyes from Me,' says God. 'Endure your Exile, and do not anticipate the End — because there is an appointed time for every event. Your eyes overwhelm Me and fill Me with compassion — but the Edict has already been proclaimed: until the pre-established time, you must faithfully bear the yoke. Rather, turn away your eyes, and if you repent, I will respond accordingly by redeeming you sooner' *(Midrash Lekach Tov; Vilna Gaon).*

¹ Where has your Beloved gone, O forsaken fairest among women? Where has your Beloved turned to rejoin you? Let us seek Him with you and build His Temple with you.

² My Beloved has descended to His Temple garden, to His incense altar, yet still He grazes my brethren remaining in gardens of exile to gather the roseate fragrance of their words of Torah. ³ I alone am my Beloved's and my Beloved is mine, He Who grazes His sheep in roselike pastures.

⁴ You are beautiful, My love, when your deeds are pleasing, as comely now as once you were in Jerusalem of old, hosts of angels stand in awe of you. ⁵ Turn your pleading eyes from Me lest I be tempted to bestow upon you holiness more than you can bear. But with all your flaws, your most common sons are as dearly beloved as the children of Jacob in the goatlike procession descending the slopes of Mount Gilead. ⁶ Your mighty leaders are perfect, as a flock of ewes come up from the washing, all of them unblemished with no miscarriage of action in them. ⁷ As many as a pomegranate's seeds are the merits of your unworthiest within your modest veil. ⁸ The queenly offspring of Abraham are sixty, compared to whom the eighty Noachides and all their countless nations are like mere concubines.

⁹ Unique is she, My constant dove, My perfect one. Unique is she, this nation striving for the truth; pure is she to Jacob who begot her. Nations saw her and acclaimed her; queens and concubines, and they praised her: ¹⁰ 'Who is this that gazes down from atop the Temple Mount, brightening like the dawn, beautiful as the moon, brilliant as the sun, awesome as the bannered hosts of kings?'

יא אֶל־גִּנַּת אֱגוֹז יָרַדְתִּי לִרְאוֹת בְּאִבֵּי הַנָּחַל, לִרְאוֹת הֲפָרְחָה הַגֶּפֶן, הֵנֵצוּ הָרִמֹּנִים.

יב לֹא יָדַעְתִּי, נַפְשִׁי שָׂמַתְנִי, מַרְכְּבוֹת עַמִּי נָדִיב.

ז

א שׁוּבִי שׁוּבִי, הַשּׁוּלַמִּית, שׁוּבִי שׁוּבִי וְנֶחֱזֶה־בָּךְ, מַה־תֶּחֱזוּ בַּשּׁוּלַמִּית, כִּמְחֹלַת הַמַּחֲנָיִם.

ב מַה־יָּפוּ פְעָמַיִךְ בַּנְּעָלִים, בַּת־נָדִיב, חַמּוּקֵי

ג יְרֵכַיִךְ כְּמוֹ חֲלָאִים, מַעֲשֵׂה יְדֵי אָמָּן. שָׁרְרֵךְ אַגַּן הַסַּהַר, אַל־יֶחְסַר הַמָּזֶג, בִּטְנֵךְ עֲרֵמַת חִטִּים,

ד סוּגָה בַּשּׁוֹשַׁנִּים. שְׁנֵי שָׁדַיִךְ כִּשְׁנֵי עֳפָרִים, תָּאֳמֵי

ה צְבִיָּה. צַוָּארֵךְ כְּמִגְדַּל הַשֵּׁן, עֵינַיִךְ בְּרֵכוֹת בְּחֶשְׁבּוֹן, עַל־שַׁעַר בַּת־רַבִּים, אַפֵּךְ כְּמִגְדַּל הַלְּבָנוֹן, צוֹפֶה פְּנֵי דַמָּשֶׂק.

ו רֹאשֵׁךְ עָלַיִךְ כַּכַּרְמֶל, וְדַלַּת רֹאשֵׁךְ כָּאַרְגָּמָן,

ז מֶלֶךְ אָסוּר בָּרְהָטִים. מַה־יָּפִית וּמַה־נָּעַמְתְּ,

ח אַהֲבָה בַּתַּעֲנוּגִים. זֹאת קוֹמָתֵךְ דָּמְתָה לְתָמָר, וְשָׁדַיִךְ לְאַשְׁכֹּלוֹת.

ט אָמַרְתִּי, אֶעֱלֶה בְתָמָר, אֹחֲזָה בְּסַנְסִנָּיו, וְיִהְיוּ־ נָא שָׁדַיִךְ כְּאֶשְׁכְּלוֹת הַגֶּפֶן, וְרֵיחַ אַפֵּךְ כַּתַּפּוּחִים.

י וְחִכֵּךְ כְּיֵין הַטּוֹב,

הוֹלֵךְ לְדוֹדִי לְמֵישָׁרִים, דּוֹבֵב שִׂפְתֵי יְשֵׁנִים.

יא־יב אֲנִי לְדוֹדִי, וְעָלַי תְּשׁוּקָתוֹ. לְכָה דוֹדִי, נֵצֵא הַשָּׂדֶה, נָלִינָה בַּכְּפָרִים.

יג נַשְׁכִּימָה לַכְּרָמִים, נִרְאֶה אִם־פָּרְחָה הַגֶּפֶן,

11 I descended upon the deceptively simple holiness of the Second Temple to see your moisture-laden deeds in valleys. Had your Torah scholars budded on the vine, had your merit-laden righteous flowered like the pomegranates filled with seeds?

12 Alas, I knew not how to guard myself from sin! My own devices harnessed me, like chariots subject to a foreign nation's mercies.

12-7:1. ISRAEL RESPONDS

Hearing God's praise of her glorious past, Israel reflects on her current plight and responds sadly.

7/1. Israel is still the speaker, recalling how the heathens tried to entice her to join with them.

1 The nations have said to me, 'Turn away, turn away from God, O nation whose faith in Him is perfect, turn away, turn away, and we shall choose nobility from you.'

But I replied to them, 'What can you bestow upon a nation whole in faith to Him commensurate even with the desert camps encircling?'

2. THE NATIONS TO ISRAEL

2 But your footsteps were so lovely when shod in pilgrim's sandals, O daughter of nobles. The rounded shafts for your libations' abysslike trenches, handiwork of the Master Craftsman. 3 At earth's very center your Sanhedrin site is an ivory basin of ceaseless, flowing teaching; your national center an indispensable heap of nourishing knowledge hedged about with roses. 4 Your twin sustainers, the Tablets of the Law, are like two fawns, twins of the gazelle. 5 Your altar and Temple, erect and stately as an ivory tower; your wise men aflow with springs of complex wisdom at the gate of the many-peopled city; your face, like a Lebanese tower, looks to your future boundary as far as Damascus.

3. A rose hedge is hardly an imposing barrier. Despite its thorns it can be trampled easily. Its true effectiveness is in its beauty; only a callous person would trample a rose bush. Thus it can only deter those who appreciate its beauty; for the esthetically blind, it is no barrier at all. Similarly, the sanctions of Torah and Rabbinic ordinances are gentle reminders to refrain from trespass against the handiwork of God and are effective only for those who understand the greatness and majesty of Torah (Harav Mordechai Gifter).

6 The Godly name on your head is as mighty as Carmel; your crowning braid is royal purple, your King is bound in nazaritic tresses. 7 How beautiful and pleasant are you, befitting the pleasures of spiritual love. 8 Such is your stature, likened to a towering palm tree, from your teachers flow sustenance like wine-filled clusters.

9-10. GOD TO ISRAEL

10-8:2. ISRAEL INTERJECTS

In love so upright, i.e., a love so intense that even my departed ancestors will rejoice in me and be thankful for their lot (Rashi).

9 I boast on High that your deeds cause Me to ascend on your palm tree, I grasp onto your branches. I beg now your teachers that they may remain like clusters of grapes from which flow strength to your weakest ones, and the fragrance of your face like apples. 10 and may your utterance be like finest wine.

I shall heed Your plea to uphold my faith before my Beloved in love so upright and honest that my slumbering fathers will move their lips in approval.

11 I say to the nations, 'I am my Beloved's and He longs for my perfection.'

12 Come, my Beloved, let us go to the fields where Your children serve You in want, there let us lodge with Esau's children who are blessed with plenty yet still deny.

13. Israel invites God to observe the fine conduct of her children.

13 Let us wake at dawn in vineyards of prayer and study. Let us see if students of Writ have budded, if students

פִּתַּח הַסְּמָדַר, הֵנֵצוּ הָרִמּוֹנִים, שָׁם אֶתֵּן אֶת־דֹּדַי לָךְ.

יד הַדּוּדָאִים נָתְנוּ־רֵיחַ, וְעַל־פְּתָחֵינוּ כָּל־מְגָדִים, חֲדָשִׁים גַּם־יְשָׁנִים, דּוֹדִי, צָפַנְתִּי לָךְ.

ח

א מִי יִתֶּנְךָ כְּאָח לִי, יוֹנֵק שְׁדֵי אִמִּי, אֶמְצָאֲךָ

ב בַחוּץ אֶשָּׁקְךָ, גַּם לֹא־יָבֻזוּ לִי. אֶנְהָגְךָ, אֲבִיאֲךָ אֶל־בֵּית אִמִּי, תְּלַמְּדֵנִי, אַשְׁקְךָ מִיַּיִן הָרֶקַח, מֵעֲסִיס רִמֹּנִי.

ג שְׂמֹאלוֹ תַּחַת רֹאשִׁי, וִימִינוֹ תְּחַבְּקֵנִי.

ד הִשְׁבַּעְתִּי אֶתְכֶם, בְּנוֹת יְרוּשָׁלָ͏ִם, מַה־תָּעִירוּ | וּמַה־תְּעֹרְרוּ אֶת־הָאַהֲבָה עַד שֶׁתֶּחְפָּץ.

ה מִי זֹאת עֹלָה מִן־הַמִּדְבָּר, מִתְרַפֶּקֶת עַל־דּוֹדָהּ,

תַּחַת הַתַּפּוּחַ עוֹרַרְתִּיךָ, שָׁמָּה חִבְּלַתְךָ אִמֶּךָ,

שָׁמָּה חִבְּלָה יְלָדַתְךָ. שִׂמֵנִי כַחוֹתָם עַל לִבֶּךָ, כַּחוֹתָם עַל־זְרוֹעֶךָ, כִּי־עַזָּה כַמָּוֶת אַהֲבָה, קָשָׁה כִשְׁאוֹל קִנְאָה, רְשָׁפֶיהָ רִשְׁפֵּי אֵשׁ, שַׁלְהֶבֶתְיָה.

ז מַיִם רַבִּים לֹא יוּכְלוּ לְכַבּוֹת אֶת־הָאַהֲבָה, וּנְהָרוֹת לֹא יִשְׁטְפוּהָ,

אִם־יִתֵּן אִישׁ אֶת־כָּל־הוֹן בֵּיתוֹ בָּאַהֲבָה, בּוֹז יָבוּזוּ לוֹ.

ח אָחוֹת לָנוּ קְטַנָּה, וְשָׁדַיִם אֵין לָהּ, מַה־נַּעֲשֶׂה לַאֲחוֹתֵנוּ בַּיּוֹם שֶׁיְּדֻבַּר־בָּהּ.

ט אִם־חוֹמָה הִיא, נִבְנֶה עָלֶיהָ טִירַת כָּסֶף, וְאִם־דֶּלֶת הִיא, נָצוּר עָלֶיהָ לוּחַ אָרֶז.

of Oral Law have blossomed, if ripened scholars have bloomed — there I will display my finest products to You.

[14] All my baskets, good and bad, emit a fragrance, all at our doors have the precious fruits of comely deeds — those the Scribes have newly ordained and Your Torah's timeless wisdom, for You, Beloved, has my heart stored them.

8/ God had earlier expressed His desire to rest His *Shechinah* upon His people once again. They now continue their response with a longing plea for His aid and comfort.

[1] If only, despite my wrongs, You could comfort me as Joseph did, like a brother nurtured at the bosom of my mother, if in the streets I found Your prophets I would kiss You and embrace You through them, nor could anyone despise me for it. [2] I would lead You, I would bring You to my mother's Temple for You to teach me as You did in Moses' Tent; to drink I'd give You spiced libations, wines like pomegranate nectar.

3-4. ISRAEL TO THE NATIONS

Know, you nations: Although I complain and lament, my Beloved holds my hand and is my support throughout my Exile *(Rashi).*

[3] Despite my laments in Exile, His left hand supports my head and His right hand embraces me in support. [4] I adjure you, O nations destined to ascend to Jerusalem — for if you violate your oath you will become defenseless — if you dare provoke God to hate me or disturb His love for me while He still desires it.

5. GOD AND THE HEAVENLY TRIBUNAL

5-7. ISRAEL INTERJECTS

'It was I and no other who sought out Your shade under the apple tree to which You are compared [see 2:3], and I jumped at the opportunity to cry out נַעֲשֶׂה וְנִשְׁמָע, 'we will do and we will obey!' *(Alshich).*

[5] How worthy she is who rises from the desert bearing Torah and His Presence, clinging to her Beloved!

Under Sinai suspended above me, there I roused Your love, there was Your people born; a mother to other nations, there she endured the travail of her birth. [6] For the sake of my love, place me like a seal on Your heart, like a seal to dedicate Your strength for me, for strong till the death is my love; though their zeal for vengeance is hard as the grave, its flashes are flashes of fire from the flame of God. [7] Many waters of heathen tribulation cannot extinguish the fire of this love, nor rivers of royal seduction or torture wash it away.

GOD REPLIES TO ISRAEL

Were any man to offer all the treasure of his home to entice you away from your love, they would scorn him to extreme.

8-9. THE HEAVENLY TRIBUNAL REFLECTS

[8] Israel desires to cleave to us, the small and humble one, but her time of spiritual maturity has not come. What shall we do for our cleaving one on the day the nations plot against her?

9. The Tribunal's response depends upon how she conducts herself in the interim while in Exile.

[9] If her faith and belief are strong as a wall withstanding incursions from without, we shall become her fortress and beauty; building her City and Holy Temple; but if she wavers like a door, succumbing to every alien knock, with fragile cedar panels shall we then enclose her.

י   אֲנִי חוֹמָה, וְשָׁדַי כַּמִּגְדָּלוֹת, אָז הָיִיתִי בְעֵינָיו כְּמוֹצְאֵת שָׁלוֹם.

יא   כֶּרֶם הָיָה לִשְׁלֹמֹה בְּבַעַל הָמוֹן, נָתַן אֶת־הַכֶּרֶם לַנֹּטְרִים, אִישׁ יָבִא בְּפִרְיוֹ אֶלֶף כָּסֶף.

יב   כַּרְמִי שֶׁלִּי לְפָנָי, הָאֶלֶף לְךָ שְׁלֹמֹה, וּמָאתַיִם לְנֹטְרִים אֶת־פִּרְיוֹ.

יג   הַיּוֹשֶׁבֶת בַּגַּנִּים, חֲבֵרִים מַקְשִׁיבִים לְקוֹלֵךְ, הַשְׁמִיעִנִי.

יד   בְּרַח | דּוֹדִי, וּדְמֵה־לְךָ לִצְבִי, אוֹ לְעֹפֶר הָאַיָּלִים, עַל הָרֵי בְשָׂמִים.

10. ISRAEL REPLIES PROUDLY ...
'Your fear is unjustified!'

¹⁰ My faith is firm as a wall, and my nourishing synagogues and study halls are strong as towers! Then, having said so, I become in His eyes like a bride found perfect.

11. ... AND REMINISCES

¹¹ Israel was vineyard of Him to Whom peace belongs in populous Jerusalem. He gave His vineyard to harsh, cruel guardians; each one came to extort his fruit, even a thousand silver pieces.

12. GOD TO THE NATIONS, ON THE DAY OF JUDGMENT

¹² The vineyard is Mine! Your iniquities are before Me!

THE NATIONS WILL REPLY
Whatever, we filched from Israel [verses] will be returned to You, for the vineyard is Yours *(Rashi)*.

The thousand silver pieces are Yours, You to Whom peace belongs, and two hundred more to the Sages who guarded the fruit of Torah from our designs.

13. GOD TO ISRAEL

¹³ O My beloved, dwelling in far-flung gardens, your fellows, the angels hearken to your voice of Torah and prayer. Let Me hear it that they may then sanctify Me.

14. ISRAEL TO GOD

¹⁴ Flee, my Beloved, from our common Exile and be like a gazelle or a young hart in Your swiftness to redeem and rest your Presence among us on the fragrant Mount Moriah, site of Your Temple.

רות

RUTH

ruth

Your People is My People

Ruth and Boaz are an unlikely pair of heroes. She was a Moabite princess who fell from honor and wealth to contempt and poverty. He
was the *Shofet,* the Judge, leader of the Jewish nation; venerable,
wealthy and revered. Much more than a hostile border separated Ruth
from Boaz. In age, they were two generations apart, he was eighty, she
was forty *(Ruth Rabbah* 6:2). In background, much further.

Yet the two came together under the most unlikely circumstances,
to create the royal family of Israel — the House of David. The Talmud
calls Ruth אִמָּא שֶׁל מַלְכוּת, *mother of royalty,* because her progeny
included David and Solomon, and the future Messiah who will end all
exiles, return Israel to its greatest glory, and lead all the world to the
destiny for which it was created.

The Book of Ruth begins with a famine in *Eretz Yisrael,* and the
departure of Elimelech and Naomi and their children from Bethlehem
to Moab. Elimelech was an aristocrat, a wealthy leader. He fled from
Bethlehem not because *he* was hungry — he had more than he
needed — but because he was afraid that the poor and hungry of his
town would knock on his door for help. In a time of crisis, he was more
concerned with the fate of his fortune than the plight of his people. As
the Midrash puts it, he struck despair into the hearts of his people
because when the famine came he fled. In his list of priorities,
responsibility to his fellow Jews came last, and for that he was
punished. Elimelech died in Moab, widowing his righteous wife Naomi.

The two surviving sons should have seen the hand of God, picked up
their fortune and returned to Bethlehem, but they did not. Typically,
they interpreted their father's death as a judgment of nature, not God,
so they stayed in Moab and even elevated their status in their
comfortable, self-imposed exile. They married Orpah and Ruth, two
Moabite princesses. How fortunate they must have regarded
themselves in escaping from famine to noble status! The two men,
Machlon and Kilion, also died, and then there were three widows.
Having lost her family and her fortune, the righteous Naomi turned her
sights back to Bethlehem where she had belonged all along.

Both daughters-in-law wanted to accompany her, but Naomi said
no. Why go to a strange land, to a life of loneliness and poverty? Orpah
kissed Naomi good-bye and went back to Moab, but Ruth clung to
Naomi with a fierce loyalty and the immortal words:

> *Wherever you go, I will go; where you lodge, I will lodge; your people are my people and your God is my God; where you die, I will die, and there I will be buried (1:16-17).*

Naomi and Ruth went back to Bethlehem where they lived as paupers. Young, vigorous Ruth cared for her aged, broken mother-in-law, begging and scrounging in the fields. There she met Boaz, who, according to the Sages *(Bava Basra* 91a), was the Judge Ivtzan *(Judges* 12:8), who had just lost his wife. His extensive properties were managed and run by his many employees. He saw Ruth gathering neglected sheaves in the field, and he admired her honesty and modesty, not to mention her devotion to Naomi, his relative. Boaz recognized his responsibilities, not only to help the two women but to preserve their self-respect while doing so.

During the harvest, while Ruth spent her time gleaning in Boaz's field and had at least limited access to him, Naomi hoped that Ruth's 'chance encounter' with Boaz was providential and that Boaz would 'redeem' Ruth by marrying her, thus perpetuating Machlon's memory.

But then the harvest was over and Boaz made no such move. The prospect that Ruth might meet Boaz again was remote, and Naomi feared that since Boaz had not taken the initiative when Ruth was near, he could hardly be expected to respond to more conventional suggestions of marriage when she was out of sight. For all they knew, Boaz might even be offended at the mere suggestion of a marriage to Ruth. After all, Naomi was destitute, Ruth was of Moabite stock, and Boaz was a man of substance, the Judge and leader of the generation. Could Naomi expect simply to ask him to redeem and marry this girl?

Naomi realized that she had to take a bold initiative. At that time, the prohibition of יִחוּד פְּנוּיָה, the seclusion of a man with an unmarried woman — later forbidden by the court of King David — had not yet been proclaimed. Naomi therefore decided that the best course — however daring and unconventional — was for Ruth herself to approach Boaz very privately and remind him of his responsibility to the family of his dead uncle, Elimelech. In a personal confrontation — convinced that her motives were sincere — his compassion for her bitter plight might be evoked. It was. As an outgrowth of these events, Boaz married Ruth and she conceived on the last day of his life. Their child was Oved, grandfather of King David.

The Book of Ruth, among its other lessons, teaches a Jewish sense of duty. Elimelech fled, Boaz stayed. Orpah wept and left, Ruth wept and stayed. Machlon and Kilion did not go back; they died. Naomi went back and lived to nurture Ruth's baby. Boaz's cousin refused to marry

Ruth, fearing that marriage to a Moabitess would contaminate his progeny; Boaz knew the Oral Law's teaching that a female convert from Moab is permitted to marry into Israel, and he became the ancestor of the Davidic dynasty and the Messianic destiny.

The Book of Ruth is read on Shavuos for a variety of reasons. One of these reasons is instructive and inspiring to us all in our everyday lives. Someone once said that the great majority of people lead lives of quiet desperation, thinking that their struggles, successes, and failures have no lasting purpose. No one had more right to feel that way than Ruth and Naomi, scratching for existence and scrounging for the next meal. Boaz surely felt that his instructions to his men to make it easier for Ruth to gather food was a small gesture with no real significance. But God looks carefully at our deeds and discerns in them layers of meaning and importance beyond our imagination. The deeds of the righteous people in the Book of Ruth achieved the greatest of all imprimaturs: God let them be recorded as part of the Torah. How great man can become! God's Torah was given on Shavuos. And the deeds of mortals, too, have become part of the Torah and are read every Shavuos. This shows us how much we can make of ourselves and our world — if we realize our full potential.

From the Book of Ruth we learn never to underestimate the importance of what we do. As the Midrash unforgettably puts it:

> Scripture teaches us that when a person performs a *mitzvah,* he should do it wholeheartedly … Had Boaz only known that the Holy One, Blessed is He, would inscribe about him, *He handed her parched grain and she ate and was satisfied, and had some left over* (2:4), he would have fed her fatted calves! …
>
> In times past, a person would perform a commandment and a prophet would inscribe it, but now who inscribes the commandment that a person performs? Elijah inscribes it, and the King Messiah and the Holy One, Blessed is He, affix their signatures to it. As it is written: *Then those who fear hashem spoke to one another, and HASHEM listened and heard* (Malachi 3:16).

א וַיְהִי בִּימֵי שְׁפֹט הַשֹּׁפְטִים וַיְהִי רָעָב בָּאָרֶץ וַיֵּלֶךְ
אִישׁ מִבֵּית לֶחֶם יְהוּדָה לָגוּר בִּשְׂדֵי מוֹאָב הוּא

ב וְאִשְׁתּוֹ וּשְׁנֵי בָנָיו: וְשֵׁם הָאִישׁ אֱלִימֶלֶךְ וְשֵׁם
אִשְׁתּוֹ נָעֳמִי וְשֵׁם שְׁנֵי־בָנָיו | מַחְלוֹן וְכִלְיוֹן
אֶפְרָתִים מִבֵּית לֶחֶם יְהוּדָה וַיָּבֹאוּ שְׂדֵי־מוֹאָב

ג וַיִּהְיוּ־שָׁם: וַיָּמָת אֱלִימֶלֶךְ אִישׁ נָעֳמִי וַתִּשָּׁאֵר

ד הִיא וּשְׁנֵי בָנֶיהָ: וַיִּשְׂאוּ לָהֶם נָשִׁים מֹאֲבִיּוֹת שֵׁם
הָאַחַת עָרְפָּה וְשֵׁם הַשֵּׁנִית רוּת וַיֵּשְׁבוּ שָׁם

ה כְּעֶשֶׂר שָׁנִים: וַיָּמֻתוּ גַם־שְׁנֵיהֶם מַחְלוֹן וְכִלְיוֹן

ו וַתִּשָּׁאֵר הָאִשָּׁה מִשְּׁנֵי יְלָדֶיהָ וּמֵאִישָׁהּ: וַתָּקָם
הִיא וְכַלֹּתֶיהָ וַתָּשָׁב מִשְּׂדֵי מוֹאָב כִּי שָׁמְעָה
בִּשְׂדֵה מוֹאָב כִּי־פָקַד יְהוָה אֶת־עַמּוֹ לָתֵת לָהֶם

ז לָחֶם: וַתֵּצֵא מִן־הַמָּקוֹם אֲשֶׁר הָיְתָה־שָּׁמָּה וּשְׁתֵּי
כַלֹּתֶיהָ עִמָּהּ וַתֵּלַכְנָה בַדֶּרֶךְ לָשׁוּב אֶל־אֶרֶץ

ח יְהוּדָה: וַתֹּאמֶר נָעֳמִי לִשְׁתֵּי כַלֹּתֶיהָ לֵכְנָה

יעש ק שֹׁבְנָה אִשָּׁה לְבֵית אִמָּהּ יַעֲשֶׂה יְהוָה עִמָּכֶם

ט חֶסֶד כַּאֲשֶׁר עֲשִׂיתֶם עִם־הַמֵּתִים וְעִמָּדִי: יִתֵּן
יְהוָה לָכֶם וּמְצֶאןָ מְנוּחָה אִשָּׁה בֵּית אִישָׁהּ

י וַתִּשַּׁק לָהֶן וַתִּשֶּׂאנָה קוֹלָן וַתִּבְכֶּינָה: וַתֹּאמַרְנָה־

יא לָּהּ כִּי־אִתָּךְ נָשׁוּב לְעַמֵּךְ: וַתֹּאמֶר נָעֳמִי שֹׁבְנָה
בְנֹתַי לָמָּה תֵלַכְנָה עִמִּי הַעוֹד־לִי בָנִים בְּמֵעַי

יב וְהָיוּ לָכֶם לַאֲנָשִׁים: שֹׁבְנָה בְנֹתַי לֵכְןָ כִּי זָקַנְתִּי
מִהְיוֹת לְאִישׁ כִּי אָמַרְתִּי יֶשׁ־לִי תִקְוָה גַּם הָיִיתִי

יג הַלַּיְלָה לְאִישׁ וְגַם יָלַדְתִּי בָנִים: הֲלָהֵן | תְּשַׂבֵּרְנָה
עַד אֲשֶׁר יִגְדָּלוּ הֲלָהֵן תֵּעָגֵנָה לְבִלְתִּי הֱיוֹת
לְאִישׁ אַל בְּנֹתַי כִּי־מַר־לִי מְאֹד מִכֶּם כִּי־יָצְאָה

RUTH 1:1-13

1/1. THE FAMINE

The story of Ruth occurred before the reign of King Saul, when the Jews were governed by Judges. According to *Seder Hadoros* and *Tzemach David,* the episode happened approximately in the year 2787 (973 B.C.E)

2. *Ephrathites.* The *Midrash* considers the word to be a title of honor, interpreting it to mean 'courtiers,' 'aristocrats.' Bethlehem was originally called 'Ephrath,' and later given the name Bethlehem.

… They were the most prominent citizens of the most prominent city in Eretz Yisrael *(Malbim).*

3. ELIMELECH DIES

An untimely death *(Midrash).* This punishment was inflicted upon the family 'because they should have begged for mercy for their generation and they did not do so' *(Bava Basra 91b)*

4. Ruth and Orpah were the daughters of Eglon King of Moab *(Talmud).*

8. NAOMI TRIES TO DISSUADE HER DAUGHTERS-IN-LAW

[The Sages rule that one must attempt to dissuade a would-be convert three times; this was the first time — the others are in verses 11 and 12.]

13. *Would you wait for them?* I.e. for the hypothetical children to whom I might give birth? *(Iggeres Shmuel).*

¹ **A**nd it happened in the days when the Judges judged, that there was a famine in the land, and a man went from Bethlehem in Judah to sojourn in the fields of Moab, he, his wife, and his two sons. ² The man's name was Elimelech, his wife's name was Naomi, and his two sons were named Machlon and Kilion, Ephrathites of Bethlehem in Judah. They came to the field of Moab and there they remained.

³ Elimelech, Naomi's husband, died; and she was left with her two sons. ⁴ They married Moabite women, one named Orpah, and the other Ruth, and they lived there about ten years. ⁵ The two of them, Machlon and Kilion, also died; and the woman was bereft of her two children and of her husband.

⁶ She then arose along with her daughter-in-law to return from the fields of Moab, for she had heard in the fields of Moab that HASHEM had remembered His people by giving them food. ⁷ She left the place where she had been, accompanied by her two daughters-in-law, and they set out on the road to return to the land of Judah.

⁸ Then Naomi said to her two daughters-in-law: 'Go, return, each of you to her mother's house. May HASHEM deal kindly with you, as you have dealt kindly with the dead and with me! ⁹ May HASHEM grant that you may find security, each in the home of her husband.' She kissed them, and they raised their voice and wept. ¹⁰ And they said to her: 'No, we will return with you to your people.' ¹¹ But Naomi said: 'Turn back, my daughters. Why should you come with me? Have I more sons in my womb who could become husbands to you? ¹² Turn back, my daughters, go along, for I am too old to have a husband. Even if I were to say: there is hope for me, and even if I were to have a husband tonight — and even bear sons — ¹³ would you wait for them until they were grown up? Would you tie yourselves down for them and not marry anyone else? No, my daughters! I am very embittered on account of you;

יד בִּי יַד־יְהֹוָה: וַתִּשֶּׂנָה קוֹלָן וַתִּבְכֶּינָה עֲוֹד וַתִּשַּׁק

טו עָרְפָּה לַחֲמוֹתָהּ וְר֫וּת דָּבְקָה בָּהּ: וַתֹּאמֶר הִנֵּה
שָׁבָה יְבִמְתֵּךְ אֶל־עַמָּהּ וְאֶל־אֱלֹהֶיהָ שׁוּבִי אַחֲרֵי

טז יְבִמְתֵּךְ: וַתֹּאמֶר רוּת אַל־תִּפְגְּעִי־בִי לְעָזְבֵךְ
לָשׁוּב מֵאַחֲרָיִךְ כִּי אֶל־אֲשֶׁר תֵּלְכִי אֵלֵךְ וּבַאֲשֶׁר

יז תָּלִינִי אָלִין עַמֵּךְ עַמִּי וֵאלֹהַיִךְ אֱלֹהָי: בַּאֲשֶׁר
תָּמוּתִי אָמוּת וְשָׁם אֶקָּבֵר כֹּה יַעֲשֶׂה יְהֹוָה לִי

יח וְכֹה יוֹסִיף כִּי הַמָּוֶת יַפְרִיד בֵּינִי וּבֵינֵךְ: וַתֵּרֶא כִּי־
מִתְאַמֶּצֶת הִיא לָלֶכֶת אִתָּהּ וַתֶּחְדַּל לְדַבֵּר

יט אֵלֶיהָ: וַתֵּלַכְנָה שְׁתֵּיהֶם עַד־בּוֹאָנָה בֵּית לָחֶם
וַיְהִי כְּבוֹאָנָה בֵּית לֶחֶם וַתֵּהֹם כָּל־הָעִיר עֲלֵיהֶן

כ וַתֹּאמַרְנָה הֲזֹאת נָעֳמִי: וַתֹּאמֶר אֲלֵיהֶן אַל־
תִּקְרֶאנָה לִי נָעֳמִי קְרֶאןָ לִי מָרָא כִּי־הֵמַר שַׁדַּי

כא לִי מְאֹד: אֲנִי מְלֵאָה הָלַכְתִּי וְרֵיקָם הֱשִׁיבַנִי יְהֹוָה
לָמָּה תִקְרֶאנָה לִי נָעֳמִי וַיהֹוה עָנָה בִי וְשַׁדַּי

כב הֵרַע־לִי: וַתָּשָׁב נָעֳמִי וְר֫וּת הַמּוֹאֲבִיָּה כַלָּתָהּ
עִמָּהּ הַשָּׁבָה מִשְּׂדֵי מוֹאָב וְהֵמָּה בָּאוּ בֵּית לֶחֶם

ב א בִּתְחִלַּת קְצִיר שְׂעֹרִים: וּלְנָעֳמִ֗י °מִידָע לְאִישָׁהּ °מוֹדַע ק׳
אִישׁ גִּבּוֹר חַיִל מִמִּשְׁפַּחַת אֱלִימֶלֶךְ וּשְׁמוֹ בֹּעַז:

ב וַתֹּאמֶר רוּת הַמּוֹאֲבִיָּה אֶל־נָעֳמִי אֵלְכָה־נָּא
הַשָּׂדֶה וַאֲלַקֳּטָה בַשִּׁבֳּלִים אַחַר אֲשֶׁר אֶמְצָא־חֵן

ג בְּעֵינָיו וַתֹּאמֶר לָהּ לְכִי בִתִּי: וַתֵּלֶךְ וַתָּבוֹא
וַתְּלַקֵּט בַּשָּׂדֶה אַחֲרֵי הַקֹּצְרִים וַיִּקֶר מִקְרֶהָ
חֶלְקַת הַשָּׂדֶה לְבֹעַז אֲשֶׁר מִמִּשְׁפַּחַת אֱלִימֶלֶךְ:

ד וְהִנֵּה־בֹעַז בָּא מִבֵּית לֶחֶם וַיֹּאמֶר לַקּוֹצְרִים יְהֹוָה
עִמָּכֶם וַיֹּאמְרוּ לוֹ יְבָרֶכְךָ יְהֹוָה: וַיֹּאמֶר בֹּעַז

14. ORPAH PARTS; RUTH CLINGS

Orpah kissed. The kiss was their parting. No words. Only a kiss. Scripture divulges no more, but the pain was intense. As Naomi watched Orpah walk towards Moab, she knew that the last vestige of her son Kilion was lost to her forever.

19. RETURN TO BETHLEHEM

The two of them. See how precious proselytes are to God! Once she decided to convert, Scriptures ranked her equally with Naomi *(Midrash; Rashi).*

'Could this be Naomi?' In the past, she used to go in a covered carriage, and now she walks barefoot; in the past, she wore a cloak of fine wool, and now she is clothed in rags; in the past, her appearance was full from food and drink, now it is shrunken from hunger — *could this be Naomi? (Midrash).*

How can you call me Naomi: How can you call me a name describing good fortune — a name which in retrospect, I was never really entitled to — seeing how afflicted I have become! *(Malbim).*

2/ RUTH MEETS BOAZ

1. *Naomi had a relative.* He was the son of Elimelech's brother *(Rashi).* Although Boaz was a close relative, Naomi avoided him even in her dire need. She did not ask him for support because she still felt shame at having deserted her people during the famine, while Boaz stayed on and supported them. In addition, she was aware that Boaz was angry that she had brought a Moabite girl back with her. He avoided them both until God brought Ruth to his fields [verse 3] and he realized how virtuous she was *(Alshich).*

4. *Boaz had arrived.* He had returned to his field after completion of the mourning period for his wife who had recently died *(Midrash).*

for the hand of HASHEM has gone forth against me.'

[14] They raised up their voice and wept again. Orpah kissed her mother-in-law, but Ruth clung to her. [15] So she said: 'Look, your sister-in-law has returned to her people and to her god; go follow your sister-in-law.' [16] But Ruth said: 'Do not urge me to leave you, to turn back and not follow you. For wherever you go, I will go; where you lodge, I will lodge; your people are my people, and your God is my God; [17] where you die, I will die, and there I will be buried. Thus may HASHEM do to me — and more! — if anything but death separates me from you.'

[18] When she saw she was determined to go with her, she stopped arguing with her, [19] and the two of them went on until they came to Bethlehem.

And it came to pass, when they arrived in Bethlehem, the whole city was tumultuous over them, and the women said: 'Could this be Naomi?' [20] 'Do not call me Naomi [pleasant one],' she replied, 'call me Mara [embittered one], for the Almighty has dealt very bitterly with me. [21] I was full when I went away, but HASHEM has brought me back empty. How can you call me Naomi — HASHEM has testified against me, the Almighty has brought misfortune upon me!'

[22] And so it was that Naomi returned, and Ruth the Moabite, her daughter-in-law, with her — who returned from the fields of Moab. They came to Bethlehem at the beginning of the barley harvest.

[1] **N**aomi had a relative through her husband, a man of substance, from the family of Elimelech, whose name was Boaz.

[2] Ruth the Moabite said to Naomi: 'Let me go out to the field, and glean among the ears of grain behind someone in whose eyes I shall find favor.' 'Go ahead, my daughter,' she said to her.

[3] So off she went. She came and gleaned in the field behind the harvesters, and her fate made her happen upon a parcel of land belonging to Boaz, who was of the family of Elimelech.

[4] Behold, Boaz arrived from Bethlehem. He greeted the harvesters, 'HASHEM be with you!' And they answered him: 'May HASHEM bless you!'

לְנַעֲרוֹ הַנִּצָּב עַל־הַקּוֹצְרֶים לְמִי הַנַּעֲרָה הַזְּאת:

ו וַיַּעַן הַנַּעַר הַנִּצָּב עַל־הַקּוֹצְרֶים וַיֹּאמַר נַעֲרָה מוֹאֲבִיָּה הִיא הַשָּׁבָה עִם־נָעֳמִי מִשְּׂדֵי מוֹאָב:

ז וַתֹּאמֶר אֲלַקֳטָה־נָּא וְאָסַפְתִּי בָעֳמָרִים אַחֲרֵי הַקּוֹצְרֵים וַתָּבוֹא וַתַּעֲמוֹד מֵאָז הַבֹּקֶר וְעַד־עַתָּה זֶה שִׁבְתָּהּ הַבַּיִת מְעָט:

ח וַיֹּאמֶר בֹּעַז אֶל־רוּת הֲלוֹא שָׁמַעַתְּ בִּתִּי אַל־תֵּלְכִי לִלְקֹט בְּשָׂדֶה אַחֵר וְגַם לֹא תַעֲבוּרִי מִזֶּה וְכֹה תִדְבָּקִין עִם־נַעֲרֹתָי:

ט עֵינַיִךְ בַּשָּׂדֶה אֲשֶׁר־יִקְצֹרוּן וְהָלַכְתְּ אַחֲרֵיהֶן הֲלוֹא צִוִּיתִי אֶת־הַנְּעָרִים לְבִלְתִּי נָגְעֵךְ וְצָמִת וְהָלַכְתְּ אֶל־הַכֵּלִים וְשָׁתִית מֵאֲשֶׁר יִשְׁאֲבוּן הַנְּעָרִים:

י וַתִּפֹּל עַל־פָּנֶיהָ וַתִּשְׁתַּחוּ אָרְצָה וַתֹּאמֶר אֵלָיו מַדּוּעַ מָצָאתִי חֵן בְּעֵינֶיךָ לְהַכִּירֵנִי וְאָנֹכִי נָכְרִיָּה:

יא וַיַּעַן בֹּעַז וַיֹּאמֶר לָהּ הֻגֵּד הֻגַּד לִי כֹּל אֲשֶׁר־עָשִׂית אֶת־חֲמוֹתֵךְ אַחֲרֵי מוֹת אִישֵׁךְ וַתַּעַזְבִי אָבִיךְ וְאִמֵּךְ וְאֶרֶץ מוֹלַדְתֵּךְ וַתֵּלְכִי אֶל־

יב עַם אֲשֶׁר לֹא־יָדַעַתְּ תְּמוֹל שִׁלְשׁוֹם: יְשַׁלֵּם יְהוָה פָּעֳלֵךְ וּתְהִי מַשְׂכֻּרְתֵּךְ שְׁלֵמָה מֵעִם יְהוָה אֱלֹהֵי יִשְׂרָאֵל אֲשֶׁר־בָּאת לַחֲסוֹת תַּחַת־כְּנָפָיו:

יג וַתֹּאמֶר אֶמְצָא־חֵן בְּעֵינֶיךָ אֲדֹנִי כִּי נִחַמְתָּנִי וְכִי דִבַּרְתָּ עַל־לֵב שִׁפְחָתֶךָ וְאָנֹכִי לֹא אֶהְיֶה כְּאַחַת שִׁפְחֹתֶיךָ:

יד וַיֹּאמֶר לָהּ בֹעַז לְעֵת הָאֹכֶל גֹּשִׁי הֲלֹם וְאָכַלְתְּ מִן־הַלֶּחֶם וְטָבַלְתְּ פִּתֵּךְ בַּחֹמֶץ וַתֵּשֶׁב מִצַּד הַקֹּצְרִים וַיִּצְבָּט־לָהּ קָלִי וַתֹּאכַל וַתִּשְׂבַּע וַתֹּתַר:

טו וַתָּקָם לְלַקֵּט וַיְצַו בֹּעַז אֶת־נְעָרָיו לֵאמֹר גַּם בֵּין הָעֳמָרִים תְּלַקֵּט וְלֹא תַכְלִימוּהָ: וְגַם שֹׁל־

5. *To whom does that young woman belong?* When he noticed her modesty he inquired about her. The other women jested with the harvesters, while she remained reserved; the other women gathered from *between* the sheaves, while she gathered only from that which was definitely abandoned *(Midrash).*

6. *'She is a Moabite girl'* — and yet you say her conduct is praiseworthy and modest? Her good manners are not her own. Her seemingly modest behavior was drilled into her by her mother-in-law *(Midrash).* Thus, the overseer tried to dissuade Boaz from showing interest in the girl.

7. *And she had said.* This is a continuation of the overseer's response to Boaz…

10. RUTH'S GRATITUDE

Then she fell on her face. In humble gratitude for his graciousness and cordiality towards her *(Alshich).*

11. BOAZ REASSURES RUTH

Boaz responds that he has heard of her extraordinary and magnanimous deeds in the exemplary way she treated her mother-in-law, and her leaving home and family to embrace Judaism.

⁵ Boaz then said to his servant who was overseeing the harvesters: 'To whom does that young woman belong?' ⁶ 'She is a Moabite girl,' the servant who was overseeing the harvesters replied, ' — the one that returned with Naomi from the fields of Moab; ⁷ and she had said: "Please let me glean, and gather among the sheaves behind the harvesters." So she came, and has been on her feet since the morning until now; except for her resting a little in the hut.'

⁸ Then Boaz said to Ruth: 'Hear me well, my daughter. Do not go to glean in another field, and don't leave here, but stay close to my maidens. ⁹ Keep your eyes on the field which they are harvesting and follow them. I have ordered the young men not to molest you. Should you get thirsty, go to the jugs and drink from what the young men have drawn.'

¹⁰ Then she fell on her face, bowing down to the ground, and said to him: 'Why have I found favor in your eyes that you should take special note of me though I am a foreigner?'

¹¹ Boaz replied and said to her: 'I have been fully informed of all that you have done for your mother-in-law after the death of your husband; how you left your father and mother and the land of your birth and went to a people you had never known before. ¹² May HASHEM reward your actions, and may your payment be full from HASHEM, the God of Israel, under whose wings you have come to seek refuge.'

¹³ Then she said: 'May I continue to find favor in your eyes, my lord, because you have comforted me, and because you have spoken to the heart of your maid-servant — though I am not even as worthy as one of your maid-servants.'

¹⁴ At mealtime, Boaz said to her, 'Come over here and partake of the bread, and dip your morsel in the vinegar.' So she sat beside the harvesters. He handed her parched grain, and she ate and was satisfied, and had some left over.

¹⁵ Then she got up to glean, and Boaz ordered his young men, saying: 'Let her glean even among the sheaves; do not embarrass her. ¹⁶ And even

תָּשֹׁלּוּ לָהּ מִן־הַצְּבָתִים וַעֲזַבְתֶּם וְלִקְּטָה וְלֹא

יז תִגְעֲרוּ־בָהּ: וַתְּלַקֵּט בַּשָּׂדֶה עַד־הָעָרֶב וַתַּחְבֹּט

יח אֵת אֲשֶׁר־לִקֵּטָה וַיְהִי כְּאֵיפָה שְׂעֹרִים: וַתִּשָּׂא

וַתָּבוֹא הָעִיר וַתֵּרֶא חֲמוֹתָהּ אֵת אֲשֶׁר־לִקֵּטָה

וַתּוֹצֵא וַתִּתֶּן־לָהּ אֵת אֲשֶׁר־הוֹתִרָה מִשָּׂבְעָהּ:

יט וַתֹּאמֶר לָהּ חֲמוֹתָהּ אֵיפֹה לִקַּטְתְּ הַיּוֹם וְאָנָה

עָשִׂית יְהִי מַכִּירֵךְ בָּרוּךְ וַתַּגֵּד לַחֲמוֹתָהּ אֵת

אֲשֶׁר־עָשְׂתָה עִמּוֹ וַתֹּאמֶר שֵׁם הָאִישׁ אֲשֶׁר

עָשִׂיתִי עִמּוֹ הַיּוֹם בֹּעַז: וַתֹּאמֶר נָעֳמִי לְכַלָּתָהּ

כ בָּרוּךְ הוּא לַיהוָה אֲשֶׁר לֹא־עָזַב חַסְדּוֹ אֶת־

הַחַיִּים וְאֶת־הַמֵּתִים וַתֹּאמֶר לָהּ נָעֳמִי קָרוֹב לָנוּ

כא הָאִישׁ מִגֹּאֲלֵנוּ הוּא: וַתֹּאמֶר רוּת הַמּוֹאֲבִיָּה גַּם |

כִּי־אָמַר אֵלַי עִם־הַנְּעָרִים אֲשֶׁר־לִי תִּדְבָּקִין עַד

כב אִם־כִּלּוּ אֵת כָּל־הַקָּצִיר אֲשֶׁר־לִי: וַתֹּאמֶר נָעֳמִי

אֶל־רוּת כַּלָּתָהּ טוֹב בִּתִּי כִּי תֵצְאִי עִם־נַעֲרוֹתָיו

כג וְלֹא יִפְגְּעוּ־בָךְ בְּשָׂדֶה אַחֵר: וַתִּדְבַּק בְּנַעֲרוֹת

בֹּעַז לְלַקֵּט עַד־כְּלוֹת קְצִיר־הַשְּׂעֹרִים וּקְצִיר

ג א הַחִטִּים וַתֵּשֶׁב אֶת־חֲמוֹתָהּ: וַתֹּאמֶר לָהּ נָעֳמִי

חֲמוֹתָהּ בִּתִּי הֲלֹא אֲבַקֶּשׁ־לָךְ מָנוֹחַ אֲשֶׁר יִיטַב־

ב לָךְ: וְעַתָּה הֲלֹא בֹעַז מֹדַעְתָּנוּ אֲשֶׁר הָיִית אֶת־

נַעֲרוֹתָיו הִנֵּה־הוּא זֹרֶה אֶת־גֹּרֶן הַשְּׂעֹרִים

ג הַלָּיְלָה: וְרָחַצְתְּ | וָסַכְתְּ וְשַׂמְתְּ °שִׂמְלֹתֵךְ עָלַיִךְ °שִׂמְלֹתַיִךְ ק׳

°וְיָרַדְתְּ הַגֹּרֶן אַל־תִּוָּדְעִי לָאִישׁ עַד כַּלֹּתוֹ °וְיָרַדְתִּי ק׳

ד לֶאֱכֹל וְלִשְׁתּוֹת: וִיהִי בְשָׁכְבוֹ וְיָדַעַתְּ אֶת־הַמָּקוֹם

אֲשֶׁר יִשְׁכַּב־שָׁם וּבָאת וְגִלִּית מַרְגְּלֹתָיו

°וְשָׁכָבְתְּ וְהוּא יַגִּיד לָךְ אֵת אֲשֶׁר תַּעֲשִׂין: °וְשָׁכַבְתִּי ק׳

deliberately pull out some for her from the heaps and leave them for her to glean; don't rebuke her.'

¹⁷ So she gleaned in the field until evening, and she beat out what she had gleaned — it came to about an ephah of barley. ¹⁸ She carried it and came to the city. Her mother-in-law saw what she had gleaned, and she took out and gave her what she had left over after eating her fill.

¹⁹ 'Where did you glean today?' her mother-in-law asked her. 'Where did you work? May the one that took such generous notice of you be blessed.' So she told her mother-in-law whom she had worked by, and said: 'The name of the man by whom I worked today is Boaz.'

²⁰ Naomi said to her daughter-in-law: 'Blessed be he of HASHEM , for not failing in his kindness to the living or to the dead! The man is closely related to us.' Naomi then said to her, 'He is one of our redeeming kinsmen.'

²¹ And Ruth the Moabite said: 'What's more, he even said to me: "Stay close to my workers, until they have finished all my harvest." ²² Naomi said to her daughter-in-law Ruth: 'It is fine, my daughter, that you go out with his young women, so that you will not be annoyed in another field.'

²³ So she stayed close to Boaz' young women to glean, until the end of the barley harvest and of the wheat harvest. Then she stayed [at home] with her mother-in-law.

3/ NAOMI'S PLAN

¹ Naomi, her mother-in-law, said to her: 'My daughter, I must seek security for you, that it may go well with you. ² Now, Boaz, our relative, with whose maidens you have been, will be winnowing barley tonight on the threshing floor. ³ Therefore, bathe and anoint yourself, don your finery, and go down to the threshing floor, but do not make yourself known to the man until he has finished eating and drinking. ⁴ And when he lies down, note the place where he lies, and go over, uncover his feet, and lie down. He will tell you what you are to do.'

---

20. *He is one of our redeeming kinsmen.* The גֹּאֵל, *redeemer,* is the next of kin who is obligated to redeem the property which his impoverished relative was compelled to sell (see *Leviticus 25:25*).

4. A brother who refuses to enter into יִבּוּם, *levirate marriage,* undergoes a ceremony of *chalitzah* which involves the removal of his shoe [see *Deut. 25:5-10*]. Although Boaz was not Machlon's brother, as his redeemer Boaz had a moral obligation to marry Ruth. Therefore Naomi suggested that Ruth 'uncover his feet,' a gesture reminiscent of *chalitzah,* in the hope that it would make Boaz aware of his moral obligation *(Malbim).*

ה וַתֹּאמֶר אֵלֶיהָ כֹּל אֲשֶׁר־תֹּאמְרִי ‪°‬ אֶעֱשֶֽׂה:

°אֵלַי קרי ולא כתיב

ו וַתֵּרֶד הַגֹּרֶן וַתַּעַשׂ כְּכֹל אֲשֶׁר־צִוַּתָּה חֲמוֹתָֽהּ:

ז וַיֹּאכַל בֹּעַז וַיֵּשְׁתְּ וַיִּיטַב לִבּוֹ וַיָּבֹא לִשְׁכַּב בִּקְצֵה הָעֲרֵמָה וַתָּבֹא בַלָּט וַתְּגַל מַרְגְּלֹתָיו וַתִּשְׁכָּֽב:

ח וַיְהִי בַּחֲצִי הַלַּיְלָה וַיֶּחֱרַד הָאִישׁ וַיִּלָּפֵת וְהִנֵּה

ט אִשָּׁה שֹׁכֶבֶת מַרְגְּלֹתָיו: וַיֹּאמֶר מִי־אָתְּ וַתֹּאמֶר אָנֹכִי רוּת אֲמָתֶךָ וּפָרַשְׂתָּ כְנָפֶךָ עַל־אֲמָתְךָ כִּי

י גֹאֵל אָֽתָּה: וַיֹּאמֶר בְּרוּכָה אַתְּ לַיהוָה בִּתִּי הֵיטַבְתְּ חַסְדֵּךְ הָאַחֲרוֹן מִן־הָרִאשׁוֹן לְבִלְתִּי

יא לֶכֶת אַחֲרֵי הַבַּחוּרִים אִם־דַּל וְאִם־עָשִׁיר: וְעַתָּה בִּתִּי אַל־תִּירְאִי כֹּל אֲשֶׁר־תֹּאמְרִי אֶעֱשֶׂה־לָּךְ כִּי

יב יוֹדֵעַ כָּל־שַׁעַר עַמִּי כִּי אֵשֶׁת חַיִל אָֽתְּ: וְעַתָּה כִּי אָמְנָם כִּי °אִם גֹּאֵל אָנֹכִי וְגַם יֵשׁ גֹּאֵל קָרוֹב

°כתיב ולא קרי

יג מִמֶּנִּי: לִינִי | הַלַּיְלָה וְהָיָה בַבֹּקֶר אִם־יִגְאָלֵךְ טוֹב יִגְאָל וְאִם־לֹא יַחְפֹּץ לְגָאֳלֵךְ וּגְאַלְתִּיךְ אָנֹכִי חַי־

יד יהוָה שִׁכְבִי עַד־הַבֹּקֶר: וַתִּשְׁכַּב מַרְגְּלוֹתָו עַד־ הַבֹּקֶר וַתָּקָם °בטרום יַכִּיר אִישׁ אֶת־רֵעֵהוּ

°בְּטֶרֶם ק'

טו וַיֹּאמֶר אַל־יִוָּדַע כִּי־בָאָה הָאִשָּׁה הַגֹּרֶן: וַיֹּאמֶר הָבִי הַמִּטְפַּחַת אֲשֶׁר־עָלַיִךְ וְאֶחֳזִי־בָהּ וַתֹּאחֶז בָּהּ וַיָּמָד שֵׁשׁ־שְׂעֹרִים וַיָּשֶׁת עָלֶיהָ וַיָּבֹא הָעִֽיר:

טז וַתָּבוֹא אֶל־חֲמוֹתָהּ וַתֹּאמֶר מִי־אַתְּ בִּתִּי וַתַּגֶּד־ לָהּ אֵת כָּל־אֲשֶׁר עָֽשָׂה־לָהּ הָאִֽישׁ: וַתֹּאמֶר שֵׁשׁ־

יז הַשְּׂעֹרִים הָאֵלֶּה נָתַן לִי כִּי אָמַר ‪°‬ אַל־תָּבוֹאִי

°אֵלַי קרי ולא כתיב

יח רֵיקָם אֶל־חֲמוֹתֵֽךְ: וַתֹּאמֶר שְׁבִי בִתִּי עַד אֲשֶׁר תֵּדְעִין אֵיךְ יִפֹּל דָּבָר כִּי לֹא יִשְׁקֹט הָאִישׁ כִּי אִם־

א כִּלָּה הַדָּבָר הַיּֽוֹם: וּבֹעַז עָלָה הַשַּׁעַר וַיֵּשֶׁב שָׁם

ד

5. The word אֵלַי, *to me,* is read, but it does not appear in the written Hebrew text. This, and all textual readings, as transmitted by the *Soferim,* are *Halachah* from Moses at Sinai (*Nedarim* 37b). The omitted אֵלַי demonstrates the extent to which Ruth left matters in the hands of Heaven — as if she excluded *herself,* and had no personal stake in their resolution; she left everything to God's beneficence (*M'lo HaOmer*).

9. *Spread your robe,* as a token of marriage. She said, 'Redeem the estate and take me as a wife, so that the name of the deceased will be perpetuated on his property. If you marry me, people will say: "She was the wife of Machlon" whenever I visit the field' (*Rashi*).

11. BOAZ REASSURES HER

12. *I am a redeemer.* The written text has כִּי אִם גֹּאֵל אָנֹכִי, *For if I am a redeemer;* but according to the *Masorah* the word אִם, *if,* is written but not read': because it implies uncertainty, while in fact there *was* definitely another redeemer (*Midrash Lekach Tov; Rashi*).

17. *For he said to me.* The word אֵלַי, *to me,* is read, but it does not appear in the written Hebrew text. By omitting אֵלַי, Ruth intimated that Boaz, in his modesty, did not even look directly at her during their conversation (*Iggeres Shmuel*).

4/ BOAZ FULFILLS HIS PROMISE

⁵ She replied, 'All that you say to me I will do.'

⁶ So she went down to the threshing floor and did everything as her mother-in-law instructed her. ⁷ Boaz ate and drank and his heart was merry. He went to lie down at the end of the grain pile, and she came stealthily, uncovered his feet, and lay down. ⁸ In the middle of the night the man was startled, and turned about — there was a woman lying at his feet!

⁹ 'Who are you?' he asked. And she answered: 'I am your handmaid, Ruth. Spread your robe over your handmaid; for you are a redeemer.'

¹⁰ And he said: 'Be blessed of HASHEM, my daughter; you have made your latest act of kindness greater than the first, in that you have not gone after the younger men, be they poor or rich. ¹¹ And now, my daughter, do not fear; whatever you say, I will do for you; for all the men in the gate of my people know that you are a worthy woman. ¹² Now while it is true that I am a redeemer; there is also another redeemer closer than I. ¹³ Stay the night, then in the morning, if he will redeem you, fine! Let him redeem. But if he does not want to redeem you, then I will redeem you "Chai HASHEM"! Lie down until the morning.'

¹⁴ So she lay at his feet until the morning and she arose before one man could recognize another, for he said: 'Let it not be known that the woman came to the threshing floor.' ¹⁵ And he said, 'Hold out the shawl you are wearing and grasp it.' She held it, and he measured out six measures of barley, and set it on her; then he went into the city.

¹⁶ She came to her mother-in-law who said: 'How do things stand with you, my daughter?' So she told her all that the man had done for her, ¹⁷ and she said: 'He gave me these six measures of barley for he said to me, "Do not go emptyhanded to your mother-in-law." '

¹⁸ Then she said, 'Sit patiently, my daughter, until you know how the matter will turn out, for the man will not rest unless he settles the matter today.'

¹ **B**oaz, meanwhile, had gone up to the gate, and sat down there. Just then, the redeemer of

וְהִנֵּה הַגֹּאֵל עֹבֵר אֲשֶׁר דִּבֶּר־בֹּעַז וַיֹּאמֶר סוּרָה

ב שְׁבָה־פֹּה פְּלֹנִי אַלְמֹנִי וַיָּסַר וַיֵּשֵׁב: וַיִּקַּח עֲשָׂרָה אֲנָשִׁים מִזִּקְנֵי הָעִיר וַיֹּאמֶר שְׁבוּ־פֹה וַיֵּשֵׁבוּ:

ג וַיֹּאמֶר לַגֹּאֵל חֶלְקַת הַשָּׂדֶה אֲשֶׁר לְאָחִינוּ לֶאֱלִימֶלֶךְ מָכְרָה נָעֳמִי הַשָּׁבָה מִשְּׂדֵה מוֹאָב:

ד וַאֲנִי אָמַרְתִּי אֶגְלֶה אָזְנְךָ לֵאמֹר קְנֵה נֶגֶד הַיֹּשְׁבִים וְנֶגֶד זִקְנֵי עַמִּי אִם־תִּגְאַל גְּאָל וְאִם־לֹא יִגְאַל הַגִּידָה לִּי וְאֵדְעָ כִּי אֵין זוּלָתְךָ לִגְאוֹל

ה וְאָנֹכִי אַחֲרֶיךָ וַיֹּאמֶר אָנֹכִי אֶגְאָל: וַיֹּאמֶר בֹּעַז בְּיוֹם־קְנוֹתְךָ הַשָּׂדֶה מִיַּד נָעֳמִי וּמֵאֵת רוּת הַמּוֹאֲבִיָּה אֵשֶׁת־הַמֵּת °קָנִיתִי לְהָקִים שֵׁם־הַמֵּת °קָנִיתָ ק

ו עַל־נַחֲלָתוֹ: וַיֹּאמֶר הַגֹּאֵל לֹא אוּכַל °לִגְאוֹל־לִי פֶּן־ °לִגְאָל ק אַשְׁחִית אֶת־נַחֲלָתִי גְּאַל־לְךָ אַתָּה אֶת־גְּאֻלָּתִי

ז כִּי לֹא־אוּכַל לִגְאֹל: וְזֹאת לְפָנִים בְּיִשְׂרָאֵל עַל־ הַגְּאוּלָּה וְעַל־הַתְּמוּרָה לְקַיֵּם כָּל־דָּבָר שָׁלַף אִישׁ נַעֲלוֹ וְנָתַן לְרֵעֵהוּ וְזֹאת הַתְּעוּדָה בְּיִשְׂרָאֵל:

ח וַיֹּאמֶר הַגֹּאֵל לְבֹעַז קְנֵה־לָךְ וַיִּשְׁלֹף נַעֲלוֹ:

ט וַיֹּאמֶר בֹּעַז לַזְּקֵנִים וְכָל־הָעָם עֵדִים אַתֶּם הַיּוֹם כִּי קָנִיתִי אֶת־כָּל־אֲשֶׁר לֶאֱלִימֶלֶךְ וְאֵת כָּל־אֲשֶׁר

י לְכִלְיוֹן וּמַחְלוֹן מִיַּד נָעֳמִי: וְגַם אֶת־רוּת הַמֹּאֲבִיָּה אֵשֶׁת מַחְלוֹן קָנִיתִי לִי לְאִשָּׁה לְהָקִים שֵׁם־הַמֵּת עַל־נַחֲלָתוֹ וְלֹא־יִכָּרֵת שֵׁם־הַמֵּת מֵעִם

יא אֶחָיו וּמִשַּׁעַר מְקוֹמוֹ עֵדִים אַתֶּם הַיּוֹם: וַיֹּאמְרוּ כָּל־הָעָם אֲשֶׁר־בַּשַּׁעַר וְהַזְּקֵנִים עֵדִים יִתֵּן יְהוָה אֶת־הָאִשָּׁה הַבָּאָה אֶל־בֵּיתֶךָ כְּרָחֵל | וּכְלֵאָה אֲשֶׁר בָּנוּ שְׁתֵּיהֶם אֶת־בֵּית יִשְׂרָאֵל וַעֲשֵׂה־חַיִל

Ploni Almoni. — A pseudonym. Sometimes translated 'So and so.' His real name was withheld because he did not discharge his duty as redeemer.

2. Ten men. From here we learn that the blessing of the bridegroom [i.e., a wedding ceremony] requires a מִנְיָן, quorum of ten (Talmud).

According to others in the Talmud, the presence of ten elders was required to publicly confirm the halachah permitting a female Moabite into the community of Israel.

5. BOAZ CLARIFIES

6. THE REDEEMER WITHDRAWS

'Then I cannot redeem it for myself.' Machlon died because he took Ruth — a Moabite woman — as a wife; shall I then go and take her? (Midrash).

'Even if I myself will not die for marrying a Moabite woman, my children may suffer. I will not cause my children to become disqualified.' He was unaware of the law newly publicized permitting a Moabitess (Midrash).

7. THE TRANSACTION IS CONSUMMATED

One would draw off his shoe. To make clear that the transference of a shoe described in this verse is not to be confused with the act of chalitzah (Deut. 29:9) where a similar symbolic act takes place, the verse describes this procedure as one accompanying every exchange and sales transaction (Meishiv Nefesh).

10. Acquisition of a wife and of property are referred to with the same legalisms, but there the similarity ends. A Jewish wife is a respected and beloved partner in the sacred task of building a home. Therefore, Boaz mentions his marriage separately to make it clear that he does not lump Ruth with his newly acquired land.

whom Boaz had spoken passed by. He said, 'Come over, sit down here, Ploni Almoni,' and he came over and sat down. ² He then took ten men of the elders of the city, and said: 'Sit here,' and they sat down.

³ Then he said to the redeemer: 'The parcel of land which belonged to our brother, Elimelech, is being offered for sale by Naomi who has returned from the fields of Moab. ⁴ I resolved that I should inform you to this effect: Buy it in the presence of those sitting here and in the presence of the elders of my people. If you are willing to redeem, redeem! But if it will not be redeemed, tell me, that I may know; for there is no one else to redeem it but you, and I after you.' And he said: 'I am willing to redeem it.'

⁵ Then Boaz said: 'The day you buy the field from Naomi, you must also buy it from Ruth the Moabite, wife of the deceased, to perpetuate the name of the deceased on his inheritance.' ⁶ The redeemer said, 'Then I cannot redeem it for myself, lest I imperil my own inheritance. Take over my redemption responsibility on yourself for I am unable to redeem.'

⁷ Formerly this was done in Israel in cases of redemption and exchange transactions to validate all matters: one would draw off his shoe, and give it to the other. This was the process of ratification in Israel. ⁸ So when the redeemer said to Boaz: 'Buy it for yourself,' he drew off his shoe.

⁹ And Boaz said to the elders, and to all the people: 'You are witness this day, that I have bought all that was Elimelech's and all that was Kilion's and Machlon's from Naomi.

¹⁰ And, what is more important, I have also "acquired" the wife of Machlon as my wife, to perpetuate the name of the deceased on his inheritance, that the name of the deceased not be cut off from among his brethren, and from the gate of his place. You are witnesses today.'

¹¹Then all the people who were at the gate, and the elders, said: 'We are witnesses! May HASHEM make the woman who is coming into your house like Rachel and like Leah, both of whom built up the House of Israel. May you prosper in Ephrath and be

יב בְּאֶפְרָ֔תָה וּקְרָא־שֵׁ֖ם בְּבֵ֥ית לָֽחֶם: וִיהִ֤י בֵֽיתְךָ֙
כְּבֵ֣ית פֶּ֔רֶץ אֲשֶׁר־יָלְדָ֥ה תָמָ֖ר לִֽיהוּדָ֑ה מִן־הַזֶּ֗רַע
יג אֲשֶׁ֨ר יִתֵּ֤ן יהוה֙ לְךָ֔ מִן־הַֽנַּעֲרָ֖ה הַזֹּֽאת: וַיִּקַּ֨ח בֹּ֜עַז
אֶת־ר֗וּת וַתְּהִי־ל֣וֹ לְאִשָּׁ֔ה וַיָּבֹ֖א אֵלֶ֑יהָ וַיִּתֵּ֨ן יהוה֥
יד לָ֛הּ הֵרָי֖וֹן וַתֵּ֥לֶד בֵּֽן: וַתֹּאמַ֤רְנָה הַנָּשִׁים֙ אֶֽל־נָעֳמִ֔י
בָּר֣וּךְ יהוה֔ אֲשֶׁ֨ר לֹ֣א הִשְׁבִּ֥ית לָ֛ךְ גֹּאֵ֖ל הַיּ֑וֹם
טו וְיִקָּרֵ֥א שְׁמ֖וֹ בְּיִשְׂרָאֵֽל: וְהָ֤יָה לָךְ֙ לְמֵשִׁ֣יב נֶ֔פֶשׁ
וּלְכַלְכֵּ֖ל אֶת־שֵׂיבָתֵ֑ךְ כִּ֣י כַלָּתֵ֤ךְ אֲשֶׁר־אֲהֵבַ֙תֶךְ֙
יְלָדַ֔תּוּ אֲשֶׁר־הִיא֙ ט֣וֹבָה לָ֔ךְ מִשִּׁבְעָ֖ה בָּנִֽים:
טז וַתִּקַּ֨ח נָעֳמִ֤י אֶת־הַיֶּ֙לֶד֙ וַתְּשִׁתֵ֣הוּ בְחֵיקָ֔הּ וַתְּהִי־ל֖וֹ
יז לְאֹמֶֽנֶת: וַתִּקְרֶ֩אנָה֩ ל֨וֹ הַשְּׁכֵנ֥וֹת שֵׁם֙ לֵאמֹ֔ר יֻלַּד־
בֵּ֖ן לְנָעֳמִ֑י וַתִּקְרֶ֤אנָה שְׁמוֹ֙ עוֹבֵ֔ד ה֥וּא אֲבִי־יִשַׁ֖י
אֲבִ֥י דָוִֽד:
יח וְאֵ֙לֶּה֙ תּוֹלְד֣וֹת פָּ֔רֶץ פֶּ֖רֶץ הוֹלִ֥יד אֶת־חֶצְרֽוֹן:
יט וְחֶצְרוֹן֙ הוֹלִ֣יד אֶת־רָ֔ם וְרָ֖ם הוֹלִ֥יד אֶת־עַמִּֽינָדָֽב:
כ וְעַמִּֽינָדָב֙ הוֹלִ֣יד אֶת־נַחְשׁ֔וֹן וְנַחְשׁ֖וֹן הוֹלִ֥יד אֶת־
כא שַׂלְמָֽה: וְשַׂלְמוֹן֙ הוֹלִ֣יד אֶת־בֹּ֔עַז וּבֹ֖עַז הוֹלִ֥יד
כב אֶת־עוֹבֵֽד: וְעֹבֵד֙ הוֹלִ֣יד אֶת־יִשַׁ֔י וְיִשַׁ֖י הוֹלִ֥יד
אֶת־דָּוִֽד:

famous in Bethlehem; [12] and may your house be like the house of Peretz, whom Tamar bore to Judah, through the offspring which HASHEM will give you by this young woman.'

13. HOLY SEEDS UNITE

With Ruth's marriage and the birth of her child, her place in Jewish history is secure. Ruth's name is no longer mentioned in the *Megillah.* The Sages maintain she enjoyed unusual longevity. She lived to see her royal descendant Solomon on the throne *(Bava Basra 91b).*

[13] And so, Boaz took Ruth and she became his wife; and he came to her. HASHEM let her conceive, and she bore a son. [14] And the women said to Naomi, 'Blessed be HASHEM who has not left you without a redeemer today! May his name be famous in Israel. [15] He will become your life-restorer, and sustain your old age; for your daughter-in-law, who loves you, has borne him, and she is better to you than seven sons.'

16. RUTH — MOTHER OF ROYALTY

17. The Talmud asks: Was it then Naomi who bore him? Surely it was Ruth who bore him! The answer: Although Ruth bore him, Naomi brought him up; hence he was called Naomi's son *(Sanhedrin 19b).*

18. Having detailed David's descent from Ruth the Moabite, the author now traces David's lineage to Judah *(Rashi).*

[16] Naomi took the child, and held it in her bosom, and she became his nurse. [17] The neighborhood women gave him a name, saying: 'A son is born to Naomi.' They named him Oved; he was the father of Jesse, the father of David.

[18] Now these are the generations of Peretz: Peretz begot Chetzron; [19] and Chetzron begot Ram, and Ram begot Aminadav; [20] and Aminadav begot Nachshon, and Nachshon begot Salman; [21] and Salmah begot Boaz, and Boaz begot Oved; [22] and Oved begot Jesse, and Jesse begot David.

אֵיכָה

eichah

Day of Tragedies

Jeremiah was a young prophet to whom God assigned a heartbreaking task. He was to warn Israel over and over again that destruction and exile were impending. The Ten Tribes of Israel, the Northern Kingdom, had been dispersed many decades before, now it was Jerusalem's turn. Warnings of destruction and pleas for repentance — these were Jeremiah's message, but they were to no avail. Prophets of doom are not popular, and Jeremiah was no exception. His written prophecies were burned, he was thrown into a dungeon, and he was accused as a false prophet and a charlatan.

He might have been excused if he had become consumed with hatred for Israel, the nation that had spurned him, but not Jeremiah. Nebuchadnezzar, the conquering Babylonian King, had given orders to his commanding general Nebuzaradan to do as he wished with the Jewish captives, but not to harm Jeremiah. The prophet sought his suffering brothers. He found their bloody footprints and weepingly knelt to kiss the blood-soaked ground. When he caught up with their famished, brutalized ranks, he embraced and kissed them. He tried to put his own head into the heavy, biting chains that held them, but Nebuzaradan forced him away.

Jeremiah bemoaned the fate that made him witness to Jewish suffering. To his weeping brethren he cried out broken-heartedly, 'If only you had wept once [in remorse over your sins] when you were still in Zion, you would not have been exiled.'

Alas, the people did not weep, but Jeremiah wept — before, during, and after his personal and the national ordeals.

Eichah is his personal elegy, his lament for his people, and it contains allusions to all Jewish woe throughout history.

※　※　※

Eichah is read on Tishah B'Av, the quintessential day of Jewish tragedy. In ancient times, five catastrophies occurred on Tishah B'Av. In the words of *Rambam:*

> On Tishah B'Av, five things occured: (1) It was decreed upon Israel in the desert that they would not enter the Land; (2-3) Both the First and Second Holy Temples were destroyed; (4) A great city named Betar was conquered ... It [Betar] fell into the hands of the Romans and its people were all killed, and it was as great a tragedy as the Destruction of the Temple; (5) And in that day that

was designated for punishment, the wicked Turnus-Rufus plowed up the area of the Temple and its surroundings to fulfill what was said by the prophet (Jeremiah 26:18) *'Zion will be plowed like a field'* (Rambam, Hilchos Ta'anis 5:3)

It is noteworthy that after cataloging the first four tragedies of the Ninth of Av, *Rambam* seems to allow a groan to escape from a heart overflowing with historic Jewish woe: *'And in that day that was designated for punishment,'* he says. It is as if he is telling us that the final brazen, gratuitous sacrilege — the plowing of the holy site where once the Holy of Holies had stood where the pillar of the Divine Presence had rested, where Abraham bound Isaac upon the altar, where all Israel ascended yearly, seasonally, daily to become saturated with holiness — could not have occurred on any other day but Tishah B'Av.

Indeed, Tishah B'Av has served that painful function throughout our history. The Spanish Inquisition reached its climax on the Ninth of Av, 1492, when the great Torah commentator and finance minister of Spain, Don Yitzchak Abarbanel led as many as 75,000 Jews out of Spain. It was their deadline: the day they had to be out of the country or face death for not converting to Christianity.

On Tishah B'Av of 1914, World War I broke out. Not only were countless Eastern European Jewish communities disrupted and hundreds of thousands of Jews turned into refugees during the war, the political, social and military upheavals of the war set in motion the Communist Revolution and Hitler's rise to power. Thus, Tishah B'Av became the root of the Holocaust that killed 6,000,000 Jews, and of the Iron Curtain that clamped shut on 3,000,000 Jews.

It is true that the day itself is destined for tragedy, but Jewish misery does not come of its own accord. Our sins cause it. Or the sins of our ancestors set forces in motion that we could have stopped had we repented — but we did not. As the Sages express it, 'If the Temple was not rebuilt during the time of any generation, it is reckoned as if it had been destroyed during its time,' because the sincere repentance of any generation would end the exile and bring about the coming of the Messiah. The Ninth of Av does not fulfill its purpose if we use it only as a reminder to look into the past and mourn its failures. That is only a first step. More important is that we should reflect upon our historic national suffering and the reasons for it, and then resolve to undo the chains that bind us to the shortcomings of our history. Only then can Tishah B'Av realize its full potential for the good.

Eichah refers to this day as a מוֹעֵד, a *festival* of sorts, a time like Pesach, Shavuos, and Succos when Israel has a spiritual rendezvous with God. This is a day that reminds us of God's watchfulness over His chosen people. Just as He does not long tolerate our sins, so He will not for a moment ignore our repentance.

The Sages teach that the Messiah will be born on Tishah B'Av, meaning that a proper understanding of and reflection upon the causes of destruction contains within it the seeds of redemption. We do not forget our tragedies nor do we dissipate our energies by mourning the past without looking to the future. Rather we always retain our optimism and cultivate the attitude: *Had I not fallen I could not have arisen; had I not sat in the darkness, God would not have been a light for me (Midrash Tehillim* ch. 22).

The prophet Amos (5:2) states a chilling, frightening prophecy: נָפְלָה לֹא תוֹסִיף קוּם בְּתוּלַת יִשְׂרָאֵל, *She has fallen; she shall not again rise the maiden of Israel.*

In *Eretz Yisrael,* they punctuated the verse differently and read it this way: נָפְלָה לֹא תוֹסִיף. קוּם בְּתוּלַת יִשְׂרָאֵל, *She has fallen, she shall not again. Rise, O Maiden of Israel (Berachos* 4b).

After more than nineteen centuries of downfall, may Messiah, born on Tishah B'Av finally come to bring us the glad news, 'You have fallen enough! Rise, O Maiden of Israel!'

א

א **אֵיכָ֣ה ׀ יָשְׁבָ֣ה בָדָ֗ד** הָעִיר֙ רַבָּ֣תִי עָ֔ם הָיְתָ֖ה כְּאַלְמָנָ֑ה רַבָּ֣תִי בַגּוֹיִ֗ם שָׂרָ֙תִי֙ בַּמְּדִינ֔וֹת הָיְתָ֖ה לָמַֽס׃ **בָּכ֧וֹ** תִבְכֶּ֣ה בַּלַּ֗יְלָה וְדִמְעָתָהּ֙ עַ֣ל לֶֽחֱיָ֔הּ אֵֽין־לָ֣הּ מְנַחֵ֔ם מִכׇּל־אֹהֲבֶ֑יהָ כׇּל־רֵעֶ֙יהָ֙ בָּ֣גְדוּ בָ֔הּ ג הָ֥יוּ לָ֖הּ לְאֹיְבִֽים׃ **גָּֽלְתָ֨ה** יְהוּדָ֤ה מֵעֹ֙נִי֙ וּמֵרֹ֣ב עֲבֹדָ֔ה הִ֚יא יָשְׁבָ֣ה בַגּוֹיִ֔ם לֹ֥א מָצְאָ֖ה מָנ֑וֹחַ כׇּל־ רֹדְפֶ֥יהָ הִשִּׂיג֖וּהָ בֵּ֥ין הַמְּצָרִֽים׃ **דַּרְכֵ֨י** צִיּ֜וֹן אֲבֵל֗וֹת מִבְּלִי֙ בָּ֣אֵי מוֹעֵ֔ד כׇּל־שְׁעָרֶ֙יהָ֙ שֽׁוֹמֵמִ֔ין כֹּהֲנֶ֖יהָ נֶאֱנָחִ֑ים בְּתוּלֹתֶ֥יהָ נּוּג֖וֹת וְהִ֥יא מַר־לָֽהּ׃ **הָי֨וּ** צָרֶ֤יהָ לְרֹאשׁ֙ אֹיְבֶ֣יהָ שָׁל֔וּ כִּֽי־יְהֹוָ֥ה הוֹגָ֖הּ עַל־רֹ֣ב פְּשָׁעֶ֑יהָ עֽוֹלָלֶ֛יהָ הָלְכ֥וּ שְׁבִ֖י לִפְנֵי־צָֽר׃ **וַיֵּצֵ֤א**

°מִבַּת ק°

מִן־בַּת־צִיּוֹן֙ כׇּל־הֲדָרָ֔הּ הָי֣וּ שָׂרֶ֗יהָ כְּאַיָּלִים֙ לֹא־ מָצְא֣וּ מִרְעֶ֔ה וַיֵּלְכ֥וּ בְלֹא־כֹ֖חַ לִפְנֵ֥י רוֹדֵֽף׃ **זָכְרָ֣ה** ז יְרוּשָׁלַ֗͏ִם יְמֵ֤י עׇנְיָהּ֙ וּמְרוּדֶ֔יהָ כֹּ֚ל מַחֲמֻדֶ֔יהָ אֲשֶׁ֥ר הָי֖וּ מִ֣ימֵי קֶ֑דֶם בִּנְפֹ֧ל עַמָּ֣הּ בְּיַד־צָ֗ר וְאֵ֤ין עוֹזֵר֙ לָ֔הּ רָא֣וּהָ צָרִ֔ים שָׂחֲק֖וּ עַ֥ל מִשְׁבַּתֶּֽהָ׃ **חֵ֤טְא חָֽטְאָה֙** ח יְר֣וּשָׁלַ֔͏ִם עַל־כֵּ֖ן לְנִידָ֣ה הָיָ֑תָה כׇּֽל־מְכַבְּדֶ֤יהָ הִזִּיל֙וּהָ֙ כִּֽי־רָא֣וּ עֶרְוָתָ֔הּ גַּם־הִ֥יא נֶאֶנְחָ֖ה וַתָּ֥שׇׁב אָחֽוֹר׃ **טֻמְאָתָ֣הּ** ט בְּשׁוּלֶ֗יהָ לֹ֤א זָֽכְרָה֙ אַחֲרִיתָ֔הּ וַתֵּ֣רֶד פְּלָאִ֔ים אֵ֥ין מְנַחֵ֖ם לָ֑הּ רְאֵ֤ה יְהֹוָה֙ אֶת־עׇנְיִ֔י כִּ֥י הִגְדִּ֖יל אוֹיֵֽב׃ **יָד֙ו** פָּ֣רַשׂ צָ֔ר עַ֖ל כׇּל־מַחֲמַדֶּ֑יהָ י כִּֽי־רָאֲתָ֣ה גוֹיִ֗ם בָּ֚אוּ מִקְדָּשָׁ֔הּ אֲשֶׁ֣ר צִוִּ֔יתָה לֹא־ יָבֹ֥אוּ בַקָּהָ֖ל לָֽךְ׃ **כׇּל־עַמָּ֤הּ** נֶאֱנָחִים֙ מְבַקְשִׁ֣ים יא

°מַחֲמַדֵּיהֶם ק°

לֶ֔חֶם נָתְנ֧וּ °מַחֲמוֹדֵּיהֶ֛ם בְּאֹ֖כֶל לְהָשִׁ֣יב נָ֑פֶשׁ רְאֵ֤ה יְהֹוָה֙ וְֽהַבִּ֔יטָה כִּ֥י הָיִ֖יתִי זֽוֹלֵלָֽה׃ **ל֣וֹא אֲלֵיכֶ֗ם** יב כׇּל־עֹ֣בְרֵי דֶ֔רֶךְ הַבִּ֣יטוּ וּרְא֔וּ אִם־יֵ֤שׁ מַכְאוֹב֙

1/1. THE DESOLATION OF JERUSALEM

The prophet Jeremiah wrote סֵפֶר קִינוֹת, the *Book of Lamentations*, which Yehoyakim burned *'on the fire that was in the brazier' [Jeremiah 36:23]*. The book consisted of three chapters [1, 2, and 4] which Jeremiah rewrote. He later added chapters 3 and 5 *(Rashi)*.

2. Many Tishah B'Av customs are inferred from the verses in *Eichah*. An example is *Maharam Rothenburg's* inference from the phrase, *she weeps bitterly in the night*, that *Eichah* is chanted publicly on Tishah B'Av only in the evening and not in the morning [unlike *Megillas Esther* which is read publicly on Purim both evening and morning] *(Sefer Minhagim 34)*.

3. Heathen nations also go into exile, however, since they eat the bread and drink the wine of their captors, they do not experience real exile and privation. For Israel, however, which is forbidden to eat their bread or drink their wine, the exile is real *(Midrash)*.

8. *Jerusalem sinned greatly.* [lit. *'Jerusalem sinned a sin.'*] A sin consists of two parts: the sinful act itself and the thoughts and satisfaction surrounding it. Each part of the sin is evaluated separately and punished separately *(Kiddushin 40a)*. Therefore the verse uses a twin expression of sin — חֵטְא חָטְאָה *(Hagaon Rav Moshe Feinstein זצ"ל)*.

9. *On her hems.* Her sins were plainly evident for all to see *(Rashi)*.

11. JERUSALEM ITSELF LAMENTS

12. Israel says to the nations: 'May there not occur to you what has occurred to me' *(Midrash)*.

¹ **A**las — she sits in solitude! The city that was great with people has become like a widow. The greatest among nations, the princess among provinces, has become a tributary. ² She weeps bitterly in the night and her tear is on her cheek. She has no comforter from all her lovers; all her friends have betrayed her, they have become her enemies. ³ Judah has gone into exile because of suffering and harsh toil. She dwelt among the nations, but found no rest; all her pursuers overtook her in narrow straits. ⁴ The roads of Zion are in mourning for lack of festival pilgrims. All her gates are desolate, her priests sigh; her maidens are aggrieved, and she herself is embittered. ⁵ Her adversaries have become her master, her enemies are at ease, for HASHEM has aggrieved her for her abundant transgressions. Her young children have gone into captivity before the enemy. ⁶ Gone from the daughter of Zion is all her splendor. Her leaders were like deer that found no pasture, but walked on without strength before the pursuer. ⁷ Jerusalem recalled the days of her affliction and sorrow — all the treasures that were hers in the days of old. With the fall of her people into the enemy's hand and none to help her, her enemies saw her and gloated at her downfall. ⁸ Jerusalem sinned greatly, she has therefore become a wanderer. All who once respected her disparage her, for they have seen her disgrace. She herself sighs and turns away. ⁹ Her impurity is on her hems, she was heedless of the consequences. She has sunk astonishingly, there is no one to comfort her. 'Look, HASHEM, at my misery, for the enemy has acted prodigiously!' ¹⁰ The enemy spread out his hand on all her treasures; indeed, she saw nations invade her sanctuary — about whom You had commanded that they should not enter Your congregation. ¹¹ All her people are sighing, searching for bread. They traded their treasures for food to keep alive. 'Look, HASHEM, and behold what a glutton I have become!' ¹² May it not befall you — all who pass by this road. Behold and see, if there is any pain

כְּמַכְאֹבִי֙ אֲשֶׁ֣ר עוֹלַ֣ל לִ֔י אֲשֶׁ֥ר הוֹגָ֖ה יְהֹוָ֑ה בְּי֖וֹם
חֲר֥וֹן אַפּֽוֹ. **מִ**מָּר֛וֹם שָֽׁלַח־אֵ֥שׁ בְּעַצְמֹתַ֖י וַיִּרְדֶּ֑נָּה יג
פָּרַ֨שׂ רֶ֤שֶׁת לְרַגְלַי֙ הֱשִׁיבַ֣נִי אָח֔וֹר נְתָנַ֙נִי֙ שֹֽׁמֵמָ֔ה
כָּל־הַיּ֖וֹם דָּוָֽה. **נִ**שְׂקַ֞ד עֹ֤ל פְּשָׁעַי֙ בְּיָד֔וֹ יִשְׂתָּֽרְג֖וּ יד
עָל֣וּ עַל־צַוָּארִ֑י הִכְשִׁ֣יל כֹּחִ֔י נְתָנַ֣נִי אֲדֹנָ֔י בִּידֵ֖י
לֹא־אוּכַ֥ל קֽוּם. **סִ**לָּ֨ה כָל־אַבִּירַ֤י | אֲדֹנָי֙ בְּקִרְבִּ֔י טו
קָרָ֥א עָלַ֛י מוֹעֵ֖ד לִשְׁבֹּ֣ר בַּחוּרָ֑י גַּ֣ת דָּרַ֣ךְ אֲדֹנָ֔י
לִבְתוּלַ֖ת בַּת־יְהוּדָֽה. **עַל**־אֵ֣לֶּה | אֲנִ֣י בֽוֹכִיָּ֗ה עֵינִ֤י | טז
עֵינִי֙ יֹ֣רְדָה מַּ֔יִם כִּֽי־רָחַ֥ק מִמֶּ֛נִּי מְנַחֵ֖ם מֵשִׁ֣יב נַפְשִׁ֑י
הָי֤וּ בָנַי֙ שֽׁוֹמֵמִ֔ים כִּ֥י גָבַ֖ר אוֹיֵֽב. **פֵּ**רְשָׂ֨ה צִיּ֜וֹן יז
בְּיָדֶ֗יהָ אֵ֤ין מְנַחֵם֙ לָ֔הּ צִוָּ֧ה יְהֹוָ֛ה לְיַעֲקֹ֖ב סְבִיבָ֣יו
צָרָ֑יו הָיְתָ֧ה יְרוּשָׁלַ֛͏ִם לְנִדָּ֖ה בֵּֽינֵיהֶֽם. **צַ**דִּ֥יק ה֛וּא יח
יְהֹוָ֖ה כִּ֣י פִ֣יהוּ מָרִ֑יתִי שִׁמְעוּ־נָ֣א כָל־°עַמִּ֗ים וּרְאוּ֙ °הָעַמִּים ק
מַכְאֹבִ֔י בְּתוּלֹתַ֥י וּבַחוּרַ֖י הָלְכ֥וּ בַשֶּֽׁבִי. **קָ**רָ֤אתִי יט
לַֽמְאַהֲבַי֙ הֵ֣מָּה רִמּ֔וּנִי כֹּהֲנַ֥י וּזְקֵנַ֖י בָּעִ֣יר גָּוָ֑עוּ כִּֽי־
בִקְשׁ֥וּ אֹ֙כֶל֙ לָ֔מוֹ וְיָשִׁ֖יבוּ אֶת־נַפְשָֽׁם. **רְ**אֵ֨ה יְהֹוָ֤ה כ
כִּֽי־צַר־לִ֙י֙ מֵעַ֣י חֳמַרְמָ֔רוּ נֶהְפַּ֤ךְ לִבִּי֙ בְּקִרְבִּ֔י כִּ֥י
מָר֖וֹ מָרִ֑יתִי מִח֥וּץ שִׁכְּלָה־חֶ֖רֶב בַּבַּ֥יִת כַּמָּֽוֶת.
שָֽׁמְע֗וּ כִּ֤י נֶֽאֱנָחָה֙ אָ֔נִי אֵ֥ין מְנַחֵ֖ם לִ֑י כָּל־אֹ֨יְבַ֜י כא
שָֽׁמְע֤וּ רָֽעָתִי֙ שָׂ֔שׂוּ כִּ֥י אַתָּ֖ה עָשִׂ֑יתָ הֵבֵ֥אתָ יוֹם־
קָרָ֖אתָ וְיִֽהְי֣וּ כָמֹֽנִי. **תָּבֹ֨א** כָל־רָֽעָתָ֤ם לְפָנֶ֙יךָ֙ כב
וְעוֹלֵ֣ל לָ֔מוֹ כַּאֲשֶׁ֥ר עוֹלַ֛לְתָּ לִ֖י עַ֣ל כָּל־פְּשָׁעָ֑י כִּֽי־
רַבּ֥וֹת אַנְחֹתַ֖י וְלִבִּ֥י דַוָּֽי.

ב

אֵיכָה֩ יָעִ֨יב בְּאַפּ֤וֹ | אֲדֹנָי֙ אֶת־בַּת־צִיּ֔וֹן הִשְׁלִ֤יךְ א
מִשָּׁמַ֙יִם֙ אֶ֔רֶץ תִּפְאֶ֖רֶת יִשְׂרָאֵ֑ל וְלֹא־זָכַ֥ר הֲדֹם־
רַגְלָ֖יו בְּי֥וֹם אַפּֽוֹ. **בִּ**לַּ֨ע °אֲדֹנָ֜י לֹ֣א חָמַ֗ל אֵ֣ת כָּל־ ב °ולא ק

14. God collected all Zion's transgressions and metaphorically 'knit' them together into a heavy garment which He thrust upon her neck in one heavy, cumulative load, effectively weighing her down, and sapping her strength until she was unable to withstand the enemy.

15. *He proclaimed a set time against me,* i.e., the Ninth of Av *(Taanis 29a).*

17. In this parenthetic verse there is a momentary shift from first person (Zion lamenting) to third person. Jeremiah becomes the speaker and acknowledges that God is the executor of the calamity.

18. [Zion itself resumes the lament, and confesses publicly and without reservation that God is righteous and justified in what He had done.]

21. Let them share my suffering, — but let them have no part in my ultimate restoration *(Midrash).*

2/1. *Daughter of Zion* is a poetic form, used to denote Jerusalem or its populace.

like my pain which befell me; which HASHEM has afflicted me on the day of His wrath. ¹³ From on high He sent a fire into my bones, and it crushed them. He spread a net for my feet hurling me backward. He made me desolate; in constant misery. ¹⁴ The burden of my transgressions was accumulated in His hand; they were knit together and thrust upon my neck — He sapped my strength. The Lord has delivered me into the hands of those I cannot withstand. ¹⁵ The Lord has trampled all my heroes in my midst; He proclaimed a set time against me to crush my young men. As in a winepress the Lord has trodden the maiden daughter of Judah. ¹⁶ Over these things I weep; my eyes run with water because a comforter to revive my spirit is far from me. My children have become forlorn, because the enemy has prevailed. ¹⁷ Zion spread out her hands; there was none to comfort her. HASHEM commanded against Jacob that his enemies should surround him; Jerusalem has become as one unclean in their midst. ¹⁸ It is HASHEM Who is righteous, for I disobeyed His utterance. Listen, all you peoples and behold my pain: My maidens and my youths have gone into captivity. ¹⁹ I called for my lovers but they deceived me. My priests and my elders perished in the city as they sought food for themselves to keep alive. ²⁰ See, HASHEM, how distressed I am; my insides churn! My heart is turned over inside me for I rebelled grievously. Outside the sword bereaved, inside was death-like. ²¹ They heard how I sighed, there was none to comfort me. All my enemies heard of my plight and rejoiced, for it was You Who did it. O bring on the day You proclaimed and let them be like me! ²² Let all their wickedness come before You, and inflict them as You inflicted me for all my transgressions. For my groans are many, and my heart is sick.

¹ **A**las — The Lord in His anger has clouded the daughter of Zion. He cast down from heaven to earth the glory of Israel. He did not remember His footstool on the day of His wrath. ² The Lord consumed without pity all the dwell-

נְא֣וֹת יַעֲקֹב֮ הָרַ֣ס בְּעֶבְרָתוֹ֒ מִבְצְרֵ֖י בַת־יְהוּדָ֑ה

ג הִגִּ֥יעַ לָאָ֖רֶץ חִלֵּ֣ל מַמְלָכָ֣ה וְשָׂרֶ֑יהָ. גָּדַ֣ע בׇּחֳרִי־
אַ֗ף כֹּ֚ל קֶ֣רֶן יִשְׂרָאֵ֔ל הֵשִׁ֥יב אָח֖וֹר יְמִינ֣וֹ מִפְּנֵ֣י
אוֹיֵ֑ב וַיִּבְעַ֤ר בְּיַעֲקֹב֙ כְּאֵ֣שׁ לֶֽהָבָ֔ה אָכְלָ֖ה סָבִֽיב.

ד דָּרַ֨ךְ קַשְׁתּ֜וֹ כְּאוֹיֵ֗ב נִצָּ֤ב יְמִינוֹ֙ כְּצָ֔ר וַֽיַּהֲרֹ֔ג כֹּ֖ל
מַחֲמַדֵּי־עָ֑יִן בְּאֹ֙הֶל֙ בַּת־צִיּ֔וֹן שָׁפַ֥ךְ כָּאֵ֖שׁ חֲמָתֽוֹ.

ה הָיָ֨ה אֲדֹנָ֤י ׀ כְּאוֹיֵב֙ בִּלַּ֣ע יִשְׂרָאֵ֔ל בִּלַּ֖ע כׇּל־
אַרְמְנוֹתֶ֑יהָ שִׁחֵ֖ת מִבְצָרָ֑יו וַיֶּ֙רֶב֙ בְּבַת־יְהוּדָ֔ה

ו תַּאֲנִיָּ֖ה וַאֲנִיָּֽה. וַיַּחְמֹ֤ס כַּגַּן֙ שֻׂכּ֔וֹ שִׁחֵ֖ת מֹעֲד֑וֹ
שִׁכַּ֣ח יְהֹוָ֣ה ׀ בְּצִיּ֗וֹן מוֹעֵד֙ וְשַׁבָּ֔ת וַיִּנְאַ֥ץ בְּזַֽעַם־אַפּ֖וֹ

ז מֶ֥לֶךְ וְכֹהֵֽן. זָנַ֨ח אֲדֹנָ֤י ׀ מִזְבְּחוֹ֙ נִאֵ֣ר מִקְדָּשׁ֔וֹ
הִסְגִּיר֙ בְּיַד־אוֹיֵ֔ב חוֹמֹ֖ת אַרְמְנוֹתֶ֑יהָ ק֛וֹל נָתְנ֥וּ

ח בְּבֵית־יְהֹוָ֖ה כְּי֥וֹם מוֹעֵֽד. חָשַׁ֨ב יְהֹוָ֤ה ׀ לְהַשְׁחִית֙
חוֹמַ֣ת בַּת־צִיּ֔וֹן נָ֣טָה קָ֔ו לֹא־הֵשִׁ֥יב יָד֖וֹ מִבַּלֵּ֑עַ

ט וַיַּֽאֲבֶל־חֵ֥ל וְחוֹמָ֖ה יַחְדָּ֥ו אֻמְלָֽלוּ. טָבְע֤וּ בָאָ֙רֶץ֙
שְׁעָרֶ֔יהָ אִבַּ֥ד וְשִׁבַּ֖ר בְּרִיחֶ֑יהָ מַלְכָּ֤הּ וְשָׂרֶ֙יהָ֙
בַגּוֹיִם֙ אֵ֣ין תּוֹרָ֔ה גַּם־נְבִיאֶ֕יהָ לֹא־מָצְא֥וּ חָז֖וֹן

י מֵיְהֹוָֽה. יֵשְׁב֨וּ לָאָ֤רֶץ יִדְּמוּ֙ זִקְנֵ֣י בַת־צִיּ֔וֹן הֶֽעֱל֤וּ
עָפָר֙ עַל־רֹאשָׁ֔ם חָגְר֖וּ שַׂקִּ֑ים הוֹרִ֤ידוּ לָאָ֙רֶץ֙

יא רֹאשָׁ֔ן בְּתוּלֹ֖ת יְרוּשָׁלָֽ͏ִם. כָּל֤וּ בַדְּמָעוֹת֙ עֵינַ֔י
חֳמַרְמְר֣וּ מֵעַ֔י נִשְׁפַּ֤ךְ לָאָ֙רֶץ֙ כְּבֵדִ֔י עַל־שֶׁ֖בֶר בַּת־

יב עַמִּ֑י בֵּעָטֵ֤ף עוֹלֵל֙ וְיוֹנֵ֔ק בִּרְחֹב֖וֹת קִרְיָֽה. לְאִמֹּתָ֣ם
יֹאמְר֔וּ אַיֵּ֖ה דָּגָ֣ן וָיָ֑יִן בְּהִֽתְעַטְּפָ֤ם כֶּֽחָלָל֙ בִּרְחֹב֣וֹת

יג עִ֔יר בְּהִשְׁתַּפֵּ֣ךְ נַפְשָׁ֔ם אֶל־חֵ֖יק אִמֹּתָֽם. מָֽה־
°אֲעִידֵ֨ךְ מָ֣ה אֲדַמֶּה־לָּ֗ךְ הַבַּת֙ יְר֣וּשָׁלַ֔͏ִם מָ֤ה
אַשְׁוֶה־לָּךְ֙ וַֽאֲנַֽחֲמֵ֔ךְ בְּתוּלַ֖ת בַּת־צִיּ֑וֹן כִּֽי־גָד֥וֹל

°אֲעִידֵ֖ךְ ק

3. *He withdrew His right hand, i.e.,* He refrained from doing battle for His children *(Rashi).*

4. In this verse God is depicted, not only in His passive role as the One who withdrew His support, but as One who actively participated in Israel's destruction.

He consumed all her citadels. He thus vented His anger by directing His actions 'on wood and stone' [i.e., on inanimate objects rather than on human lives] so as to avoid the total slaughter of the Jews themselves *(Palgei Mayim).*

7. *As though it were a festival day.* The heathens clamored joyously at the destruction of the Temple, matching the fervor of Israel's joyous chants on its holidays *(Alshich; Rashi).*

9. *Minchas Shay* explains that the ט of טָבְעוּ, *sunk,* is written as a smaller letter in *Megillah* scrolls to allude to ט, *the Ninth,* of Av when the Temple was destroyed.

10. This verse is cited as a basis for the Halachic customs of sitting on the ground on Tishah B'Av. The 12th-century *Sefer HaEshkol* says: After the final meal, we go to the synagogue without shoes and sit on the ground as it is written: *'sit on the ground in silence.'*

ings of Jacob; in His anger He razed the fortresses of the daughter of Judah down to the ground; He profaned the kingdom and its leaders. ³ He cut down, in fierce anger, all the dignity of Israel; He withdrew His right hand in the presence of the enemy. He burned through Jacob like a flaming fire, consuming on all sides. ⁴ He bent His bow like an enemy. His right hand poised like a foe, He slew all who were of pleasant appearance. In the tent of the daughter of Zion He poured out His wrath like fire. ⁵ The Lord became like an enemy. He consumed Israel; He consumed all her citadels, He destroyed its fortresses. He increased within the daughter of Judah moaning and mourning. ⁶ He stripped His Booth like a garden, He destroyed his place of assembly. HASHEM made Zion oblivious of festival and Sabbath, and in His fierce anger He spurned king and priest. ⁷ The Lord rejected His altar, abolished His Sanctuary; He handed over to the enemy the walls of her citadels. They raised a clamor in the House of HASHEM as though it were a festival. ⁸ HASHEM resolved to destroy the wall of the daughter of Zion. He stretched out the line and did not relent from devouring. Indeed, He made rampart and wall mourn; together they languished. ⁹ Her gates have sunk into the earth, He has utterly shattered her bars; her king and officers are among the heathen, there is no Torah; her prophets, too, find no vision from HASHEM. ¹⁰ The elders of the daughter of Zion sit on the ground in silence; they have strewn ashes on their heads, and wear sackcloth. The maidens of Jerusalem have bowed their heads to the ground. ¹¹ My eyes fail with tears, my insides churn; my liver spills on the ground at the shattering of my people, while babes and sucklings swoon in the streets of the city. ¹² They say to their mothers, 'Where is bread and wine?' as they swoon like a dying man in the streets of the town; as their soul ebbs away in their mothers' laps. ¹³ With what shall I bear witness for you? To what can I compare you, O daughter of Jerusalem? To what can I liken you to comfort you, O maiden daughter of Zion? — Your ruin is as vast as the sea; who can

יד כַּיָּ֣ם שִׁבְרֵ֔ךְ מִ֖י יִרְפָּא־לָ֑ךְ. נְבִיאַ֗יִךְ חָ֤זוּ לָךְ֙ שָׁ֣וְא
°שְׁבוּתֵךְ ק וְתָפֵ֔ל וְלֹֽא־גִלּ֥וּ עַל־עֲוֺנֵ֖ךְ לְהָשִׁ֣יב °שביתך וַיֶּ֣חֱזוּ
טו לָ֔ךְ מַשְׂא֥וֹת שָׁ֖וְא וּמַדּוּחִֽם. סָֽפְק֨וּ עָלַ֤יִךְ כַּפַּ֨יִם֙
כָּל־עֹ֣בְרֵי דֶ֔רֶךְ שָֽׁרְקוּ֙ וַיָּנִ֣עוּ רֹאשָׁ֔ם עַל־בַּ֖ת
יְרוּשָׁלָ֑͏ִם הֲזֹ֣את הָעִ֗יר שֶׁיֹּֽאמְרוּ֙ כְּלִ֣ילַת יֹ֔פִי
טז מָשׂ֖וֹשׂ לְכָל־הָאָֽרֶץ. פָּצ֨וּ עָלַ֤יִךְ פִּיהֶם֙ כָּל־אֹ֣יְבַ֔יִךְ
שָֽׁרְקוּ֙ וַיַּֽחַרְקוּ־שֵׁ֔ן אָֽמְר֖וּ בִּלָּ֑עְנוּ אַ֣ךְ זֶ֧ה הַיּ֛וֹם
יז שֶׁקִּוִּינֻ֖הוּ מָצָ֥אנוּ רָאִֽינוּ. עָשָׂ֨ה יְהֹוָ֜ה אֲשֶׁ֣ר זָמָ֗ם
בִּצַּ֤ע אֶמְרָתוֹ֙ אֲשֶׁ֣ר צִוָּ֣ה מִֽימֵי־קֶ֔דֶם הָרַ֖ס וְלֹ֣א
יח חָמָ֑ל וַיְשַׂמַּ֤ח עָלַ֨יִךְ֙ אוֹיֵ֔ב הֵרִ֖ים קֶ֥רֶן צָרָֽיִךְ. צָעַ֥ק
לִבָּ֖ם אֶל־אֲדֹנָ֑י חוֹמַ֣ת בַּת־צִיּ֗וֹן הוֹרִ֤ידִי כַנַּ֨חַל֙
דִּמְעָה֙ יוֹמָ֣ם וָלַ֔יְלָה אַֽל־תִּתְּנִ֤י פוּגַת֙ לָ֔ךְ אַל־תִּדֹּ֖ם
יט בַּת־עֵינֵֽךְ. ק֣וּמִי ׀ רֹ֣נִּי בַלַּ֗יְלָה לְרֹאשׁ֙ אַשְׁמֻר֔וֹת
שִׁפְכִ֤י כַמַּ֨יִם֙ לִבֵּ֔ךְ נֹ֖כַח פְּנֵ֣י אֲדֹנָ֑י שְׂאִ֧י אֵלָ֣יו כַּפַּ֗יִךְ
עַל־נֶ֨פֶשׁ֙ עֽוֹלָלַ֔יִךְ הָעֲטוּפִ֥ים בְּרָעָ֖ב בְּרֹ֥אשׁ כָּל־
כ חוּצֽוֹת. רְאֵ֤ה יְהֹוָה֙ וְֽהַבִּ֔יטָה לְמִ֖י עוֹלַ֣לְתָּ כֹּ֑ה אִם־
תֹּאכַ֨לְנָה נָשִׁ֤ים פִּרְיָם֙ עֹֽלְלֵ֣י טִפֻּחִ֔ים אִם־יֵהָרֵ֛ג
כא בְּמִקְדַּ֥שׁ אֲדֹנָ֖י כֹּהֵ֣ן וְנָבִֽיא. שָֽׁכְב֨וּ לָאָ֤רֶץ חוּצוֹת֙
נַ֣עַר וְזָקֵ֔ן בְּתֽוּלֹתַ֥י וּבַֽחוּרַ֖י נָֽפְל֣וּ בֶחָ֑רֶב הָרַ֨גְתָּ֙
כב בְּי֣וֹם אַפֶּ֔ךָ טָבַ֖חְתָּ לֹ֥א חָמָֽלְתָּ. תִּקְרָא֩ כְי֨וֹם מוֹעֵ֤ד
מְגוּרַי֙ מִסָּבִ֔יב וְלֹ֥א הָיָ֛ה בְּי֥וֹם אַף־יְהֹוָ֖ה פָּלִ֣יט
וְשָׂרִ֑יד אֲשֶׁר־טִפַּ֥חְתִּי וְרִבִּ֖יתִי אֹֽיְבִ֥י כִלָּֽם.

ג א אֲנִ֤י הַגֶּ֨בֶר֙ רָאָ֣ה עֳנִ֔י בְּשֵׁ֖בֶט עֶבְרָתֽוֹ. אֹתִ֥י נָהַ֛ג
ג וַיֹּלַ֖ךְ חֹ֥שֶׁךְ וְלֹא־אֽוֹר. אַ֣ךְ בִּ֥י יָשֻׁ֛ב יַהֲפֹ֥ךְ יָד֖וֹ כָּל־
דה הַיּֽוֹם. בִּלָּ֤ה בְשָׂרִי֙ וְעוֹרִ֔י שִׁבַּ֖ר עַצְמוֹתָֽי. בָּנָ֥ה עָלַ֛י
ו וַיַּקַּ֥ף רֹ֖אשׁ וּתְלָאָֽה. בְּמַֽחֲשַׁכִּ֥ים הֽוֹשִׁיבַ֖נִי כְּמֵתֵ֥י

15. They hiss and wag their head ... In mock and derision, not over your loss, Jerusalem, but for themselves, as the Sages proclaimed: Had the heathens known how much they would lose by destroying the Temple, they would not have done it. The Divine blessing that had rested upon Israel and, through it, upon the entire world, left with the Destruction *(Alshich).*

18. The greatest sin of all is that we, in our time, stopped mourning properly for Jerusalem. I am convinced that, in punishment for this, our exile has lasted so long, we have never been able to find rest, and we are always being persecuted. Historically, whenever we found some security in any of the lands of our exile, we forgot Jerusalem and did not set it at the foremost place in our minds *(Rav Yaakov Emden).*

21. Had the Destruction come on a day other than 'the day of Your wrath,' i.e., Tishah B'Av, it would have been tempered with mercy and restraint. Having come on the day You specifically set aside for display of Your anger, it was untempered and complete *(Lechem Dimah).*

3/1. JEREMIAH'S PERSONAL LAMENT.

Jeremiah laments that he saw more affliction than the other prophets who foretold the Destruction. For it was destroyed not in their days, but in his *(Rashi).* Thus this chapter begins, אֲנִי הַגֶּבֶר, *I am the man,* which has the same numerical value [271] as יִרְמְיָהוּ, Jeremiah *[Tzfunos Yisrael]).*

heal you? [14] Your prophets envisioned for you vanity and foolishness, and they did not expose your iniquity to bring you back in repentance; they prophesied to you oracles of vanity and deception. [15] All who pass along the way clap hands at you; they hiss and wag their head at the daughter of Jerusalem: 'Could this be the city that was called Perfect in Beauty, Joy of All the Earth?' [16] All your enemies jeered at you; they hiss and gnash their teeth. They say: 'We have devoured her! Indeed, this is the day we longed for; we have actually seen it!' [17] HASHEM has done what He planned; He carried out His decree which He ordained long ago; He devastated without pity. He let the enemy rejoice over you; He raised the pride of your foes. [18] Their heart cried out to the Lord. O wall of the daughter of Zion: Shed tears like a river, day and night; give yourself no respite, do not let your eyes be still. [19] Arise, cry out at night in the beginning of the watches! Pour out your heart like water in the Presence of the Lord; lift up your hands to Him for the life of your young children, who swoon from hunger at every street corner. [20] Look, HASHEM, and behold, whom You have treated so. Should women eat their own offspring, the babes of their care? Should priest and prophet be slain in the Sanctuary of the Lord? [21] Out on the ground, in the streets they lie, young and old; my maidens and my young men have fallen by the sword. You slew them on the day of Your wrath; You slaughtered them and showed no mercy. [22] You invited, as though at festival time, my evil neighbors round about. So that, at the day of HASHEM'S wrath, there were none who survived or escaped. Those who I cherished and brought up, my enemy has wiped out.

I am the man who has seen affliction by the rod of His anger. [2] He has driven me on and on into unrelieved darkness. [3] Only against me did He turn His hand repeatedly all day long. [4] He has worn away my flesh and skin; He broke my bones. [5] He besieged and encircled me with bitterness and travail. [6] He has placed me in darkness like the

ז־ח עוֹלָם. גָּדַר בַּעֲדִי וְלֹא אֵצֵא הִכְבִּיד נְחָשְׁתִּי. גַּם

ט כִּי אֶזְעַק וַאֲשַׁוֵּעַ שָׂתַם תְּפִלָּתִי. גָּדַר דְּרָכַי בְּגָזִית

י נְתִיבֹתַי עִוָּה. דֹּב אֹרֵב הוּא לִי °אֲרִי °אֲרִיה ק'

יא בְּמִסְתָּרִים. דְּרָכַי סוֹרֵר וַיְפַשְּׁחֵנִי שָׂמַנִי שֹׁמֵם.

יב־יג דָּרַךְ קַשְׁתּוֹ וַיַּצִּיבֵנִי כַּמַּטָּרָא לַחֵץ. הֵבִיא בְּכִלְיוֹתַי

יד בְּנֵי אַשְׁפָּתוֹ. הָיִיתִי שְּׂחֹק לְכָל־עַמִּי נְגִינָתָם כָּל־

טו־טז הַיּוֹם. הִשְׂבִּיעַנִי בַמְּרוֹרִים הִרְוַנִי לַעֲנָה. וַיַּגְרֵס

יז בֶּחָצָץ שִׁנָּי הִכְפִּישַׁנִי בָּאֵפֶר. וַתִּזְנַח מִשָּׁלוֹם

יח נַפְשִׁי נָשִׁיתִי טוֹבָה. וָאֹמַר אָבַד נִצְחִי וְתוֹחַלְתִּי

יט־כ מֵיהוָה. זְכָר־עָנְיִי וּמְרוּדִי לַעֲנָה וָרֹאשׁ. זָכוֹר

כא תִּזְכּוֹר °וְתָשִׂיחַ עָלַי נַפְשִׁי. זֹאת אָשִׁיב אֶל־לִבִּי °וְתָשׁוֹחַ ק'

כב עַל־כֵּן אוֹחִיל. חַסְדֵי יהוה כִּי לֹא־תָמְנוּ כִּי לֹא־

כג כָלוּ רַחֲמָיו. חֲדָשִׁים לַבְּקָרִים רַבָּה אֱמוּנָתֶךָ.

כד־כה חֶלְקִי יהוה אָמְרָה נַפְשִׁי עַל־כֵּן אוֹחִיל לוֹ. טוֹב

כו יהוה לְקֹוָו לְנֶפֶשׁ תִּדְרְשֶׁנּוּ. טוֹב וְיָחִיל וְדוּמָם

כז לִתְשׁוּעַת יהוה. טוֹב לַגֶּבֶר כִּי־יִשָּׂא עֹל בִּנְעוּרָיו.

כח־כט יֵשֵׁב בָּדָד וְיִדֹּם כִּי נָטַל עָלָיו. יִתֵּן בֶּעָפָר פִּיהוּ

ל אוּלַי יֵשׁ תִּקְוָה. יִתֵּן לְמַכֵּהוּ לֶחִי יִשְׂבַּע בְּחֶרְפָּה.

לא־לב כִּי לֹא יִזְנַח לְעוֹלָם אֲדֹנָי. כִּי אִם־הוֹגָה וְרִחַם

לג כְּרֹב חֲסָדָו. כִּי לֹא עִנָּה מִלִּבּוֹ וַיַּגֶּה בְּנֵי־אִישׁ.

לד־לה לְדַכֵּא תַּחַת רַגְלָיו כֹּל אֲסִירֵי אָרֶץ. לְהַטּוֹת

לו מִשְׁפַּט־גֶּבֶר נֶגֶד פְּנֵי עֶלְיוֹן. לְעַוֵּת אָדָם בְּרִיבוֹ

לז אֲדֹנָי לֹא רָאָה. מִי זֶה אָמַר וַתֶּהִי אֲדֹנָי לֹא צִוָּה.

לח־לט מִפִּי עֶלְיוֹן לֹא תֵצֵא הָרָעוֹת וְהַטּוֹב. מַה־יִּתְאוֹנֵן

מ אָדָם חָי גֶּבֶר עַל־חֲטָאָו. נַחְפְּשָׂה דְרָכֵינוּ

מא וְנַחְקֹרָה וְנָשׁוּבָה עַד־יהוה. נִשָּׂא לְבָבֵנוּ אֶל־

Or the first-person narrative refers to the suffering of the entire nation as a collective entity personified as an individual (Midrash).

14. Jeremiah is lamenting how, whenever he prophesied impending disaster, the Jews would laugh at him and taunt him. Because of their inattentiveness to his prophecies, disaster befell them (Palgei Mayim).

16. The Talmud relates that on the eve of Tishah B'Av, after Rav would complete his regular meal, he would dip a morsel of bread into ashes and say 'This is the essence of the Erev Tishah B'Av meal, in fulfillment of the verse: ... He made me cower in ashes' (Yerushalmi Taanis 4:6).

22. Rashi, whose translation we followed, gives an alternate translation: 'חַסְדֵי ה, it is due to HASHEM's kindness, כִּי לֹא תָמְנוּ, that we were not annihilated for our transgressions, כִּי לֹא כָלוּ רַחֲמָיו — because His mercies are not exhausted [see Numbers 17:28].

26-27. Since we are certain that God will not eternally neglect us, we accept God's afflictions in quiet resignation, and silently anticipate God's ultimate salvation. As for our suffering in the interim ... It is better to bear the yoke in one's youth — while one has the vigor to withstand the tribulations, rather than when old and lacking the stamina (Alshich).

31. In the last several verses, the prophet exhorted man to completely debase himself in resignation before God. Now, he justifies his advice by extolling the compassion of God.

37-40. Rashi groups together four verses and explains: One should never ascribe his suffering to chance, because from whom else but from God do good and evil emanate? Therefore a man should not complain — but should blame his own sins, search his ways and repent.

eternally dead. [7] He has walled me in so I cannot escape; He has weighed me down with chains. [8] Though I would cry out and plead, He shut out my prayer. [9] He has walled up my roads with hewn stones; He tangled up my paths. [10] He is a lurking bear to me, a lion in hiding. [11] He has strewn my paths with thorns and made me tread carefully; He made me desolate. [12] He bent His bow and set me up as a target for the arrow. [13] He shot into my vitals the arrows of His quiver. [14] I have become a laughing stock to all my people; object of their jibes all day long. [15] He filled me with bitterness, sated me with wormwood. [16] He ground my teeth on gravel, He made me cower in ashes. [17] My soul despaired of having peace, I have forgotten goodness. [18] And I said, 'Gone is my strength and my expectation from HASHEM.' [19] Remember my afflictions and my sorrow; the wormwood and bitterness. [20] My soul remembers well — and makes me despondent. [21] Yet, this I bear in mind; therefore I still hope: [22] HASHEM's kindness surely has not ended, nor are His mercies exhausted. [21] They are new every morning; great is Your faithfulness! [24] 'HASHEM is my portion,' says my soul, therefore I have hope in Him. [25] HASHEM as good to those who trust in Him; to the soul that seeks Him. [26] It is good to hope submissively for HASHEM's salvation. [27] It is good for a man that he bear a yoke in his youth. [28] Let one sit in solitude and be submissive, for He has laid it upon him. [29] Let him put his mouth to the dust — there may yet be hope. [30] Let one offer his cheek to his smiter, let him be filled with disgrace. [31] — For the Lord does not reject forever; [32] He first afflicts, then pities according to His abundant kindness. [33] For He does not torment capriciously, nor afflict man ... [34] Nor crush under His feet all the prisoners of the earth; [35] nor deny a man justice in the presence of the Most High. [36] To wrong a man in his conflict — the Lord does not approve. [37] Whose decree was ever fulfilled unless the Lord ordained it? [38] Is it not from the mouth of the Most High that evil and good emanate? [39] Of what shall a living man complain? A strong man for his sins! [40] Let us search and examine our ways and return to HASHEM. [41] Let us lift our hearts with our hands to

מב כַּפָּיִם אֶל־אֵל בַּשָּׁמָיִם. נַחְנוּ פָשַׁעְנוּ וּמָרִינוּ אַתָּה

מג לֹא סָלָחְתָּ. סַכּוֹתָה בָאַף וַתִּרְדְּפֵנוּ הָרַגְתָּ לֹא

מד-מה חָמָלְתָּ. סַכּוֹתָה בֶעָנָן לָךְ מֵעֲבוֹר תְּפִלָּה. סְחִי

מו וּמָאוֹס תְּשִׂימֵנוּ בְּקֶרֶב הָעַמִּים. פָּצוּ עָלֵינוּ פִּיהֶם

מז כָּל־אֹיְבֵינוּ. פַּחַד וָפַחַת הָיָה לָנוּ הַשֵּׁאת וְהַשָּׁבֶר.

מח-מט פַּלְגֵי־מַיִם תֵּרַד עֵינִי עַל־שֶׁבֶר בַּת־עַמִּי. עֵינִי

נ נִגְּרָה וְלֹא תִדְמֶה מֵאֵין הֲפֻגוֹת. עַד־יַשְׁקִיף וְיֵרֶא

נא יְהוָה מִשָּׁמָיִם. עֵינִי עוֹלְלָה לְנַפְשִׁי מִכֹּל בְּנוֹת

נב-נג עִירִי. צוֹד צָדוּנִי כַּצִּפּוֹר אֹיְבַי חִנָּם. צָמְתוּ בַבּוֹר

נד חַיָּי וַיַּדּוּ־אֶבֶן בִּי. צָפוּ־מַיִם עַל־רֹאשִׁי אָמַרְתִּי

נה-נו נִגְזָרְתִּי. קָרָאתִי שִׁמְךָ יְהוָה מִבּוֹר תַּחְתִּיּוֹת. קוֹלִי

שָׁמָעְתָּ אַל־תַּעְלֵם אָזְנְךָ לְרַוְחָתִי לְשַׁוְעָתִי.

נז-נח קָרַבְתָּ בְּיוֹם אֶקְרָאֶךָּ אָמַרְתָּ אַל־תִּירָא. רַבְתָּ

נט אֲדֹנָי רִיבֵי נַפְשִׁי גָּאַלְתָּ חַיָּי. רָאִיתָה יְהוָה עַוָּתָתִי

שְׁפְטָה מִשְׁפָּטִי. רָאִיתָה כָּל־נִקְמָתָם כָּל־

סא מַחְשְׁבֹתָם לִי. שָׁמַעְתָּ חֶרְפָּתָם יְהוָה כָּל־

סב מַחְשְׁבֹתָם עָלָי. שִׂפְתֵי קָמַי וְהֶגְיוֹנָם עָלַי כָּל־

סג הַיּוֹם. שִׁבְתָּם וְקִימָתָם הַבִּיטָה אֲנִי מַנְגִּינָתָם.

סד-סה תָּשִׁיב לָהֶם גְּמוּל יְהוָה כְּמַעֲשֵׂה יְדֵיהֶם. תִּתֵּן

סו לָהֶם מְגִנַּת־לֵב תַּאֲלָתְךָ לָהֶם. תִּרְדֹּף בְּאַף

וְתַשְׁמִידֵם מִתַּחַת שְׁמֵי יְהוָה.

ד

א אֵיכָה יוּעַם זָהָב יִשְׁנֶא הַכֶּתֶם הַטּוֹב תִּשְׁתַּפֵּכְנָה

ב אַבְנֵי־קֹדֶשׁ בְּרֹאשׁ כָּל־חוּצוֹת. בְּנֵי צִיּוֹן הַיְקָרִים

הַמְסֻלָּאִים בַּפָּז אֵיכָה נֶחְשְׁבוּ לְנִבְלֵי־חֶרֶשׂ

ג מַעֲשֵׂה יְדֵי יוֹצֵר. גַּם־תַנִּין חָלְצוּ שַׁד הֵינִיקוּ °תַנִים ק׳

ד גּוּרֵיהֶן בַּת־עַמִּי לְאַכְזָר °כִּי עֵנִים בַּמִּדְבָּר. דָּבַק °כַּיְעֵנִים ק׳

46. Instead of completely ignoring us — as one would normally ignore *'filth and refuse'* — our enemies taunted and jeered at us giving us no peace; not even allowing us to wallow, undisturbed, in our misery *(Ibn Yachya).*

51. This is a personal lament of Jeremiah who was of an aristocratic priestly family. He anguished that his weeping contorted his face and aggrieved his spirit more than any inhabitant of the city. His family was particularly affected, and suffered more than others because, as priests, they had been selected for holiness and the service of God *(Rashi).*

57. The phrase *'Do not be afraid!'* appears throughout Scripture. It was said not only on isolated occasions, but to virtually every one of the fathers of our people; it is a divine promise that Israel need not fear.

64-66. In these verses God is asked to mete out retribution to Israel's enemies, in kind, for all their evil.

4/2. *Midrash Lekach Tov,* commenting on the precious character of the people of Jerusalem, notes that when residents of Jerusalem sat down to eat they would hang a cloth over their door as a signal to the poor that they might come to share their meal [see also *Bava Basra* 93b].

God in heaven: ⁴² 'We have transgressed and rebelled — You have not forgiven. ⁴³ You have enveloped Yourself in anger and pursued us; You have slain mercilessly. ⁴⁴ You wrapped Yourself in a cloud that no prayer can pierce. ⁴⁵ You made us a filth and refuse among the nations.' ⁴⁶ All our enemies jeered at us; ⁴⁷ panic and pitfall were ours, ravage and ruin. ⁴⁸ My eye shed streams of water at the shattering of my people. ⁴⁹ My eye will flow and will not cease — without relief — until HASHEM looks down and takes notice from heaven. ⁵¹ My eyes have brought me grief over all the daughters of my city. ⁵² I have been constantly ensnared like a bird by my enemies without cause. ⁵³ They cut off my life in a pit and threw stones at me. ⁵⁴ Waters flowed over my head; I thought, ' I am doomed!' ⁵⁵ I called on Your name, HASHEM, from the depths of the pit. ⁵⁶ You have heard my voice; do not shut your ear from my prayer for my relief when I cry out. ⁵⁷ You always drew near on the day I would call You; You said, 'Do not be afraid.' ⁵⁸ You always championed my cause, O Lord, you redeemed my life. ⁵⁹ You have seen, HASHEM, the injustices I suffer; judge my cause. ⁶⁰ You have seen all their vengeance, all their designs against me. ⁶¹ You have heard their insults, HASHEM; all their designs regarding me. ⁶² The speech and thoughts of my enemies are against me all day long. ⁶³ Look, in everything they do, I am the butt of their taunts. ⁶⁴ Pay them back their due, HASHEM, as they have done. ⁶⁵ Give them a broken heart; may Your curse be upon them! ⁶⁶ Pursue them in anger and destroy them from under the heavens of HASHEM.

¹ **A**las — The gold is dimmed! The finest gold is changed! Sacred stones are scattered at every street corner! ² The precious children of Zion, who are comparable to fine gold — alas, are now treated like earthen jugs, work of a potter. ³ Even 'Tanim' will offer the breast and suckle their young; the daughter of my people has become cruel, like ostriches in the desert. ⁴ The tongue of the suckling

לְשׁוֹן יוֹנֵק אֶל־חִכּוֹ בַּצָּמָא עוֹלָלִים שָׁאֲלוּ לֶחֶם

ה פֹּרֵשׂ אֵין לָהֶם. הָאֹכְלִים לְמַעֲדַנִּים נָשַׁמּוּ בַּחוּצוֹת הָאֱמֻנִים עֲלֵי תוֹלָע חִבְּקוּ אַשְׁפַּתּוֹת.

ו וַיִּגְדַּל עֲוֺן בַּת־עַמִּי מֵחַטַּאת סְדֹם הַהֲפוּכָה כְמוֹ־

ז רָגַע וְלֹא־חָלוּ בָהּ יָדָיִם. זַכּוּ נְזִירֶיהָ מִשֶּׁלֶג צַחוּ

ח מֵחָלָב אָדְמוּ עֶצֶם מִפְּנִינִים סַפִּיר גִּזְרָתָם. חָשַׁךְ מִשְּׁחוֹר תָּאֳרָם לֹא נִכְּרוּ בַּחוּצוֹת צָפַד עוֹרָם

ט עַל־עַצְמָם יָבֵשׁ הָיָה כָעֵץ. טוֹבִים הָיוּ חַלְלֵי־חֶרֶב מֵחַלְלֵי רָעָב שֶׁהֵם יָזֻבוּ מְדֻקָּרִים מִתְּנוּבֹת שָׂדָי.

י יְדֵי נָשִׁים רַחֲמָנִיּוֹת בִּשְּׁלוּ יַלְדֵיהֶן הָיוּ לְבָרוֹת

יא לָמוֹ בְּשֶׁבֶר בַּת־עַמִּי. כִּלָּה יהוה אֶת־חֲמָתוֹ שָׁפַךְ

יב חֲרוֹן אַפּוֹ וַיַּצֶּת־אֵשׁ בְּצִיּוֹן וַתֹּאכַל יְסֹדֹתֶיהָ. לֹא הֶאֱמִינוּ מַלְכֵי־אֶרֶץ °וְכֹל יֹשְׁבֵי תֵבֵל כִּי יָבֹא צַר °כל ק

יג וְאוֹיֵב בְּשַׁעֲרֵי יְרוּשָׁלָ͏ִם. מֵחַטֹּאת נְבִיאֶיהָ עֲוֺנֹת

יד כֹּהֲנֶיהָ הַשֹּׁפְכִים בְּקִרְבָּהּ דַּם צַדִּיקִים. נָעוּ עִוְרִים בַּחוּצוֹת נְגֹאֲלוּ בַּדָּם בְּלֹא יוּכְלוּ יִגְּעוּ בִּלְבֻשֵׁיהֶם.

טו סוּרוּ טָמֵא קָרְאוּ לָמוֹ סוּרוּ סוּרוּ אַל־תִּגָּעוּ כִּי

טז נָצוּ גַּם־נָעוּ אָמְרוּ בַּגּוֹיִם לֹא יוֹסִפוּ לָגוּר. פְּנֵי יהוה חִלְּקָם לֹא יוֹסִיף לְהַבִּיטָם פְּנֵי כֹהֲנִים לֹא נָשָׂאוּ °זְקֵנִים לֹא חָנָנוּ. °עוֹדֵינָה תִּכְלֶינָה עֵינֵינוּ °זקנים ק / °עודינו ק יז

אֶל־עֶזְרָתֵנוּ הָבֶל בְּצִפִּיָּתֵנוּ צִפִּינוּ אֶל־גּוֹי לֹא

יח יוֹשִׁעַ. צָדוּ צְעָדֵינוּ מִלֶּכֶת בִּרְחֹבֹתֵינוּ קָרַב קִצֵּנוּ

יט מָלְאוּ יָמֵינוּ כִּי־בָא קִצֵּנוּ. קַלִּים הָיוּ רֹדְפֵינוּ מִנִּשְׁרֵי שָׁמָיִם עַל־הֶהָרִים דְּלָקֻנוּ בַּמִּדְבָּר אָרְבוּ

כ לָנוּ. רוּחַ אַפֵּינוּ מְשִׁיחַ יהוה נִלְכַּד בִּשְׁחִיתוֹתָם

כא אֲשֶׁר אָמַרְנוּ בְּצִלּוֹ נִחְיֶה בַגּוֹיִם. שִׂישִׂי וְשִׂמְחִי

5. In the verse Jeremiah further laments the fall of the people from their previous heights to the nethermost depths to which they have fallen. People who were brought up eating only the finest delicacies and dressed only in the most luxurious clothing, now lay faint from hunger in the streets, and scrounged through garbage heaps for the most meager scraps of food *(Lechem Dimah).*

10. The impending Destruction, and the ravages and famine of war, caused compassionate mothers to become so depraved that with their own hands they boiled their children and they consumed them without even leaving flesh for other members of the family *(Alshich).*

The *Shelah* comments that this phrase also contains moralistic criticism of overly compassionate and over-indulgent mothers who, for example, let their children sleep late rather than go to synagogue or to school. With this 'misplaced compassion' they 'roast' and destroy their children's souls.

18. *So we could not walk in our streets.* When a Jew went to market they would pounce on him screaming 'Jew! Jew!' *(Lekach Tov).*

21. The words 'rejoice and exult' are spoken sarcastically: 'Rejoice while you can because you will not escape punishment for your sins' *(Midrash Lekach Tov).*

cleaves to its palate for thirst; young children beg for bread, no one extends it to them. ⁵ Those who feasted extravagantly lie destitute in the streets; those who were brought up in scarlet clothing wallow garbage. ⁶ The iniquity of the daughter of my people is greater than the sin of Sodom, which was overturned in a moment without mortal hands being laid on her. ⁷ Her princes were purer than snow, whiter than milk; their appearance was ruddier than rubies, their outline was like sapphire. ⁸ Their appearance has become blacker than soot, they are not recognized in the streets; their skin has shriveled on their bones, it became dry as wood. ⁹ More fortunate were the victims of the sword than the victims of famine, for they pine away, stricken, lacking the fruits of the field. ¹⁰ Hands of compassionate women have boiled their own children; they became their food when the daughter of my people was shattered. ¹¹ HASHEM vented His fury, He poured out His fierce anger; He kindled a fire in Zion which consumed its foundations. ¹² The kings of the earth did not believe, nor did any of the world's inhabitants, that the adversary or enemy could enter the gates of Jerusalem. ¹³ It was for the sins of her prophets, the iniquities of her priests, who had shed in her midst the blood of the righteous. ¹⁴ The blind wandered through the streets, defiled with blood, so that none could touch their garments. ¹⁵ 'Away, unclean one!' people shouted at them; 'Away! Away! Don't touch! For they are loathsome and wander about.' The nations had said: 'They will not sojourn again.' ¹⁶ The anger of HASHEM has divided them, caring for them no longer; they showed no regard for the priests nor favor for the elders. ¹⁷ Our eyes still strained in vain for our deliverance; in our expectations we watched for a nation that could not save. ¹⁸ They dogged our steps so we could not walk in our streets; our end drew near, our days are done, for our end has come. ¹⁹ Our pursuers were swifter than eagles in the sky; they chased us in the mountains, ambushed us in the desert. ²⁰ The breath of our nostrils, HASHEM's anointed, was caught in their traps; he, under whose protection, we had thought, we would live among the nations. ²¹ Rejoice and exult, O daughter of Edom, who

°יוֹשֶׁבֶת ק׳ בַּת־אֱדוֹם °יוֹשַׁבְתִּי בְּאֶרֶץ עוּץ גַּם־עָלַיִךְ תַּעֲבָר־

כב כּוֹס תִּשְׁכְּרִי וְתִתְעָרִי. תַּם־עֲוֺנֵךְ בַּת־צִיּוֹן לֹא
יוֹסִיף לְהַגְלוֹתֵךְ פָּקַד עֲוֺנֵךְ בַּת־אֱדוֹם גִּלָּה עַל־
חַטֹּאתָיִךְ.

ה

א זְכֹר יהוה מֶה־הָיָה לָנוּ הַבֵּיט וּרְאֵה אֶת־
ב חֶרְפָּתֵנוּ. נַחֲלָתֵנוּ נֶהֶפְכָה לְזָרִים בָּתֵּינוּ לְנָכְרִים.
°וְאֵין ק׳ ג יְתוֹמִים הָיִינוּ °אֵין אָב אִמֹּתֵינוּ כְּאַלְמָנוֹת.
ד־ה מֵימֵינוּ בְּכֶסֶף שָׁתִינוּ עֵצֵינוּ בִּמְחִיר יָבֹאוּ. עַל
°וְלֹא ק׳ ו צַוָּארֵנוּ נִרְדָּפְנוּ יָגַעְנוּ °לֹא הוּנַח־לָנוּ. מִצְרַיִם
ז נָתַנּוּ יָד אַשּׁוּר לִשְׂבֹּעַ לָחֶם. אֲבֹתֵינוּ חָטְאוּ
°וְאֵינָם ק׳ / °וַאֲנַחְנוּ ק׳ ח °אֵינָם °אֲנַחְנוּ עֲוֺנֹתֵיהֶם סָבָלְנוּ. עֲבָדִים מָשְׁלוּ
ט בָנוּ פֹּרֵק אֵין מִיָּדָם. בְּנַפְשֵׁנוּ נָבִיא לַחְמֵנוּ מִפְּנֵי
י חֶרֶב הַמִּדְבָּר. עוֹרֵנוּ כְּתַנּוּר נִכְמָרוּ מִפְּנֵי
יא זַלְעֲפוֹת רָעָב. נָשִׁים בְּצִיּוֹן עִנּוּ בְּתֻלֹת בְּעָרֵי
יב יְהוּדָה. שָׂרִים בְּיָדָם נִתְלוּ פְּנֵי זְקֵנִים לֹא נֶהְדָּרוּ.
יג־יד בַּחוּרִים טְחוֹן נָשָׂאוּ וּנְעָרִים בָּעֵץ כָּשָׁלוּ. זְקֵנִים
טו מִשַּׁעַר שָׁבָתוּ בַּחוּרִים מִנְּגִינָתָם. שָׁבַת מְשׂוֹשׂ
טז לִבֵּנוּ נֶהְפַּךְ לְאֵבֶל מְחוֹלֵנוּ. נָפְלָה עֲטֶרֶת רֹאשֵׁנוּ
יז אוֹי־נָא לָנוּ כִּי חָטָאנוּ. עַל־זֶה הָיָה דָוֶה לִבֵּנוּ עַל־
יח אֵלֶּה חָשְׁכוּ עֵינֵינוּ. עַל הַר־צִיּוֹן שֶׁשָּׁמֵם שׁוּעָלִים
יט הִלְּכוּ־בוֹ. אַתָּה יהוה לְעוֹלָם תֵּשֵׁב כִּסְאֲךָ לְדֹר
כ וָדוֹר. לָמָּה לָנֶצַח תִּשְׁכָּחֵנוּ תַּעַזְבֵנוּ לְאֹרֶךְ יָמִים.
כא הֲשִׁיבֵנוּ יהוה | אֵלֶיךָ וְנָשׁוּבָ וְחַדֵּשׁ יָמֵינוּ כְּקֶדֶם.
כב כִּי אִם־מָאֹס מְאַסְתָּנוּ קָצַפְתָּ עָלֵינוּ עַד־מְאֹד.

The following verse is recited aloud by the congregation,
then repeated by the reader:

הֲשִׁיבֵנוּ יהוה אֵלֶיךָ וְנָשׁוּבָה, חַדֵּשׁ יָמֵינוּ כְּקֶדֶם.

dwells in the land of Uz; to you, too, will the cup pass, you will be drunk and will vomit. ²²Your iniquity is expiated, O daughter of Zion, He will not exile you again; He remembers your iniquity, daughter of Edom, He will uncover your sins.

5/1. Chapter Five is composed of 22 verses like chapters 1, 2 and 4. It differs from the previous four chapters in that it is not alphabetically arranged.

7. Our misfortune is the result of our sins which intermingled with the sins of our ancestors. This follows the doctrine of *punishing the iniquity of the fathers upon the children … of those that hate Me* (Exodus 20:5). God punishes children for the sins of the fathers only if the children 'hate Me,' i.e., they persist in committing those same sins (Sanhedrin 27b).

Rav Yisrael Salanter explained this verse morally: Fathers who do not train their children in the ways of Torah are considered sinners, even when *they are no more*, i.e., after their deaths. Because their children continue the sinful ways for which their fathers are responsible, they, the children *suffer for their father's iniquities*, suffering for which the parents bear the onus.

18. Mount Zion's desolation is so utter, that foxes, which usually dwell in ruins, prowl freely and undisturbed over it *(Ibn Ezra).*

¹ **R**emember, HASHEM, what has befallen us; look and see our disgrace. ² Our inheritance has been turned over to strangers; our houses to foreigners. ³ We have become orphans, fatherless; our mothers are like widows. ⁴ We pay money to drink our own water, obtain our wood at a price. ⁵ Upon our necks we are pursued; we toil, but nothing is left us. ⁶ We stretched out a hand to Egypt, and to Assyria to be satisfied with bread. ⁷ Our fathers have sinned and are no more, and we have suffered for their iniquities. ⁸ Slaves ruled us, there is no rescuer from their hands. ⁹ In mortal danger we bring out bread, because of the sword of the wilderness. ¹⁰ Our skin was scorched like an oven, with the fever of famine. ¹¹ They ravaged women in Zion; maidens in the towns of Judah. ¹² Leaders were hanged by their hand, elders were shown no respect. ¹³ Young men drag the millstone, and youths stumble under the wood. ¹⁴ The elders are gone from the gate, the young men from their music. ¹⁵ Gone is the joy of our hearts, our dancing has turned into mourning. ¹⁶ The crown of our head has fallen; woe to us, for we have sinned. ¹⁷ For this our heart was faint, for these our eyes dimmed: ¹⁸ for Mount Zion which lies desolate, foxes prowled over it. ¹⁹ Yet You, HASHEM, are enthroned forever, Your throne is ageless. ²⁰ Why do You ignore us eternally, forsake us for so long? ²¹ Bring us back to You, HASHEM, and we shall return, renew our days as of old. ²² For even if You had utterly rejected us, You have already raged sufficiently against us.

The following verse is recited aloud by the congregation, then repeated by the reader:

Bring us back …. It is customary to repeat verse 21 rather than end with the rebuke of verse 22 (Rashi).

Bring us back to You, HASHEM, and we shall return, renew our days as of old.

קֹהֶלֶת

koheles

A Sense of Values

Succos is זְמַן שִׂמְחָתֵנוּ, *the time of our gladness.* In *Eretz Yisrael,* the harvest is complete. For everyone, the stressful period of the Days of Awe is over and we prepare to celebrate and express our gratitude for God's blessing, bounty, and protection. It is not surprising that unrestrained joy does not bring out the best in people. We may forget ourselves and fail to live up to our responsibilities as servants of God. To help us retain our perspectives during this season of happiness, major segments of the Jewish people have adopted the custom of reading the sobering Book of Koheles during the services on the Sabbath of the Intermediate Days, or — if all the Intermediate days fall during the week — on Shemini Atzeres. Thinking people cannot be carried away to excess frivolity after listening carefully to Solomon, the wisest of men, proclaiming 'Futility of futilities! All is futile!'

❀   ❀   ❀

Anyone who reads *Koheles* casually would be confused by its apparent gloom and contradictions. The Sages, too, were troubled, and they considered the possiblity of concealing *Koheles,* of removing it from the list of the Sacred Writings. They feared its effect on unlearned people who could not or would not try to understand the deeper meaning of Solomon's difficult pronouncements. There was even fear that the unlearned or uncaring might make heretical interpretations of parts of *Koheles.*

Finally, they decided to let *Koheles* remain in its place of honor, 'because it commences with words of Torah and it concludes with words of Torah' and, as *Rashi* explains, surely the balance of the Book must be understood as following the same pattern of Torah *(Shabbos* 30b). Its opening and its conclusion show beyond a doubt that it is a book filled with fear of God and the spirit of Torah. Indeed there may be those who will refuse to understand it, those who will read false meanings into it. That did not frighten the Sages. It was clear to them that honest, sincere people would understand or, if they did not, that they would seek the guidance of those who did. If there should still be people who persisted in misunderstanding the meaning of the Torah — such as those who insist on prattling about a literal interpretation of 'an eye for an eye' despite the Talmud's explanation that it refers to monetary compensation — then it can only be because they *wish* to

err. No matter how a verse could be rephrased, they would find some pretext to deny its validity, if that is their wish (*Michtav MeEliyahu*).

The fear of those who preferred to conceal Koheles was that the text presented such difficulties that it was inevitable that people would find contradictions or worse. To this objection, the Sages cited the opening and conclusion of the book. It is clearly a statement of Torah, an exposition of fear of God. No one who read its introductory and closing statements could doubt the purity of the entire book.

What are these beginning and closing verses that shed such a favorable light on a book that would otherwise have been feared? The message of the final verse is obvious:

סוֹף דָּבָר הַכֹּל נִשְׁמָע, אֶת הָאֱלֹהִים יְרָא וְאֶת מִצְוֹתָיו שְׁמוֹר, כִּי זֶה כָּל הָאָדָם.

The sum of the matter, when all has been considered: Fear God and keep His commandments, for that is man's whole duty (12:13).

The message of the beginning verse, however, is not so clear. The Talmud tells us that it refers to the third verse of the book:

מַה יִּתְרוֹן לָאָדָם בְּכָל עֲמָלוֹ שֶׁיַּעֲמֹל תַּחַת הַשָּׁמֶשׁ.

What profit does man have for all his labor which he toils beneath the sun? (1:3).

The Talmud (ibid.) explains that man's striving is futile if his concern is to triumph in what is *under* the sun, but if he strives to advance in matters of the Torah and the spirit — which *preceded* and surpass the sun and everything upon which it casts its rays — then whatever man does is hardly futile. It is of the greatest possible importance. *Koheles* is telling us that man should not let himself be blinded by 'the sun' and all the dazzling earthly splendor that occupies so much of our time and energy. Rather we should maintain our sense of values, and always remember that our work and striving, our happiness and gratification on earth should be utilized to help us carry out our mission as the only creature with a Godly soul. If we always bear that in mind, then we have a perspective on what is futile and what is valuable.

Shortly before *Ramban* left Spain to settle in *Eretz Yisrael* in 5027 (1266 C.E.), he delivered a sermon on *Koheles*, in which he set forth the three themes of the Book. As *Ramban* explained them, they are:

(1) Man should avoid the striving after the pleasures of this world, because — for all their allures — they are fleeting and valueless. Pointing to his own material attainments, Solomon speaks of himself as the one who should know this better than anyone else. He could have

anything he wanted — homes, wealth, entertainment, respect, the obeisance of other rulers and wise men. Despite it all, he concludes that all such striving is הֶבֶל, *futility*. *Ramban* defines הֶבֶל as a *mist,* like breath turned to vapor on a cold day, or the stagnant air at the bottom of a pit. One can see the vapor, feel the air, but both have no substance and swiftly disappear.

(2) The spiritual essence is eternal, and the Creator made man to have a vital role in His master plan. It is with this in mind that man should ply his earthly existence. He should satisfy his physical and emotional needs, but his purpose should always be that the purpose of health and prosperity is so that he should be able to serve God better.

(3) How do we respond to the troubling question of why the righteous suffer and wicked prosper? That is a question we can answer only after we know the whole picture. When the final reckoning is made, at the end of a person's lifetime and after his reward and punishment have been totaled, the ledger will show that God's ways are just. No human being can ever know all the facts and all the calculations, because we are trying to apply our human intelligence to the ways of God. But God's intelligence is beyond our capacity — how, then, can we doubt His justice on the basis of our lack of understanding? When the Messiah leads the world to its future state of spiritual grandeur, all will perceive God's mercy in every event. Until then, we must keep our faith and accept the fact that our mortal shortcomings prevent us from comprehending His ways.

Seen this way, *Koheles* hardly dampens the festivity of Succos, rather it deepens our enjoyment of the festival because it helps us focus on what our goals in life should be. And, as in many areas, a clear knowledge of one's goal is half the job of getting there.

א

דִּבְרֵי֙ קֹהֶ֣לֶת בֶּן־דָּוִ֔ד מֶ֖לֶךְ בִּירוּשָׁלָֽ͏ִם: הֲבֵ֤ל א-ב
הֲבָלִים֙ אָמַ֣ר קֹהֶ֔לֶת הֲבֵ֥ל הֲבָלִ֖ים הַכֹּ֥ל הָֽבֶל:
מַה־יִּתְר֖וֹן לָֽאָדָ֑ם בְּכָל־עֲמָל֔וֹ שֶֽׁיַּעֲמֹ֖ל תַּ֥חַת ג
הַשָּֽׁמֶשׁ: דּ֤וֹר הֹלֵךְ֙ וְד֣וֹר בָּ֔א וְהָאָ֖רֶץ לְעוֹלָ֥ם ד
עֹמָֽדֶת: וְזָרַ֤ח הַשֶּׁ֙מֶשׁ֙ וּבָ֣א הַשָּׁ֔מֶשׁ וְאֶ֨ל־מְקוֹמ֔וֹ ה
שׁוֹאֵ֛ף זוֹרֵ֥חַֽ ה֖וּא שָֽׁם: הוֹלֵךְ֙ אֶל־דָּר֔וֹם וְסוֹבֵ֖ב ו
אֶל־צָפ֑וֹן סוֹבֵ֤ב ׀ סֹבֵב֙ הוֹלֵ֣ךְ הָר֔וּחַ וְעַל־סְבִיבֹתָ֖יו
שָׁ֥ב הָרֽוּחַ: כָּל־הַנְּחָלִים֙ הֹלְכִ֣ים אֶל־הַיָּ֔ם וְהַיָּ֖ם ז
אֵינֶ֣נּוּ מָלֵ֑א אֶל־מְק֗וֹם שֶׁ֤הַנְּחָלִים֙ הֹֽלְכִ֔ים שָׁ֛ם הֵ֥ם
שָׁבִ֖ים לָלָֽכֶת: כָּל־הַדְּבָרִ֣ים יְגֵעִ֔ים לֹא־יוּכַ֥ל אִ֖ישׁ ח
לְדַבֵּ֑ר לֹא־תִשְׂבַּ֥ע עַ֙יִן֙ לִרְא֔וֹת וְלֹא־תִמָּלֵ֥א אֹ֖זֶן
מִשְּׁמֹֽעַ: מַה־שֶּֽׁהָיָה֙ ה֣וּא שֶׁיִּֽהְיֶ֔ה וּמַה־שֶּֽׁנַּעֲשָׂ֔ה ט
ה֖וּא שֶׁיֵּעָשֶׂ֑ה וְאֵ֥ין כָּל־חָדָ֖שׁ תַּ֥חַת הַשָּֽׁמֶשׁ: יֵ֣שׁ י
דָּבָ֛ר שֶׁיֹּאמַ֥ר רְאֵה־זֶ֖ה חָדָ֣שׁ ה֑וּא כְּבָר֙ הָיָ֣ה
לְעֹֽלָמִ֔ים אֲשֶׁ֥ר הָיָ֖ה מִלְּפָנֵ֑נוּ: אֵ֤ין זִכְרוֹן֙ יא
לָרִ֣אשֹׁנִ֔ים וְגַ֛ם לָאַחֲרֹנִ֥ים שֶׁיִּהְי֖וּ לֹֽא־יִהְיֶ֣ה לָהֶ֑ם
זִכָּר֕וֹן עִ֥ם שֶׁיִּהְי֖וּ לָאַחֲרֹנָֽה:
אֲנִ֣י קֹהֶ֗לֶת הָיִ֥יתִי מֶ֛לֶךְ עַל־יִשְׂרָאֵ֖ל בִּירוּשָׁלָֽ͏ִם: יב
וְנָתַ֣תִּי אֶת־לִבִּ֗י לִדְר֤וֹשׁ וְלָתוּר֙ בַּֽחָכְמָ֔ה עַ֖ל כָּל־ יג
אֲשֶׁ֥ר נַעֲשָׂ֖ה תַּ֣חַת הַשָּׁמָ֑יִם ה֣וּא ׀ עִנְיַ֣ן רָ֗ע נָתַ֤ן
אֱלֹהִים֙ לִבְנֵ֣י הָֽאָדָ֔ם לַעֲנ֖וֹת בּֽוֹ: רָאִ֙יתִי֙ אֶת־כָּל־ יד
הַֽמַּעֲשִׂ֔ים שֶֽׁנַּעֲשׂ֖וּ תַּ֣חַת הַשָּׁ֑מֶשׁ וְהִנֵּ֥ה הַכֹּ֛ל הֶ֥בֶל
וּרְע֥וּת רֽוּחַ: מְעֻוָּ֖ת לֹֽא־יוּכַ֣ל לִתְקֹ֑ן וְחֶסְר֖וֹן לֹֽא־ טו
יוּכַ֥ל לְהִמָּנֽוֹת: דִּבַּ֤רְתִּי אֲנִי֙ עִם־לִבִּ֣י לֵאמֹ֔ר אֲנִ֗י טז
הִנֵּ֨ה הִגְדַּ֤לְתִּי וְהוֹסַ֙פְתִּי֙ חָכְמָ֔ה עַ֥ל כָּל־אֲשֶׁר־הָיָ֥ה
לְפָנַ֖י עַל־יְרוּשָׁלָ֑͏ִם וְלִבִּ֛י רָאָ֥ה הַרְבֵּ֖ה חָכְמָ֥ה

1/1. In Solomon's old age — shortly before his death — the Divine Spirit rested upon him and he 'uttered' the three Books: *Proverbs, Song of Songs, and Koheles. (Seder Olam Rabbah).*

The *Talmud* notes that King Hezekiah and his colleagues committed this book to writing *(Bava Basra 15a).*

Koheles. He was called by three names: Yedidiah [*II Samuel* 12:25], Koheles and Solomon. Why was he called Koheles? [not his proper name, but a title *(Ibn Ezra on 12:8)*] — Because his words were uttered בְּהַקְהֵל [*b'hikahel], in public assembly,* as is written, *then Solomon assembled ... (I Kings* 8:1). In addition, droves of peoples constantly assembled to hear his wisdom *(Midrash).*

Solomon was called *Koheles* because קִיהֵל חָכְמוֹת הַרְבֵּה, *he assembled much wisdom (Rashi).*

13. In this verse Solomon relates how he totally immersed himself in the study of philosophy and in material quests until he realized that the *evil* mentioned in the Torah refers to this obsessive quest for mundanity and riches with which man is perpetually preoccupied. Although man must seek a livelihood, it should not totally consume him to the point of exhaustion *(Taalumos Chachmah).*

15. One who was 'crooked' in his life time [and did not repent] cannot expect to 'straighten himself' after he dies *(Almosnino).*

¹ The words of Koheles son of David, King in Jerusalem:

² Futility of futilities! — said Koheles — Futility of futilities! All is futile! ³ What profit does man have for all his labor which he toils beneath the sun? ⁴ A generation goes and a generation comes, but the earth endures forever. ⁵ And the sun rises and the sun sets — then to its place it rushes; there it rises again. ⁶ It goes toward the south and veers toward the north; the wind goes round and round, and on its rounds the wind returns. ⁷ All the rivers flow into the sea, yet the sea is not full; to the place where the rivers flow, there they flow once more.

⁸ All words are wearying, one becomes speechless; the eye is never sated with seeing, nor the ear filled with hearing. ⁹ Whatever has been, is what will be; and whatever has been done is what will be done. There is nothing new beneath the sun! ¹⁰ Sometimes there is something of which one says: 'Look, this is new!' — It has already existed in the ages before us. ¹¹ As there is no recollection of the former ones; so too the latter ones that are yet to be, there will be no recollection among those of a still later time.

¹² I, Koheles, was king over Israel in Jerusalem. ¹³ I applied my mind to seek and probe by wisdom all that happens beneath the sky — it is a sorry task that God has given to the sons of man with which to be concerned. ¹⁴ I have seen all the deeds done beneath the sun, and behold all is futile and a vexation of the spirit. ¹⁵ A twisted thing cannot be made straight; and what is not there cannot be numbered.

¹⁶ I said to myself: Here I have acquired great wisdom, more than any of my predecessors over Jerusalem, and my mind has had much experience

יז וְיָדַעְתִּי: וָאֶתְּנָה לִבִּי לָדַעַת חָכְמָה וְדַעַת הוֹלֵלוֹת

יח וְשִׂכְלוּת יָדַעְתִּי שֶׁגַּם־זֶה הוּא רַעְיוֹן רוּחַ: כִּי
בְּרֹב חָכְמָה רָב־כָּעַס וְיוֹסִיף דַּעַת יוֹסִיף מַכְאוֹב:

ב

א אָמַרְתִּי אֲנִי בְּלִבִּי לְכָה־נָּא אֲנַסְּכָה בְשִׂמְחָה

ב וּרְאֵה בְטוֹב וְהִנֵּה גַם־הוּא הָבֶל: לִשְׂחוֹק אָמַרְתִּי

ג מְהוֹלָל וּלְשִׂמְחָה מַה־זֹּה עֹשָׂה: תַּרְתִּי בְלִבִּי
לִמְשׁוֹךְ בַּיַּיִן אֶת־בְּשָׂרִי וְלִבִּי נֹהֵג בַּחָכְמָה וְלֶאֱחֹז
בְּסִכְלוּת עַד אֲשֶׁר־אֶרְאֶה אֵי־זֶה טוֹב לִבְנֵי
הָאָדָם אֲשֶׁר יַעֲשׂוּ תַּחַת הַשָּׁמַיִם מִסְפַּר יְמֵי

ד חַיֵּיהֶם: הִגְדַּלְתִּי מַעֲשָׂי בָּנִיתִי לִי בָתִּים נָטַעְתִּי

ה לִי כְּרָמִים: עָשִׂיתִי לִי גַּנּוֹת וּפַרְדֵּסִים וְנָטַעְתִּי

ו בָהֶם עֵץ כָּל־פֶּרִי: עָשִׂיתִי לִי בְּרֵכוֹת מָיִם
לְהַשְׁקוֹת מֵהֶם יַעַר צוֹמֵחַ עֵצִים: קָנִיתִי עֲבָדִים

ז וּשְׁפָחוֹת וּבְנֵי־בַיִת הָיָה לִי גַּם מִקְנֶה בָקָר וָצֹאן
הַרְבֵּה הָיָה לִי מִכֹּל שֶׁהָיוּ לְפָנַי בִּירוּשָׁלָם:

ח כָּנַסְתִּי לִי גַּם־כֶּסֶף וְזָהָב וּסְגֻלַּת מְלָכִים
וְהַמְּדִינוֹת עָשִׂיתִי לִי שָׁרִים וְשָׁרוֹת וְתַעֲנוּגֹת בְּנֵי

ט הָאָדָם שִׁדָּה וְשִׁדּוֹת: וְגָדַלְתִּי וְהוֹסַפְתִּי מִכֹּל
שֶׁהָיָה לְפָנַי בִּירוּשָׁלָם אַף חָכְמָתִי עָמְדָה לִּי:

י וְכֹל אֲשֶׁר שָׁאֲלוּ עֵינַי לֹא אָצַלְתִּי מֵהֶם לֹא־
מָנַעְתִּי אֶת־לִבִּי מִכָּל־שִׂמְחָה כִּי־לִבִּי שָׂמֵחַ

יא מִכָּל־עֲמָלִי וְזֶה־הָיָה חֶלְקִי מִכָּל־עֲמָלִי: וּפָנִיתִי
אֲנִי בְּכָל־מַעֲשַׂי שֶׁעָשׂוּ יָדַי וּבֶעָמָל שֶׁעָמַלְתִּי
לַעֲשׂוֹת וְהִנֵּה הַכֹּל הֶבֶל וּרְעוּת רוּחַ וְאֵין יִתְרוֹן

יב תַּחַת הַשָּׁמֶשׁ: וּפָנִיתִי אֲנִי לִרְאוֹת חָכְמָה
וְהוֹלֵלוֹת וְסִכְלוּת כִּי | מֶה הָאָדָם שֶׁיָּבוֹא אַחֲרֵי

with wisdom and knowledge. ¹⁷ I applied my mind to know wisdom and to know madness and folly. I perceived that this, too, is a vexation of the spirit. ¹⁸ For with much wisdom comes much grief, and he who increases knowledge increases pain.

2/1. Having achieved little satisfaction with his previous pursuits, Koheles seeks new areas of experimentation.

3. He resolved to attempt grasping them all: merry-making, wisdom, and folly, and to stimulate and pamper his flesh by imbibing in wine *(Rashi).*
But he will indulge in each of these life-styles only long enough to establish its merit *(Metzudas David).*

9. Still, despite these vast undertakings, I did not neglect wisdom *(Rashi; Sforno).*

10. *And this was my reward.* All these efforts yielded me nothing more than this *(Rashi);* i.e., this satisfaction, alone, was all that remained with me as reward for all my endeavors *(Ibn Ezra).*

12. Coming after the king, what more could anyone hope to accomplish than the king has already done? [i.e., the king is best equipped to institute the comparison between wisdom and folly on the basis of personal experience; there is no need for anyone to follow him and repeat the experiment] *(Ibn Ezra).*

¹ I said to myself, Come, I will experiment with joy and enjoy pleasure. That, too, turned out to be futile. ² I said of laughter, It is mad! And of joy, What does it accomplish!

³ I ventured to stimulate my body with wine — while my heart is involved with wisdom — and to grasp folly, until I can discern which is best for mankind to do under the heavens during the brief span of their lives. ⁴ I acted in grand style: I built myself houses, I planted vineyards; ⁵ I made for myself gardens and orchards and planted in them every kind of fruit tree; ⁶ I constructed pools from which to irrigate a grove of young trees; ⁷ I bought slaves — male and female — and I acquired stewards; I also owned more possessions, both cattle and sheep, than all of my predecessors in Jerusalem; ⁸ I amassed even silver and gold for myself, and the treasure of kings and the provinces; I provided myself with various musical instruments, and with every human luxury — chests and chests of them. ⁹ Thus, I grew and surpassed any of my predecessors in Jerusalem; still, my wisdom stayed with me. ¹⁰ Whatever my eyes desired I did not deny them; I did not deprive myself of any kind of joy. Indeed, my heart drew joy from all my activities, and this was my reward for all my endeavors.

¹¹ Then I looked at all the things that I had done and the energy I had expended in doing them; it was clear that it was all futile and a vexation of the spirit — and there is no real profit under the sun.

¹² Then I turned my attention to appraising wisdom with madness and folly — for what can man who comes after the king do? It has

יג הַמֶּלֶךְ אֵת אֲשֶׁר־כְּבָר עָשׂוּהוּ: וְרָאִיתִי אָנִי שֶׁיֵּשׁ
יִתְרוֹן לַחָכְמָה מִן־הַסִּכְלוּת כִּיתְרוֹן הָאוֹר מִן־
יד הַחֹשֶׁךְ: הֶחָכָם עֵינָיו בְּרֹאשׁוֹ וְהַכְּסִיל בַּחֹשֶׁךְ
הוֹלֵךְ וְיָדַעְתִּי גַם־אָנִי שֶׁמִּקְרֶה אֶחָד יִקְרֶה אֶת־
טו כֻּלָּם: וְאָמַרְתִּי אֲנִי בְּלִבִּי כְּמִקְרֵה הַכְּסִיל גַּם־אֲנִי
יִקְרֵנִי וְלָמָּה חָכַמְתִּי אֲנִי אָז יֹתֵר וְדִבַּרְתִּי בְלִבִּי
טז שֶׁגַּם־זֶה הָבֶל: כִּי אֵין זִכְרוֹן לֶחָכָם עִם־הַכְּסִיל
לְעוֹלָם בְּשֶׁכְּבָר הַיָּמִים הַבָּאִים הַכֹּל נִשְׁכָּח וְאֵיךְ
יז יָמוּת הֶחָכָם עִם־הַכְּסִיל: וְשָׂנֵאתִי אֶת־הַחַיִּים כִּי
רַע עָלַי הַמַּעֲשֶׂה שֶׁנַּעֲשָׂה תַּחַת הַשָּׁמֶשׁ כִּי־הַכֹּל
יח הֶבֶל וּרְעוּת רוּחַ: וְשָׂנֵאתִי אֲנִי אֶת־כָּל־עֲמָלִי
שֶׁאֲנִי עָמֵל תַּחַת הַשָּׁמֶשׁ שֶׁאַנִּיחֶנּוּ לָאָדָם
יט שֶׁיִּהְיֶה אַחֲרָי: וּמִי יוֹדֵעַ הֶחָכָם יִהְיֶה אוֹ סָכָל
וְיִשְׁלַט בְּכָל־עֲמָלִי שֶׁעָמַלְתִּי וְשֶׁחָכַמְתִּי תַּחַת
כ הַשָּׁמֶשׁ גַּם־זֶה הָבֶל: וְסַבּוֹתִי אֲנִי לְיַאֵשׁ אֶת־לִבִּי
כא עַל כָּל־הֶעָמָל שֶׁעָמַלְתִּי תַּחַת הַשָּׁמֶשׁ: כִּי־יֵשׁ
אָדָם שֶׁעֲמָלוֹ בְּחָכְמָה וּבְדַעַת וּבְכִשְׁרוֹן וּלְאָדָם
שֶׁלֹּא עָמַל־בּוֹ יִתְּנֶנּוּ חֶלְקוֹ גַּם־זֶה הֶבֶל וְרָעָה
כב רַבָּה: כִּי מֶה־הֹוֶה לָאָדָם בְּכָל־עֲמָלוֹ וּבְרַעְיוֹן
כג לִבּוֹ שֶׁהוּא עָמֵל תַּחַת הַשָּׁמֶשׁ: כִּי כָל־יָמָיו
מַכְאֹבִים וָכַעַס עִנְיָנוֹ גַּם־בַּלַּיְלָה לֹא־שָׁכַב לִבּוֹ
כד גַּם־זֶה הֶבֶל הוּא: אֵין־טוֹב בָּאָדָם שֶׁיֹּאכַל וְשָׁתָה
וְהֶרְאָה אֶת־נַפְשׁוֹ טוֹב בַּעֲמָלוֹ גַּם־זֹה רָאִיתִי אָנִי
כה כִּי מִיַּד הָאֱלֹהִים הִיא: כִּי מִי יֹאכַל וּמִי יָחוּשׁ
כו חוּץ מִמֶּנִּי: כִּי לְאָדָם שֶׁטּוֹב לְפָנָיו נָתַן חָכְמָה
וְדַעַת וְשִׂמְחָה וְלַחוֹטֶא נָתַן עִנְיָן לֶאֱסֹף וְלִכְנוֹס

14. The wise man clearly sees the way ahead of him and takes the most direct route to his destination, unlike the fool who goes about uncertainly as if groping in the darkness; not even knowing over what he stumbles *(Ibn Ezra).*

16. The wise man's memory is praised and the fool's is disgraced *(Metzudas David).*

19. That wise men should toil and fools inherit is one of the futile aspects of life *(Rashi).*

25. This verse modifies the previous one: If all my property will eventually pass on to strangers, is it not right that I should view my possessions as a Divine gift and perform lofty spiritual deeds with them while I am still alive? Why should only others benefit from my wealth (next verse)? This is all part of God's Master Plan.

already been done. [13] And I perceived that wisdom excels folly as light excels darkness. [14] The wise man has his eyes in his head, whereas a fool walks in darkness. But I also realized that the same fate awaits them all. [15] So I said to myself: The fate of the fool will befall me also; to what advantage, then, have I become wise? But I concluded that this, too, was futility, [16] for there is no comparison between the remembrance of the wise man and of the fool at all, for as the succeeding days roll by, is all forgotten? How can the wise man's death be like the fool's?

[17] So I hated life, for I was depressed by all that goes on under the sun, because everything is futile and a vexation of the spirit.

[18] Thus I hated all my achievements laboring under the sun, for I must leave it to the man who succeeds me [19] — and who knows whether he will be wise or foolish? — and he will control all my possessions for which I toiled and have shown myself wise beneath the sun. This, too, is futility. [20] So I turned my heart to despair of all that I had achieved by laboring under the sun, [21] for there is a man who labored with wisdom, knowledge and skill, yet he must hand on his portion to one who has not toiled for it. This, too, is futility and a great evil. [22] For what has a man of all his toil and his stress in which he labors beneath the sun? [23] For all his days are painful, and his business is a vexation; even at night his mind has no rest. This, too, is futility!

[24] Is it not good for man that he eats and drinks and shows his soul satisfaction in his labor? And even that, I perceived, is from the hand of God. — [25] For who should eat and who should make haste except me? — [26] To the man who pleases Him He has given wisdom, knowledge and joy; but to the sinner He has given the urge to gather and amass

לָתֵת לְטוֹב לִפְנֵי הָאֱלֹהִים גַּם־זֶה הֶבֶל וּרְעוּת

ג א רוּחַ: לַכֹּל זְמָן וְעֵת לְכָל־חֵפֶץ תַּחַת הַשָּׁמָיִם:

וְעֵת לָמוּת	ב עֵת לָלֶדֶת
וְעֵת לַעֲקוֹר נָטוּעַ:	עֵת לָטַעַת
וְעֵת לִרְפּוֹא	ג עֵת לַהֲרוֹג
וְעֵת לִבְנוֹת:	עֵת לִפְרוֹץ
וְעֵת לִשְׂחוֹק	ד עֵת לִבְכּוֹת
וְעֵת רְקוֹד:	עֵת סְפוֹד
וְעֵת כְּנוֹס אֲבָנִים	ה עֵת לְהַשְׁלִיךְ אֲבָנִים
וְעֵת לִרְחֹק מֵחַבֵּק:	עֵת לַחֲבוֹק
וְעֵת לְאַבֵּד	ו עֵת לְבַקֵּשׁ
וְעֵת לְהַשְׁלִיךְ:	עֵת לִשְׁמוֹר
וְעֵת לִתְפּוֹר	ז עֵת לִקְרוֹעַ
וְעֵת לְדַבֵּר:	עֵת לַחֲשׁוֹת
וְעֵת לִשְׂנֹא	ח עֵת לֶאֱהֹב
וְעֵת שָׁלוֹם:	עֵת מִלְחָמָה

ט-י מַה־יִּתְרוֹן הָעוֹשֶׂה בַּאֲשֶׁר הוּא עָמֵל: רָאִיתִי
אֶת־הָעִנְיָן אֲשֶׁר נָתַן אֱלֹהִים לִבְנֵי הָאָדָם לַעֲנוֹת

יא בּוֹ: אֶת־הַכֹּל עָשָׂה יָפֶה בְעִתּוֹ גַּם אֶת־הָעֹלָם נָתַן
בְּלִבָּם מִבְּלִי אֲשֶׁר לֹא־יִמְצָא הָאָדָם אֶת־
הַמַּעֲשֶׂה אֲשֶׁר־עָשָׂה הָאֱלֹהִים מֵרֹאשׁ וְעַד־סוֹף:

יב יָדַעְתִּי כִּי אֵין טוֹב בָּם כִּי אִם־לִשְׂמוֹחַ וְלַעֲשׂוֹת

יג טוֹב בְּחַיָּיו: וְגַם כָּל־הָאָדָם שֶׁיֹּאכַל וְשָׁתָה וְרָאָה

יד טוֹב בְּכָל־עֲמָלוֹ מַתַּת אֱלֹהִים הִיא: יָדַעְתִּי כִּי
כָּל־אֲשֶׁר יַעֲשֶׂה הָאֱלֹהִים הוּא יִהְיֶה לְעוֹלָם
עָלָיו אֵין לְהוֹסִיף וּמִמֶּנּוּ אֵין לִגְרֹעַ וְהָאֱלֹהִים

— that he may hand it on to one who is pleasing to God. That, too, is futility and a vexation of the spirit.

¹ **E**verything has its season, and there is a time for everything under the heaven:

² A time to be born   and a time to die;

a time to plant   and a time to uproot the planted.

³ A time to kill   and a time to heal;

a time to wreck   and a time to build.

⁴ A time to weep   and a time to laugh;

a time to wail   and a time to dance.

⁵ A time to scatter stones

and a time to gather stones;

a time to embrace   and a time to shun embraces.

⁶ A time to seek   and a time to lose;

a time to keep   and a time to discard.

⁷ A time to rend   and a time to mend;

a time to be silent   and a time to speak.

⁸ A time to love   and a time to hate;

a time for war   and a time for peace.

⁹ What gain, then, has the worker by his toil?

¹⁰ I have observed the task which God has given the sons of man to be concerned with: ¹¹ He made everything beautiful in its time; He has also put an enigma into their minds so that man cannot comprehend what God has done from beginning to end. ¹² Thus I perceived that there is nothing better for each of them than to rejoice and do good in his life. ¹³ Indeed, every man who eats and drinks and finds satisfaction in all his labor — it is a gift of God.

¹⁴ I realized that whatever God does will endure forever: Nothing can be added to it and nothing can be subtracted from it, and God has acted

3/2. Is then all the wisdom which Solomon uttered simply that there is *A time to be born and a time to die?* Rather, the meaning is: Happy is the man whose hour of death is like the hour of his birth; just as he was pure in the hour of his birth, so should he be pure in the hour of his death *(Midrash).*

11. Although God instilled worldly wisdom into the hearts of man, He did not instill all wisdom into all men. Rather He dispensed small amounts to each person so no one would grasp fully the workings of God, or foresee the future. This is to ensure that, not knowing when they will die or what would befall them, people will repent *(Rashi).*

13. *It is a gift of God.* Since rejoicing is regulated by time [verse 4], man must realize that he would not be able to rejoice in his lot were it not so ordained by God at the time of his birth *(Ibn Ezra).*

עָשָׂה שֶׁיִּֽרְאוּ מִלְּפָנָיו: מַה־שֶּֽׁהָיָה כְּבָר הוּא
וַאֲשֶׁר לִהְיוֹת כְּבָר הָיָה וְהָאֱלֹהִים יְבַקֵּשׁ אֶת־
נִרְדָּף: וְעוֹד רָאִיתִי תַּחַת הַשָּׁמֶשׁ מְקוֹם הַמִּשְׁפָּט
שָׁמָּה הָרֶשַׁע וּמְקוֹם הַצֶּדֶק שָׁמָּה הָרָשַׁע:
אָמַרְתִּי אֲנִי בְּלִבִּי אֶת־הַצַּדִּיק וְאֶת־הָרָשָׁע
יִשְׁפֹּט הָאֱלֹהִים כִּי־עֵת לְכָל־חֵפֶץ וְעַל כָּל־
הַמַּעֲשֶׂה שָׁם: אָמַרְתִּי אֲנִי בְּלִבִּי עַל־דִּבְרַת בְּנֵי
הָאָדָם לְבָרָם הָאֱלֹהִים וְלִרְאוֹת שְׁהֶם־בְּהֵמָה
הֵמָּה לָהֶם: כִּי מִקְרֶה בְנֵי־הָאָדָם וּמִקְרֶה
הַבְּהֵמָה וּמִקְרֶה אֶחָד לָהֶם כְּמוֹת זֶה כֵּן מוֹת זֶה
וְרוּחַ אֶחָד לַכֹּל וּמוֹתַר הָאָדָם מִן־הַבְּהֵמָה אָיִן
כִּי הַכֹּל הָבֶל: הַכֹּל הוֹלֵךְ אֶל־מָקוֹם אֶחָד הַכֹּל
הָיָה מִן־הֶעָפָר וְהַכֹּל שָׁב אֶל־הֶעָפָר: מִי יוֹדֵעַ
רוּחַ בְּנֵי הָאָדָם הָעֹלָה הִיא לְמָעְלָה וְרוּחַ
הַבְּהֵמָה הַיֹּרֶדֶת הִיא לְמַטָּה לָאָרֶץ: וְרָאִיתִי כִּי
אֵין טוֹב מֵאֲשֶׁר יִשְׂמַח הָאָדָם בְּמַעֲשָׂיו כִּי־הוּא
חֶלְקוֹ כִּי מִי יְבִיאֶנּוּ לִרְאוֹת בְּמֶה שֶׁיִּהְיֶה אַחֲרָיו:
וְשַׁבְתִּי אֲנִי וָאֶרְאֶה אֶת־כָּל־הָעֲשֻׁקִים אֲשֶׁר
נַעֲשִׂים תַּחַת הַשָּׁמֶשׁ וְהִנֵּה | דִּמְעַת הָעֲשֻׁקִים
וְאֵין לָהֶם מְנַחֵם וּמִיַּד עֹשְׁקֵיהֶם כֹּחַ וְאֵין לָהֶם
מְנַחֵם: וְשַׁבֵּחַ אֲנִי אֶת־הַמֵּתִים שֶׁכְּבָר מֵתוּ מִן־
הַחַיִּים אֲשֶׁר הֵמָּה חַיִּים עֲדֶנָה: וְטוֹב מִשְּׁנֵיהֶם
אֵת אֲשֶׁר־עֲדֶן לֹא הָיָה אֲשֶׁר לֹא־רָאָה אֶת
הַמַּעֲשֶׂה הָרָע אֲשֶׁר נַעֲשָׂה תַּחַת הַשָּׁמֶשׁ:
וְרָאִיתִי אֲנִי אֶת־כָּל־עָמָל וְאֵת כָּל־כִּשְׁרוֹן
הַמַּעֲשֶׂה כִּי הִיא קִנְאַת־אִישׁ מֵרֵעֵהוּ גַּם־זֶה הֶבֶל

טו

טז

יז

יח

יט

כ

כא

כב

א

ב

ג

ד

ד

15. God never changes His ways: *God will always seek* [i.e., be on the side of] *the pursued,* and exact retribution from the pursuer. Therefore, of what benefit are the evil ways in which one toils? He will ultimately be held to account for his deeds.

16-22. Koheles now enters into a discussion on corrupt practices in the administration of justice; eventual divine retribution against the wicked; and the *seeming* similarity between man and beast.

17. A man can do what he pleases in this world, but in the hereafter there will be judgment and reckoning *(Midrash).*

4/2-3. The dead, who are no longer exposed to social injustices, are more fortunate than the living. But most fortunate of all are the unborn who were never exposed to any form of human cruelty *(Rav Yosef Kara).*

4. Even though most people are basically sincere and are without criminal motives, they are nevertheless impelled by competition, greed and jealously. These factors are themselves 'futility and a vexation of the spirit' *(Ibn Latif).*

so that [man] should stand in awe of Him. ¹⁵ What has been, already exists, and what is still to be, has already been, and God always seeks the pursued.

¹⁶ Furthermore, I have observed beneath the sun: In the place of justice there is wickedness, and in the place of righteousness there is wickedness. ¹⁷ I mused: God will judge the righteous and the wicked, for there is a time for everything and for every deed, there.

¹⁸ Then I said to myself concerning men: 'God has chosen them out, but only to see that they themselves are as beasts.' ¹⁹ For the fate of men and the fate of beast — they have one and the same fate: as one dies, so dies the other, and they all have the same spirit. Man has no superiority over the beast, for all is futile. ²⁰ All go to the same place; all originate from dust and all return to dust. ²¹ Who perceived that the spirit of man is the one that ascends on high while the spirit of the beast is the one that descends down into the earth? ²² I therefore observed that there is nothing better for man than to be happy in what he is doing, for that is his lot. For who can enable him to see what will be after him?

¹ And I returned and contemplated all the acts of oppression that are committed beneath the sun: Behold! Tears of the oppressed with none to comfort them, and their oppressors have the power — with none to comfort them. ² So I consider more fortunate the dead who have already died, than the living who are still alive; ³ but better than either of them is he who has not yet been, and has never witnessed the evil that is committed beneath the sun.

⁴ And I saw that all labor and skillful enterprise spring from man's rivalry with his neighbor. This, too, is futility and a vexation of the spirit!

ה   וּרְעוּת רֽוּחַ: הַכְּסִיל֙ חֹבֵ֣ק אֶת־יָדָ֔יו וְאֹכֵ֖ל אֶת־

ו   בְּשָׂרֽוֹ: ט֕וֹב מְלֹ֥א כַ֖ף נָ֑חַת מִמְּלֹ֥א חׇפְנַ֛יִם עָמָ֖ל

ז   וּרְעוּת רֽוּחַ: וְשַׁ֧בְתִּי אֲנִ֛י וָאֶרְאֶ֥ה הֶ֖בֶל תַּ֥חַת

ח   הַשָּֽׁמֶשׁ: יֵ֣שׁ אֶחָד֩ וְאֵ֨ין שֵׁנִ֜י גַּ֣ם בֵּ֧ן וָאָ֣ח אֵֽין־ל֗וֹ

°עֵינ֣וֹ ק׳   וְאֵ֥ין קֵץ֙ לְכׇל־עֲמָל֔וֹ גַּם־°עֵינָ֖יו לֹא־תִשְׂבַּ֣ע עֹ֑שֶׁר

    וּלְמִ֣י ׀ אֲנִ֣י עָמֵ֗ל וּמְחַסֵּ֤ר אֶת־נַפְשִׁי֙ מִטּוֹבָ֔ה גַּם־זֶ֥ה

ט   הֶ֛בֶל וְעִנְיַ֥ן רָ֖ע הֽוּא: טוֹבִ֥ים הַשְּׁנַ֖יִם מִן־הָאֶחָ֑ד

י   אֲשֶׁ֧ר יֵשׁ־לָהֶ֛ם שָׂכָ֥ר ט֖וֹב בַּעֲמָלָֽם: כִּ֣י אִם־יִפֹּ֔לוּ

    הָאֶחָ֖ד יָקִ֣ים אֶת־חֲבֵר֑וֹ וְאִ֣יל֗וֹ הָֽאֶחָד֙ שֶׁיִּפּ֔וֹל וְאֵ֥ין

יא   שֵׁנִ֖י לַהֲקִימֽוֹ: גַּ֛ם אִם־יִשְׁכְּב֥וּ שְׁנַ֖יִם וְחַ֣ם לָהֶ֑ם

יב   וּלְאֶחָ֖ד אֵ֣יךְ יֵחָֽם: וְאִֽם־יִתְקְפוֹ֙ הָאֶחָ֔ד הַשְּׁנַ֖יִם

    יַעַמְד֣וּ נֶגְדּ֑וֹ וְהַחוּט֙ הַֽמְשֻׁלָּ֔שׁ לֹ֥א בִמְהֵרָ֖ה יִנָּתֵֽק:

יג   ט֛וֹב יֶ֥לֶד מִסְכֵּ֖ן וְחָכָ֑ם מִמֶּ֤לֶךְ זָקֵן֙ וּכְסִ֔יל אֲשֶׁ֛ר

יד   לֹא־יָדַ֥ע לְהִזָּהֵ֖ר עֽוֹד: כִּֽי־מִבֵּ֥ית הָסוּרִ֖ים יָצָ֣א

טו   לִמְלֹ֑ךְ כִּ֛י גַּ֥ם בְּמַלְכוּת֖וֹ נוֹלַ֥ד רָֽשׁ: רָאִ֙יתִי֙ אֶת־

    כׇּל־הַ֣חַיִּ֔ים הַֽמְהַלְּכִ֖ים תַּ֣חַת הַשָּׁ֑מֶשׁ עִ֚ם הַיֶּ֣לֶד

טז   הַשֵּׁנִ֔י אֲשֶׁ֥ר יַעֲמֹ֖ד תַּחְתָּֽיו: אֵֽין־קֵ֣ץ לְכׇל־הָעָ֗ם

    לְכֹ֤ל אֲשֶׁר־הָיָה֙ לִפְנֵיהֶ֔ם גַּ֥ם הָאַחֲרוֹנִ֖ים לֹ֣א

יז   יִשְׂמְחוּ־ב֑וֹ כִּֽי־גַם־זֶ֥ה הֶ֖בֶל וְרַעְי֥וֹן רֽוּחַ: שְׁמֹ֣ר

°רַגְלֶ֣יךָ ק׳   °רַגְלְךָ֗ כַּאֲשֶׁ֤ר תֵּלֵךְ֙ אֶל־בֵּ֣ית הָֽאֱלֹהִ֔ים וְקָר֣וֹב

    לִשְׁמֹ֔עַ מִתֵּ֥ת הַכְּסִילִ֖ים זָ֑בַח כִּֽי־אֵינָ֥ם יוֹדְעִ֖ים

ה   א   לַעֲשׂ֥וֹת רָֽע: אַל־תְּבַהֵ֨ל עַל־פִּ֜יךָ וְלִבְּךָ֧ אַל־יְמַהֵ֣ר

    לְהוֹצִ֥יא דָבָ֖ר לִפְנֵ֣י הָאֱלֹהִ֑ים כִּ֣י הָאֱלֹהִ֤ים

    בַּשָּׁמַ֙יִם֙ וְאַתָּ֣ה עַל־הָאָ֔רֶץ עַל־כֵּ֛ן יִהְי֥וּ דְבָרֶ֖יךָ

ב   מְעַטִּֽים: כִּ֛י בָּ֥א הַחֲל֖וֹם בְּרֹ֣ב עִנְיָ֑ן וְק֥וֹל כְּסִ֖יל

ג   בְּרֹ֥ב דְּבָרִֽים: כַּאֲשֶׁר֩ תִּדֹּ֨ר נֶ֜דֶר לֵֽאלֹהִים֙ אַל־

5 The fool folds his hands and eats his own flesh. 6 Better is one handful of pleasantness than two fistfuls of labor and vexation of the spirit.

7 Then I returned and contemplated [another] futility beneath the sun: 8 a lone and solitary man who has neither son nor brother, yet there is no end to his toil, nor is his eye ever sated with riches [nor does he ask himself], 'For whom am I toiling and depriving myself of goodness.' This, too, is futility; indeed, it is a sorry task.

9 Two are better than one, for they get a greater return for their labor. 10 For should they fall, one can raise the other; but woe to him who is alone when he falls and there is no one to raise him! 11 Also, if two sleep together they keep warm, but how can one be warm alone? 12 Where one can be overpowered, two can resist attack: A three-ply cord is not easily severed! 13 Better is a poor but wise youth than an old and foolish king who no longer knows how to take care of himself; 14 because from the prison-house he emerged to reign, while even in his reign he was born poor. 15 I saw all the living that wander beneath the sun throng to the succeeding youth who steps into his place. 16 There is no end to the entire nation, to all that was before them; similarly the ones that come later will not rejoice in him. For this, too, is futility and a vexation of the spirit.

17 Guard your tongue when you go to the House of God; better to draw near and hearken than to offer the sacrifices of fools, for they do not consider that they do evil.

1 Be not rash with your mouth, and let not your heart be hasty to utter a word before God; for God is in heaven and you are on earth, so let your words be few. 2 For a dream comes from much concern, and foolish talk from many words. 3 When you make a vow to God, do not

9. Two can accomplish more than one, because there are projects that an individual would never attempt alone (Rashi).

12. If one is a scholar, and his son and grandson are scholars as well, the Torah will nevermore cease from his descendants. These three generations are alluded to by the strength of the *three-ply cord* in our verse (*Bava Metzia* 85a).

14. The verse further describes Solomon's allegory and explains why he feels that the wise young child is superior to the old king: because such a wise youth would manage to find his way to the throne even if he were imprisoned (Ibn Ezra).

5/1. God rules the world, and lowly man cannot presume to fathom His method of ruling His creatures (Lekach Tov).

תְּאַחֵר֙ לְשַׁלְּמ֔וֹ כִּ֣י אֵ֥ין חֵ֖פֶץ בַּכְּסִילִ֑ים אֵ֥ת אֲשֶׁר־

ד תִּדֹּ֖ר שַׁלֵּֽם: ט֤וֹב אֲשֶׁ֣ר לֹֽא־תִדֹּ֔ר מִשֶּׁתִּדּ֖וֹר וְלֹ֥א

ה תְשַׁלֵּֽם: אַל־תִּתֵּ֤ן אֶת־פִּ֙יךָ֙ לַחֲטִ֣יא אֶת־בְּשָׂרֶ֔ךָ וְאַל־תֹּאמַר֙ לִפְנֵ֣י הַמַּלְאָ֔ךְ כִּ֥י שְׁגָגָ֖ה הִ֑יא לָ֣מָּה יִקְצֹ֤ף הָֽאֱלֹהִים֙ עַל־קוֹלֶ֔ךָ וְחִבֵּ֖ל אֶת־מַעֲשֵׂ֥ה

ו יָדֶֽיךָ: כִּ֣י בְרֹ֤ב חֲלֹמוֹת֙ וַהֲבָלִ֔ים וּדְבָרִ֖ים הַרְבֵּ֑ה כִּ֥י

ז אֶת־הָאֱלֹהִ֖ים יְרָֽא: אִם־עֹ֣שֶׁק רָ֠שׁ וְגֵ֨זֶל מִשְׁפָּ֤ט וָצֶ֙דֶק֙ תִּרְאֶ֣ה בַמְּדִינָ֔ה אַל־תִּתְמַ֖הּ עַל־הַחֵ֑פֶץ כִּ֣י

ח גָבֹ֜הַּ מֵעַ֤ל גָּבֹ֙הַּ֙ שֹׁמֵ֔ר וּגְבֹהִ֖ים עֲלֵיהֶֽם: וְיִתְר֥וֹן

°הוּא ק׳   ט אֶ֖רֶץ בַּכֹּ֣ל °הִ֑יא מֶ֥לֶךְ לְשָׂדֶ֖ה נֶעֱבָֽד: אֹהֵ֥ב כֶּ֙סֶף֙ לֹא־יִשְׂבַּ֣ע כֶּ֔סֶף וּמִֽי־אֹהֵ֥ב בֶּהָמ֖וֹן לֹ֣א תְבוּאָ֑ה גַּם־

י זֶ֖ה הָֽבֶל: בִּרְבוֹת֙ הַטּוֹבָ֔ה רַבּ֖וּ אוֹכְלֶ֑יהָ וּמַה־

°רְאוּת ק׳   יא כִּשְׁרוֹן֙ לִבְעָלֶ֔יהָ כִּ֥י אִם־°רְא֖וּת עֵינָֽיו: מְתוּקָה֙ שְׁנַ֣ת הָעֹבֵ֔ד אִם־מְעַ֥ט וְאִם־הַרְבֵּ֖ה יֹאכֵ֑ל וְהַשָּׂבָע֙

יב לֶֽעָשִׁ֔יר אֵינֶ֛נּוּ מַנִּ֥יחַֽ ל֖וֹ לִישֽׁוֹן: יֵ֚שׁ רָעָ֣ה חוֹלָ֔ה רָאִ֖יתִי תַּ֣חַת הַשָּׁ֑מֶשׁ עֹ֛שֶׁר שָׁמ֥וּר לִבְעָלָ֖יו

יג לְרָעָתֽוֹ: וְאָבַ֛ד הָעֹ֥שֶׁר הַה֖וּא בְּעִנְיַ֣ן רָ֑ע וְהוֹלִ֣יד בֵּ֔ן וְאֵ֥ין בְּיָד֖וֹ מְאֽוּמָה: כַּאֲשֶׁ֤ר יָצָא֙ מִבֶּ֣טֶן אִמּ֔וֹ עָר֛וֹם

יד יָשׁ֥וּב לָלֶ֖כֶת כְּשֶׁבָּ֑א וּמְא֙וּמָה֙ לֹא־יִשָּׂ֣א בַעֲמָל֔וֹ שֶׁיֹּלֵ֖ךְ בְּיָדֽוֹ: וְגַם־זֹה֙ רָעָ֣ה חוֹלָ֔ה כָּל־עֻמַּ֥ת שֶׁבָּ֖א

טו כֵּ֣ן יֵלֵ֑ךְ וּמַה־יִּתְר֣וֹן ל֔וֹ שֶֽׁיַּעֲמֹ֖ל לָרֽוּחַ: גַּ֥ם כָּל־יָמָ֛יו

טז בַּחֹ֥שֶׁךְ יֹאכֵ֖ל וְכָעַ֣ס הַרְבֵּ֑ה וְחָלְי֖וֹ וָקָֽצֶף: הִנֵּ֞ה אֲשֶׁר־רָאִ֣יתִי אָ֗נִי ט֣וֹב אֲשֶׁר־יָפֶ֣ה לֶֽאֱכוֹל־ וְלִשְׁתּ֗וֹת וְלִרְא֤וֹת טוֹבָה֙ בְּכָל־עֲמָל֣וֹ | שֶֽׁיַּעֲמֹ֣ל תַּֽחַת־הַשֶּׁ֗מֶשׁ מִסְפַּ֧ר יְמֵי־חַיָּ֛ו אֲשֶׁר־נָֽתַן־ל֥וֹ

יח הָאֱלֹהִ֖ים כִּי־ה֣וּא חֶלְק֑וֹ: גַּ֣ם כָּל־הָאָדָ֗ם אֲשֶׁ֨ר

4. Hence the praiseworthy custom of saying בְּלִי נֶדֶר, *without a vow.'* Thereby, although the speaker still obligates himself to keep his word, he avoids the transgression of breaking a vow in the event he is unable to do so.

7. Do not despair at the impunity and freedom from retribution with which unscrupulous wielders of power oppress the helpless. Know that the most august of all beings, God, who is *higher than high,* sees what they do and will avenge the victims when the proper time comes *(Rav Saadiah Gaon; Sforno).*

11. The man who is not indolent, and who does not work merely to hoard riches, but who tills the ground earnestly to support his family, is extolled in this verse. He has neither large estates nor fortunes over which to worry constantly. Whether he eats little or much, he is able to sleep undisturbed by business worries *(Rav Yosef Kara).*

17-18. Essentially these verses restate an earlier conclusion (2:24; 3:12,22): Since man must depart exactly as he came, financial pursuits are worthless. Let man involve himself in Torah pursuits *(Rashi),* and let him eat of God's bounty and be content *(Ibn Ezra).*

For that is his lot, i.e., God bequeathed these few pleasures to man so that man may harness them and, by utilitizing them for the proper spiritual goals, lift himself up to the greater service of God *(Almosnino).*

delay paying it, for He has no liking for fools; what you vow, pay. ⁴ Better that you not vow at all than that you vow and not pay. ⁵ Let not your mouth bring guilt on your flesh, and do not tell the messenger that it was an error. Why should God be angered by your speech and destroy the work of your hands? ⁶ In spite of all dreams, futility and idle chatter, rather: Fear God!

⁷ If you see oppression of the poor, and the suppression of justice and right in the State, do not be astonished at the fact, for there is One higher than high Who watches and there are high ones above them.

⁸ The advantage of land is supreme; even a king is indebted to the soil.

⁹ A lover of money will never be satisfied with money; a lover of abundance has no wheat. This, too, is futility! ¹⁰ As goods increase, so do those who consume them; what advantage, then, has the owner except what his eyes see? ¹¹ Sweet is the sleep of the laborer, whether he eats little or much; the satiety of the rich does not let him sleep.

¹² There is a sickening evil which I have seen under the sun: riches hoarded by their owner to his misfortune, ¹³ and he loses those riches in some bad venture. If he begets a son, he has nothing in hand. ¹⁴ As he had come from his mother's womb, naked will he return, as he has come; he can salvage nothing from his labor to take with him. ¹⁵ This, too, is a sickening evil: Exactly as he came he must depart, and what did he gain by toiling for the wind? ¹⁶ Indeed, all his life he eats in darkness; he is greatly grieved, and has illness and anger.

¹⁷ So what I have seen to be good is that it is suitable to eat and drink and enjoy pleasure with all one's labor that he toils beneath the sun during the brief span of his life that God has given him, for that is his lot. ¹⁸ Furthermore, every man to whom

נָֽתַן־ל֣וֹ הָאֱלֹהִ֗ים עֹ֤שֶׁר וּנְכָסִים֙ וְהִשְׁלִיט֣וֹ לֶאֱכֹ֣ל
מִמֶּ֔נּוּ וְלָשֵׂ֥את אֶת־חֶלְק֖וֹ וְלִשְׂמֹ֣חַ בַּעֲמָל֑וֹ זֹ֕ה

יט מַתַּ֥ת אֱלֹהִ֖ים הִֽיא: כִּ֚י לֹ֣א הַרְבֵּ֔ה יִזְכֹּ֖ר אֶת־
יְמֵ֣י חַיָּ֑יו כִּ֧י הָאֱלֹהִ֛ים מַעֲנֶ֖ה בְּשִׂמְחַ֥ת לִבּֽוֹ:

ו א יֵ֣שׁ רָעָ֔ה אֲשֶׁ֥ר רָאִ֖יתִי תַּ֣חַת הַשָּׁ֑מֶשׁ וְרַבָּ֥ה הִ֖יא
עַל־הָאָדָֽם: ב אִ֗ישׁ אֲשֶׁ֨ר יִתֶּן־ל֣וֹ הָאֱלֹהִ֡ים עֹשֶׁר֩
וּנְכָסִ֨ים וְכָב֜וֹד וְֽאֵינֶ֨נּוּ חָסֵ֥ר לְנַפְשׁ֣וֹ ׀ מִכֹּ֣ל אֲשֶׁר־
יִתְאַוֶּ֗ה וְלֹֽא־יַשְׁלִיטֶ֤נּוּ הָֽאֱלֹהִים֙ לֶאֱכֹ֣ל מִמֶּ֔נּוּ כִּ֛י

ג אִ֥ישׁ נׇכְרִ֖י יֹֽאכְלֶ֑נּוּ זֶ֥ה הֶ֛בֶל וׇחֳלִ֥י רָ֖ע הֽוּא: אִם־
יוֹלִ֨יד אִ֜ישׁ מֵאָ֣ה וְשָׁנִים֩ רַבּ֨וֹת יִֽחְיֶ֜ה וְרַ֣ב ׀ שֶׁיִּהְי֣וּ
יְמֵֽי־שָׁנָ֗יו וְנַפְשׁוֹ֙ לֹא־תִשְׂבַּ֣ע מִן־הַטּוֹבָ֔ה וְגַם־
קְבוּרָ֖ה לֹא־הָ֣יְתָה לּ֑וֹ אָמַ֕רְתִּי ט֥וֹב מִמֶּ֖נּוּ הַנָּֽפֶל:

ד כִּֽי־בַהֶ֣בֶל בָּ֔א וּבַחֹ֖שֶׁךְ יֵלֵ֑ךְ וּבַחֹ֖שֶׁךְ שְׁמ֥וֹ יְכֻסֶּֽה:
ה גַּם־שֶׁ֥מֶשׁ לֹא־רָאָ֖ה וְלֹ֣א יָדָ֑ע נַ֥חַת לָזֶ֖ה מִזֶּֽה:
ו וְאִלּ֣וּ חָיָ֗ה אֶ֤לֶף שָׁנִים֙ פַּעֲמַ֔יִם וְטוֹבָ֖ה לֹ֣א רָאָ֑ה
ז הֲלֹ֛א אֶל־מָק֥וֹם אֶחָ֖ד הַכֹּ֥ל הוֹלֵֽךְ: כׇּל־עֲמַ֤ל
הָֽאָדָם֙ לְפִ֔יהוּ וְגַם־הַנֶּ֖פֶשׁ לֹ֥א תִמָּלֵֽא: ח כִּ֛י מַה־
יּוֹתֵ֥ר לֶחָכָ֖ם מִן־הַכְּסִ֑יל מַה־לֶּעָנִ֣י יוֹדֵ֔עַ לַהֲלֹ֖ךְ
ט נֶ֥גֶד הַֽחַיִּֽים: ט֛וֹב מַרְאֵ֥ה עֵינַ֖יִם מֵֽהֲלׇךְ־נָ֑פֶשׁ גַּם־
י זֶ֥ה הֶ֖בֶל וּרְע֥וּת רֽוּחַ: מַה־שֶּֽׁהָיָ֗ה כְּבָר֙ נִקְרָ֣א שְׁמ֔וֹ
וְנוֹדָ֖ע אֲשֶׁר־ה֣וּא אָדָ֑ם וְלֹֽא־יוּכַ֣ל לָדִ֔ין עִ֚ם

°שֶׁתַּקִּיף ק׳ יא
שֶׁהַתְּקִיף֙ מִמֶּ֔נּוּ: כִּ֛י יֵשׁ־דְּבָרִ֥ים הַרְבֵּ֖ה מַרְבִּ֣ים
יב הָ֑בֶל מַה־יֹּתֵ֖ר לָאָדָֽם: כִּ֣י מִֽי־יוֹדֵ֩עַ֩ מַה־טּ֨וֹב
לָֽאָדָ֜ם בַּחַיִּ֗ים מִסְפַּ֛ר יְמֵי־חַיֵּ֥י הֶבְל֖וֹ וְיַעֲשֵׂ֣ם כַּצֵּ֑ל
אֲשֶׁ֣ר מִֽי־יַגִּ֣יד לָֽאָדָ֔ם מַה־יִּהְיֶ֥ה אַחֲרָ֖יו תַּ֥חַת

ז א הַשָּֽׁמֶשׁ: ט֣וֹב שֵׁ֗ם מִשֶּׁ֣מֶן ט֑וֹב וְי֣וֹם

God has given riches and possessions and has given him the power to enjoy them, possess his share and be happy in his work: this is the gift of God. ¹⁹ For he shall remember that the days of his life are not many, while God provides him with the joy of his heart.

6/1. Solomon now bemoans those who have wealth, but whom God has denied the opportunity of enjoying it.

¹There is an evil I have observed beneath the sun, and it is prevalent among mankind: ² a man to whom God has given riches, wealth and honor, and he lacks nothing that the heart could desire, yet God did not give him the power to enjoy it; instead, a stranger will enjoy it. This is futility and an evil disease. ³ If a man begets a hundred children and lives many years — great being the days of his life — and his soul is not content with the good — and he even is deprived of burial; I say, the stillborn is better off than he. ⁴ Though its coming is futile and it departs in darkness, though its very name is enveloped in darkness, ⁵ though it never saw the sun nor knew; it has more satisfaction than he.

6. The subject of this verse is again the rich man described in verse 3. Even if he lives to two thousand years [more than twice as old as anyone recorded in the Bible], of what benefit is this longevity to him since *'he found no contentment'?* Ultimately he will return to the dust just like all paupers! *(Rashi).*

⁶ Even if he should live a thousand years twice over, but find no contentment — do not all go to the same place?

⁷ All man's toil is for his mouth, yet his wants are never satisfied. ⁸ What advantage, then, has the wise man over the fool? What [less] has the pauper who knows how to conduct himself among the living? ⁹ Better is what the eyes see than what is imagined. That, too, is futility and a vexation of the spirit.

8. *What advantage…?* A rhetorical question. There is no advantage to the wise. Both must toil for what they achieve. The difference lies in how the fruits of the labor are utilized and appreciated.

¹⁰ What has been was already named, and it is known that he is but a man. He cannot contend with one who is mightier than he. ¹¹ There are many things that increase futility; how does it benefit man? ¹² Who can possibly know what is good for man in life, during the short span of his futile existence which he should consider like a shadow; who can tell a man what will be after him beneath the sun?

7/1. As the *Midrash* notes at the end of the last chapter, these verses might be, in part, Solomon's own answer to the question (6:12), *'Who knows what is good for man in life?'*
A fine reputation — acquired with diligence and good deeds *(Sforno)* — is a more valuable possession than precious oil *(Rashi).*

¹A good name is better than good oil, and the day

ב הַמָּ֫וֶת מִיּ֣וֹם הִוָּלְד֑וֹ: ט֞וֹב לָלֶ֣כֶת אֶל־בֵּֽית־אֵ֗בֶל
מִלֶּ֨כֶת֙ אֶל־בֵּ֣ית מִשְׁתֶּ֔ה בַּאֲשֶׁ֖ר ה֣וּא ס֣וֹף כָּל־
ג הָאָדָ֑ם וְהַחַ֖י יִתֵּ֥ן אֶל־לִבּֽוֹ: ט֥וֹב כַּ֖עַס מִשְּׂחֹ֑ק כִּֽי־
ד בְרֹ֥עַ פָּנִ֖ים יִ֣יטַב לֵֽב: לֵ֤ב חֲכָמִים֙ בְּבֵ֣ית אֵ֔בֶל וְלֵ֥ב
ה כְּסִילִ֖ים בְּבֵ֥ית שִׂמְחָֽה: ט֕וֹב לִשְׁמֹ֖עַ גַּעֲרַ֣ת חָכָ֑ם
ו מֵאִ֕ישׁ שֹׁמֵ֖עַ שִׁ֥יר כְּסִילִֽים: כִּ֣י כְק֤וֹל הַסִּירִים֙
ז תַּ֣חַת הַסִּ֔יר כֵּ֖ן שְׂחֹ֣ק הַכְּסִ֑יל וְגַם־זֶ֖ה הָֽבֶל: כִּ֤י
ח הָעֹ֨שֶׁק֙ יְהוֹלֵ֣ל חָכָ֔ם וִֽיאַבֵּ֥ד אֶת־לֵ֖ב מַתָּנָֽה: ט֚וֹב
אַחֲרִ֣ית דָּבָ֔ר מֵרֵֽאשִׁית֑וֹ ט֥וֹב אֶֽרֶךְ־ר֖וּחַ מִגְּבַהּ־
ט ר֑וּחַ: אַל־תְּבַהֵ֥ל בְּרֽוּחֲךָ֖ לִכְע֑וֹס כִּ֣י כַ֔עַס בְּחֵ֥יק
י כְּסִילִ֖ים יָנֽוּחַ: אַל־תֹּאמַר֙ מֶ֣ה הָיָ֔ה שֶׁ֤הַיָּמִים֙
הָרִ֣אשֹׁנִ֔ים הָי֥וּ טוֹבִ֖ים מֵאֵ֑לֶּה כִּ֛י לֹ֥א מֵֽחָכְמָ֖ה
יא שָׁאַ֥לְתָּ עַל־זֶֽה: טוֹבָ֣ה חָכְמָ֖ה עִֽם־נַחֲלָ֑ה וְיֹתֵ֖ר
יב לְרֹאֵ֥י הַשָּֽׁמֶשׁ: כִּ֚י בְּצֵ֣ל הַֽחָכְמָ֔ה בְּצֵ֖ל הַכָּ֑סֶף
יג וְיִתְר֣וֹן דַּ֔עַת הַֽחָכְמָ֖ה תְּחַיֶּ֣ה בְעָלֶ֑יהָ: רְאֵה֙ אֶת־
מַעֲשֵׂ֣ה הָאֱלֹהִ֑ים כִּ֣י מִ֤י יוּכַל֙ לְתַקֵּ֔ן אֵ֥ת אֲשֶׁ֖ר
יד עִוְּתֽוֹ: בְּי֤וֹם טוֹבָה֙ הֱיֵ֣ה בְט֔וֹב וּבְי֥וֹם רָעָ֖ה רְאֵ֑ה
גַּ֣ם אֶת־זֶ֤ה לְעֻמַּת־זֶה֙ עָשָׂ֣ה הָֽאֱלֹהִ֔ים עַל־דִּבְרַ֗ת
טו שֶׁלֹּ֨א יִמְצָ֧א הָֽאָדָ֛ם אַחֲרָ֖יו מְא֑וּמָה: אֶת־הַכֹּ֥ל
רָאִ֖יתִי בִּימֵ֣י הֶבְלִ֑י יֵ֤שׁ צַדִּיק֙ אֹבֵ֣ד בְּצִדְק֔וֹ וְיֵ֣שׁ
טז רָשָׁ֔ע מַאֲרִ֖יךְ בְּרָעָתֽוֹ: אַל־תְּהִ֤י צַדִּיק֙ הַרְבֵּ֔ה
יז וְאַל־תִּתְחַכַּ֖ם יוֹתֵ֑ר לָ֥מָּה תִּשּׁוֹמֵֽם: אַל־תִּרְשַׁ֥ע
הַרְבֵּ֖ה וְאַל־תְּהִ֣י סָכָ֑ל לָ֥מָּה תָמ֖וּת בְּלֹ֥א עִתֶּֽךָ:
יח ט֚וֹב אֲשֶׁ֣ר תֶּאֱחֹ֣ז בָּזֶ֔ה וְגַם־מִזֶּ֖ה אַל־תַּנַּ֣ח אֶת־יָדֶ֑ךָ
יט כִּֽי־יְרֵ֥א אֱלֹהִ֖ים יֵצֵ֥א אֶת־כֻּלָּֽם: הַֽחָכְמָ֖ה תָּעֹ֣ז
כ לֶֽחָכָ֑ם מֵֽעֲשָׂרָה֙ שַׁלִּיטִ֔ים אֲשֶׁ֥ר הָי֖וּ בָעִ֑יר: כִּ֣י

The man who has lived an exemplary life and acquired a *good name* views his death as a culmination of a life well spent and as a transition to the World of Peace and Reward. Unlike the time of his birth when he is uncertain of how his life will unfold (*Akeidas Yitzchak; Ibn Ezra*).

of death than the day of birth.

² It is better to go to the house of mourning than to go to a house of feasting, for that is the end of all man, and the living should take it to heart.

³ Grief is better than gaiety — for through a sad countenance the heart is improved. ⁴ The thoughts of the wise turn to the house of mourning, but the thoughts of fools to the house of feasting.

⁵ It is better to listen to the rebuke of a wise man than for one to listen to the song of fools, ⁶ for like the crackling of thorns under a pot, so is the laughter of the fool; ⁷ for oppression makes the wise foolish, and a gift corrupts the heart.

8. Only by its outcome can a matter be properly evaluated (*Rashi*).

⁸ The end of a matter is better than its beginning; patience is better than pride. ⁹ Do not be hastily upset, for anger lingers in the bosom of fools.

10. The *Kobriner Rebbe* said: Some people think, 'In former times it was easier to serve God; there were more *tzadikim* whose example could be imitated.' This is absurd. Has anyone ever endeavored to seek God without avail? Endeavor to seek Him in the manner of those in former days and you too will find Him, just as they did.

¹⁰ Do not say, 'How was it that former times were better than these?' For that is not a question prompted by wisdom.

¹¹ Wisdom is good with an inheritance, and a boon to those who see the sun, ¹² for to sit in the shelter of wisdom is to sit in the shelter of money, and the advantage of knowledge is that wisdom preserves the life of its possessors.

¹³ Observe God's doing! For who can straighten what He has twisted? ¹⁴ Be pleased when things go well, but in a time of misfortune reflect: God has made the one as well as the other so that man should find nothing after Him.

15. This describes the paradox of צַדִּיק וְרַע לוֹ רָשָׁע וְטוֹב לוֹ, *righteous people who suffer while the wicked are fortunate*. In truth, God deals strictly with the righteous to atone for their sins so that they will not be punished in the Hereafter, and He delays punishing the wicked to allow them time to repent (*Alshich*).

16. The Talmud calls an overly righteous person חָסִיד שׁוֹטֶה, a *pious fool*. The classic example is one who would not save a drowning woman because 'It's improper to look upon her' (*Sotah* 21b).

17. Even if you have been wicked, do not persist in your evil ways [thinking that there is no hope of repentance] (*Rashi*).

¹⁵ I have seen everything during my futile existence: Sometimes a righteous man perishes for all his righteousness, and sometimes a wicked man endures for all his wickedness. ¹⁶ Do not be overly righteous or excessively wise: why be left desolate? ¹⁷ Be not overly wicked nor be a fool: why die before your time? ¹⁸ It is best to grasp the one and not let go of the other; he who fears God performs them all. ¹⁹ Wisdom strengthens the wise more than ten rulers who are in the city. ²⁰ For

אָדָ֤ם אֵ֣ין צַדִּ֔יק בָּאָ֑רֶץ אֲשֶׁ֥ר יַעֲשֶׂה־טּ֖וֹב וְלֹ֥א

כא יֶחֱטָֽא: גַּ֤ם לְכָל־הַדְּבָרִים֙ אֲשֶׁ֣ר יְדַבֵּ֔רוּ אַל־תִּתֵּ֣ן

כב לִבֶּ֑ךָ אֲשֶׁ֥ר לֹֽא־תִשְׁמַ֛ע אֶֽת־עַבְדְּךָ֖ מְקַלְלֶֽךָ: כִּ֛י

גַּם־פְּעָמִ֥ים רַבּ֖וֹת יָדַ֣ע לִבֶּ֑ךָ אֲשֶׁ֥ר גַּם־[אַתְּ] (את) קִלַּ֖לְתָּ

כג אֲחֵרִֽים: כָּל־זֹ֖ה נִסִּ֣יתִי בַֽחָכְמָ֑ה אָמַ֣רְתִּי אֶחְכָּ֔מָה

כד וְהִ֖יא רְחוֹקָ֣ה מִמֶּֽנִּי: רָח֥וֹק מַה־שֶּׁהָיָ֖ה וְעָמֹ֥ק ׀

כה עָמֹ֖ק מִ֥י יִמְצָאֶֽנּוּ: סַבּ֨וֹתִֽי אֲנִ֤י וְלִבִּי֙ לָדַ֣עַת וְלָת֔וּר

וּבַקֵּ֥שׁ חָכְמָ֖ה וְחֶשְׁבּ֑וֹן וְלָדַ֗עַת רֶ֚שַׁע כֶּ֔סֶל

כו וְהַסִּכְל֖וּת הוֹלֵלֽוֹת: וּמוֹצֶ֨א אֲנִ֜י מַ֣ר מִמָּ֗וֶת אֶת־

הָֽאִשָּׁה֙ אֲשֶׁר־הִ֣יא מְצוֹדִ֧ים וַחֲרָמִ֛ים לִבָּ֖הּ

אֲסוּרִ֣ים יָדֶ֑יהָ ט֞וֹב לִפְנֵ֤י הָאֱלֹהִים֙ יִמָּלֵ֣ט מִמֶּ֔נָּה

כז וְחוֹטֵ֖א יִלָּ֣כֶד בָּֽהּ: רְאֵ֤ה זֶה֙ מָצָ֔אתִי אָמְרָ֖ה קֹהֶ֑לֶת

כח אַחַ֥ת לְאַחַ֖ת לִמְצֹ֥א חֶשְׁבּֽוֹן: אֲשֶׁ֛ר עוֹד־בִּקְשָׁ֥ה

נַפְשִׁ֖י וְלֹ֣א מָצָ֑אתִי אָדָ֞ם אֶחָ֤ד מֵאֶ֙לֶף֙ מָצָ֔אתִי

כט וְאִשָּׁ֥ה בְכָל־אֵ֖לֶּה לֹ֣א מָצָֽאתִי: לְבַ֞ד רְאֵה־זֶ֣ה

מָצָ֗אתִי אֲשֶׁ֨ר עָשָׂ֧ה הָאֱלֹהִ֛ים אֶת־הָאָדָ֖ם יָשָׁ֑ר

ח א וְהֵ֥מָּה בִקְשׁ֖וּ חִשְּׁבֹנ֥וֹת רַבִּֽים: מִ֣י כְּהֶ֣חָכָ֔ם וּמִ֥י

יוֹדֵ֖עַ פֵּ֣שֶׁר דָּבָ֑ר חָכְמַ֤ת אָדָם֙ תָּאִ֣יר פָּנָ֔יו וְעֹ֥ז פָּנָ֖יו

ב יְשֻׁנֶּֽא: אֲנִי֙ פִּי־מֶ֣לֶךְ שְׁמֹ֔ר וְעַ֕ל דִּבְרַ֖ת שְׁבוּעַ֥ת

ג אֱלֹהִֽים: אַל־תִּבָּהֵ֤ל מִפָּנָיו֙ תֵּלֵ֔ךְ אַֽל־תַּעֲמֹ֖ד

בְּדָבָ֣ר רָ֑ע כִּ֛י כָּל־אֲשֶׁ֥ר יַחְפֹּ֖ץ יַעֲשֶֽׂה: בַּאֲשֶׁ֥ר

ד דְּבַר־מֶ֖לֶךְ שִׁלְט֑וֹן וּמִ֥י יֹֽאמַר־ל֖וֹ מַֽה־תַּעֲשֶֽׂה:

ה שׁוֹמֵ֣ר מִצְוָ֔ה לֹ֥א יֵדַ֖ע דָּבָ֣ר רָ֑ע וְעֵ֣ת וּמִשְׁפָּ֔ט יֵדַ֖ע

ו לֵ֥ב חָכָֽם: כִּ֣י לְכָל־חֵ֔פֶץ יֵ֖שׁ עֵ֣ת וּמִשְׁפָּ֑ט כִּֽי־רָעַ֥ת

ז הָאָדָ֖ם רַבָּ֥ה עָלָֽיו: כִּֽי־אֵינֶ֤נּוּ יֹדֵ֙עַ֙ מַה־שֶּׁיִּֽהְיֶ֔ה כִּ֚י

ח כַּאֲשֶׁ֣ר יִֽהְיֶ֔ה מִ֖י יַגִּ֣יד ל֑וֹ: אֵ֣ין אָדָ֞ם שַׁלִּ֤יט בָּר֙וּחַ֙

there is no man so wholly righteous on earth that he [always] does good and never sins.

²¹ Moreover, pay no attention to everything men say, lest you hear your own servant disparaging you, ²² for your own conscience knows that many times you yourself disparaged others.

²³ All this I tested with wisdom; I thought I could become wise, but it is beyond me. ²⁴ What existed is elusive; and so very deep, who can find it? ²⁵ So I turned my attention to study and probe and seek wisdom and reckoning, and to know the wickedness of folly, and the foolishness which is madness:

²⁶ And I have discovered more bitter than death: the woman whose heart is snares and nets; her arms are chains. He who is pleasing to God escapes her but the sinner is caught by her.

²⁷ See, this is what I found, said Koheles, adding one to another to reach a conclusion, ²⁸ which yet my soul seeks but I have not found. One man in a thousand I have found, but one woman among them I have not found. ²⁹ But, see, this I did find: God has made man simple, but they sought many intrigues.

¹ Who is like the wise man? And who knows what things mean? A man's wisdom lights up his face, and the boldness of his face is transformed.

² I counsel you: Obey the king's command, and that in the manner of an oath of God. ³ Do not hasten to leave his presence, do not persist in an evil thing; for he can do whatever he pleases. ⁴ Since a king's word is law, who dare say to him, 'What are you doing?' ⁵ He who obeys the commandment will know no evil; and a wise man will know time and justice. ⁶ For everything has its time and justice, for man's evil overwhelms him. ⁷ Indeed, he does not know what will happen, for when it happens, who will tell him? ⁸ Man is powerless over the spirit — to restrain

26. It is abundantly clear that in this verse Solomon refers only to evil, licentious women, who erotically trap man into evil ways. This is not a wholesale condemnation of all women. His praise of the God-fearing women in *Proverbs* 18:22 מָצָא אִשָּׁה מָצָא טוֹב, *he who has found a wife found good;* as well as in the famous 'Aishes Chayil' (ibid. 31:10-31); and his statement below (9:9) leave no room for doubt.

29. Many commentators apply this verse to mankind as a whole; *God created mankind upright* — i.e., with a perfect nature capable of high attainments. Man's perversions spring from his own devices, which, in turn, cause his downfall *(Rambam).*

8/2. *And that in the manner of an oath of God.* [An ambiguous phrase which can be variously interpreted:] Because of the oath of allegiance to God's commandments that we took at Horeb *(Rashi);* The king's command must be obeyed — but only when his command is in consonance with the *Oath to God,* i.e., that his requests are not contrary to the Laws of the Torah *(Metzudas David).*

8. A man cannot say to the Angel of Death, 'Wait for me until I finish my business and then I will come' *(Midrash).*

לִכְל֣וֹא אֶת־הָר֗וּחַ וְאֵ֤ין שִׁלְטוֹן֙ בְּי֣וֹם הַמָּ֔וֶת וְאֵ֥ין
מִשְׁלַ֖חַת בַּמִּלְחָמָ֑ה וְלֹֽא־יְמַלֵּ֥ט רֶ֖שַׁע אֶת־בְּעָלָֽיו׃

ט אֶת־כָּל־זֶ֤ה רָאִ֙יתִי֙ וְנָת֣וֹן אֶת־לִבִּ֔י לְכָל־מַעֲשֶׂ֕ה
אֲשֶׁ֥ר נַעֲשָׂ֖ה תַּ֣חַת הַשָּׁ֑מֶשׁ עֵ֗ת אֲשֶׁ֨ר שָׁלַ֧ט הָאָדָ֛ם
י בְּאָדָ֖ם לְרַ֥ע לֽוֹ׃ וּבְכֵ֡ן רָאִ֩יתִי֩ רְשָׁעִ֨ים קְבֻרִ֜ים
וָבָ֗אוּ וּמִמְּק֤וֹם קָדוֹשׁ֙ יְהַלֵּ֔כוּ וְיִֽשְׁתַּכְּח֥וּ בָעִ֖יר
יא אֲשֶׁ֣ר כֵּן־עָשׂ֑וּ גַּם־זֶ֖ה הָֽבֶל׃ אֲשֶׁר֙ אֵין־נַעֲשָׂ֣ה
פִתְגָ֗ם מַעֲשֵׂ֤ה הָֽרָעָה֙ מְהֵרָ֔ה עַל־כֵּ֡ן מָלֵ֞א לֵ֣ב בְּנֵֽי־
יב הָאָדָ֥ם בָּהֶ֖ם לַעֲשׂ֥וֹת רָֽע׃ אֲשֶׁ֣ר חֹטֶ֗א עֹשֶׂ֥ה רָ֛ע
מְאַ֖ת וּמַאֲרִ֣יךְ ל֑וֹ כִּ֚י גַּם־יוֹדֵ֣עַ אָ֔נִי אֲשֶׁ֤ר יִֽהְיֶה־
יג טּ֙וֹב֙ לְיִרְאֵ֣י הָאֱלֹהִ֔ים אֲשֶׁ֥ר יִֽירְא֖וּ מִלְּפָנָ֑יו׃ וְטוֹב֙
לֹֽא־יִֽהְיֶ֣ה לָֽרָשָׁ֔ע וְלֹֽא־יַאֲרִ֥יךְ יָמִ֖ים כַּצֵּ֑ל אֲשֶׁ֛ר
יד אֵינֶ֥נּוּ יָרֵ֖א מִלִּפְנֵ֥י אֱלֹהִֽים׃ יֶשׁ־הֶ֙בֶל֙ אֲשֶׁ֣ר נַעֲשָׂ֣ה
עַל־הָאָ֔רֶץ אֲשֶׁ֣ר ׀ יֵ֣שׁ צַדִּיקִ֗ים אֲשֶׁ֨ר מַגִּ֤יעַ אֲלֵהֶם֙
כְּמַעֲשֵׂ֣ה הָרְשָׁעִ֔ים וְיֵ֣שׁ רְשָׁעִ֔ים שֶׁמַּגִּ֥יעַ אֲלֵהֶ֖ם
כְּמַעֲשֵׂ֣ה הַצַּדִּיקִ֑ים אָמַ֕רְתִּי שֶׁגַּם־זֶ֖ה הָֽבֶל׃
טו וְשִׁבַּ֤חְתִּֽי אֲנִי֙ אֶת־הַשִּׂמְחָ֔ה אֲשֶׁ֨ר אֵֽין־ט֤וֹב לָֽאָדָם֙
תַּ֣חַת הַשֶּׁ֔מֶשׁ כִּ֛י אִם־לֶאֱכ֥וֹל וְלִשְׁתּ֖וֹת וְלִשְׂמ֑וֹחַ
וְה֞וּא יִלְוֶ֣נּוּ בַעֲמָל֗וֹ יְמֵ֥י חַיָּ֛יו אֲשֶׁר־נָתַן־ל֥וֹ
טז הָאֱלֹהִ֖ים תַּ֣חַת הַשָּֽׁמֶשׁ׃ כַּאֲשֶׁ֨ר נָתַ֤תִּי אֶת־לִבִּי֙
לָדַ֣עַת חָכְמָ֔ה וְלִרְאוֹת֙ אֶת־הָ֣עִנְיָ֔ן אֲשֶׁ֥ר נַעֲשָׂ֖ה
עַל־הָאָ֑רֶץ כִּ֣י גַ֤ם בַּיּוֹם֙ וּבַלַּ֔יְלָה שֵׁנָ֕ה בְּעֵינָ֖יו אֵינֶ֥נּוּ
יז רֹאֶֽה׃ וְרָאִ֙יתִי֙ אֶת־כָּל־מַעֲשֵׂ֣ה הָאֱלֹהִ֔ים כִּ֣י לֹ֥א
יוּכַ֣ל הָאָדָ֗ם לִמְצוֹא֙ אֶת־הַֽמַּעֲשֶׂה֙ אֲשֶׁ֣ר נַעֲשָׂ֣ה
תַֽחַת־הַשֶּׁ֔מֶשׁ בְּ֠שֶׁל אֲשֶׁ֨ר יַעֲמֹ֧ל הָאָדָ֛ם לְבַקֵּ֖שׁ
וְלֹ֣א יִמְצָ֑א וְגַ֨ם אִם־יֹאמַ֤ר הֶֽחָכָם֙ לָדַ֔עַת לֹ֥א יוּכַ֖ל

the spirit; nor is there authority over the day of death; nor discharge in war; and wickedness cannot save the wrongdoer.

⁹ All this have I seen; and I applied my mind to every deed that is done under the sun: there is a time when one man rules over another to his detriment.

10. The anomaly is how the good deeds of the righteous are forgotten, but the wicked die peacefully and leave a legacy of evil behind them. This is a great futility. (See verse 14).

¹⁰ And then I saw the wicked buried and newly come while those who had done right were gone from the Holy place and were forgotten in the city. This, too, is futility! ¹¹ Because the sentence for wrongdoing is not executed quickly — that is why men are encouraged to do evil, ¹² because a sinner does what is wrong a hundred times and He is patient with him, yet nevertheless I am aware that it will be well with those who fear God that they may fear Him, ¹³ and that it will not be well with the wicked, and he will not long endure — like a shadow — because he does not fear God.

12-13. These verses continue the thought of the previous verse. They elaborate on what the wicked see that encourages them to sin with impunity. Nevertheless, Solomon disavows this evidence and affirms his faith in the Divine Justice which rewards the righteous and punishes the sinner.

¹⁴ There is a futility that takes place on earth: Sometimes there are righteous men who are treated as if they had done according to the deeds of the wicked; and there are wicked men who are treated as if they had done the deeds of the righteous. I declared, this, too, is vanity.

14. The maintenance of Free Will — a necessary ingredient of God's plan — requires a certain amount of suffering for the righteous and prosperity for the wicked. For, if all wickedness were to be punished immediately, there would be no room for choice and everyone would be righteous. Thus, the wicked often prosper, but they misinterpret this prosperity as sanction to continue their wicked ways. They should realize that it is futility — that in reality there is justice, but that God allows them to flourish in order to confuse mankind (Meam Loez).

¹⁵ So I praised enjoyment, for man has no other goal under the sun but to eat, drink and be joyful; and this will accompany him in his toil during the days of his life which God has given him beneath the sun.

¹⁶ When I set my mind to know wisdom and to observe the activity which takes place on earth — for even day or night its eyes see no sleep. — ¹⁷ And I perceived all the work of God. Indeed, man cannot fathom the events that occur under the sun, inasmuch as man tries strenuously to search, but cannot fathom it. And even though a wise man should presume to know, he cannot fathom it.

17. Although Koheles opened this chapter implying that the wise man 'knows what things mean,' — he concludes that certain divine matters remain hidden even to the wisest of men.

ט

א לִמְצֹא: כִּי אֶת־כָּל־זֶה נָתַתִּי אֶל־לִבִּי וְלָבוּר אֶת־
כָּל־זֶה אֲשֶׁר הַצַּדִּיקִים וְהַחֲכָמִים וַעֲבָדֵיהֶם בְּיַד
הָאֱלֹהִים גַּם־אַהֲבָה גַם־שִׂנְאָה אֵין יוֹדֵעַ הָאָדָם
ב הַכֹּל לִפְנֵיהֶם: הַכֹּל כַּאֲשֶׁר לַכֹּל מִקְרֶה אֶחָד
לַצַּדִּיק וְלָרָשָׁע לַטּוֹב וְלַטָּהוֹר וְלַטָּמֵא וְלַזֹּבֵחַ
וְלַאֲשֶׁר אֵינֶנּוּ זֹבֵחַ כַּטּוֹב כַּחֹטֶא הַנִּשְׁבָּע כַּאֲשֶׁר
ג שְׁבוּעָה יָרֵא: זֶה | רָע בְּכֹל אֲשֶׁר־נַעֲשָׂה תַּחַת
הַשֶּׁמֶשׁ כִּי־מִקְרֶה אֶחָד לַכֹּל וְגַם לֵב בְּנֵי־הָאָדָם
מָלֵא־רָע וְהוֹלֵלוֹת בִּלְבָבָם בְּחַיֵּיהֶם וְאַחֲרָיו אֶל־
ד הַמֵּתִים: כִּי־מִי אֲשֶׁר °יְבַחַר אֶל כָּל־הַחַיִּים יֵשׁ יְחֻבַּר ק°
בִּטָּחוֹן כִּי־לְכֶלֶב חַי הוּא טוֹב מִן־הָאַרְיֵה הַמֵּת:
ה כִּי הַחַיִּים יוֹדְעִים שֶׁיָּמֻתוּ וְהַמֵּתִים אֵינָם יוֹדְעִים
ו מְאוּמָה וְאֵין־עוֹד לָהֶם שָׂכָר כִּי נִשְׁכַּח זִכְרָם: גַּם
אַהֲבָתָם גַּם־שִׂנְאָתָם גַּם־קִנְאָתָם כְּבָר אָבָדָה
וְחֵלֶק אֵין־לָהֶם עוֹד לְעוֹלָם בְּכֹל אֲשֶׁר־נַעֲשָׂה
ז תַּחַת הַשָּׁמֶשׁ: לֵךְ אֱכֹל בְּשִׂמְחָה לַחְמֶךָ וּשְׁתֵה
בְלֶב־טוֹב יֵינֶךָ כִּי כְבָר רָצָה הָאֱלֹהִים אֶת־
ח מַעֲשֶׂיךָ: בְּכָל־עֵת יִהְיוּ בְגָדֶיךָ לְבָנִים וְשֶׁמֶן עַל־
ט רֹאשְׁךָ אַל־יֶחְסָר: רְאֵה חַיִּים עִם־אִשָּׁה אֲשֶׁר־
אָהַבְתָּ כָּל־יְמֵי חַיֵּי הֶבְלֶךָ אֲשֶׁר נָתַן־לְךָ תַּחַת
הַשֶּׁמֶשׁ כֹּל יְמֵי הֶבְלֶךָ כִּי הוּא חֶלְקְךָ בַּחַיִּים
י וּבַעֲמָלְךָ אֲשֶׁר־אַתָּה עָמֵל תַּחַת הַשָּׁמֶשׁ: כֹּל
אֲשֶׁר תִּמְצָא יָדְךָ לַעֲשׂוֹת בְּכֹחֲךָ עֲשֵׂה כִּי אֵין
מַעֲשֶׂה וְחֶשְׁבּוֹן וְדַעַת וְחָכְמָה בִּשְׁאוֹל אֲשֶׁר
יא אַתָּה הֹלֵךְ שָׁמָּה: שַׁבְתִּי וְרָאֹה תַחַת־הַשֶּׁמֶשׁ כִּי
לֹא לַקַּלִּים הַמֵּרוֹץ וְלֹא לַגִּבּוֹרִים הַמִּלְחָמָה וְגַם

9/2. Everyone knows that death, the common equalizer, is the fate that awaits all men in this world. Nevertheless, [those with intellect] choose to take the proper path because they realize that there is a distinction between good and evil people in the Hereafter *(Rashi).*

3. *The same fate awaits all,* therefore man is emboldened to presume that there is no Providence and no justice *(Metzudas David).*

5. Once men die they no longer perform *mitzvos* worthy of reward, and 'he who has not prepared on the eve of Sabbath what shall he eat on Sabbath?' *(Rashi).*

8. Solomon exhorts man to conduct his life constantly as if he were wearing white garments and carrying a full pitcher of oil on his head. He must therefore concentrate on keeping his balance and not approach anything which can soil the whiteness of his garments. Man must live a life of spiritual and moral purity, always on guard lest he besmirch himself with a careless sin, for man, like a white garment is easy to soil and hard to cleanse *(Olelos Ephraim).*

10. Repent while you have the ability. While the wick is still lit, add oil to keep it kindled. Once the light is extinguished, oil no longer helps *(Yalkut Shimoni).*

11. These verses are Solomon's affirmation of his principles that this world is transitory and man is governed by God *(Rashi).*

¹ For all this I noted and I sought to ascertain all this: that the righteous and the wise together with their actions are in the Hand of God; whether love or hate, man does not know; all preceded them.

² All things come alike to all; the same fate awaits the righteous and the wicked, the good and the clean and the unclean, the one who brings a sacrifice and the one who does not. As is the good man so is the sinner, as is the one who swears, so is the one who fears an oath.

³ This is an evil about all things that go on under the sun: that the same fate awaits all. Therefore, the heart of man is full of evil; and madness is in their heart while they love; and after that, they go to the dead.

⁴ For he who is attached to all the living has hope, a live dog being better than a dead lion. ⁵ For the living know that they will die, but the dead know nothing at all; there is no more reward for them, their memory is forgotten. ⁶ Their love, their hate, their jealousy have already perished — nor will they ever again have a share in whatever is done beneath the sun.

⁷ Go, eat your bread with joy and drink your wine with a glad heart, for God has already approved your deeds. ⁸ Let your garments always be white, and your head never lack oil.

⁹ Enjoy life with the wife you love through all the fleeting days of your life that He has granted you beneath the sun, all of your futile existence; for that is your compensation in life and in your toil which you exert beneath the sun. ¹⁰ Whatever you are able to do with your might, do it. For there is neither doing nor reckoning nor knowledge nor wisdom in the grave where you are going.

¹¹ Once more I saw under the sun that the race is not won by the swift; nor the battle by the strong,

לֹא לַחֲכָמִים לֶחֶם וְגַם לֹא לַנְּבֹנִים עֹשֶׁר וְגַם לֹא
לַיֹּדְעִים חֵן כִּי־עֵת וָפֶגַע יִקְרֶה אֶת־כֻּלָּם: כִּי גַם
לֹא־יֵדַע הָאָדָם אֶת־עִתּוֹ כַּדָּגִים שֶׁנֶּאֱחָזִים
בִּמְצוֹדָה רָעָה וְכַצִּפֳּרִים הָאֲחֻזוֹת בַּפָּח כָּהֵם
יוּקָשִׁים בְּנֵי הָאָדָם לְעֵת רָעָה כְּשֶׁתִּפּוֹל עֲלֵיהֶם
פִּתְאֹם: גַּם־זֶה רָאִיתִי חָכְמָה תַּחַת הַשָּׁמֶשׁ
וּגְדוֹלָה הִיא אֵלָי: עִיר קְטַנָּה וַאֲנָשִׁים בָּהּ מְעָט
וּבָא־אֵלֶיהָ מֶלֶךְ גָּדוֹל וְסָבַב אֹתָהּ וּבָנָה עָלֶיהָ
מְצוֹדִים גְּדֹלִים: וּמָצָא בָהּ אִישׁ מִסְכֵּן חָכָם
וּמִלַּט־הוּא אֶת־הָעִיר בְּחָכְמָתוֹ וְאָדָם לֹא זָכַר
אֶת־הָאִישׁ הַמִּסְכֵּן הַהוּא: וְאָמַרְתִּי אָנִי טוֹבָה
חָכְמָה מִגְּבוּרָה וְחָכְמַת הַמִּסְכֵּן בְּזוּיָה וּדְבָרָיו
אֵינָם נִשְׁמָעִים: דִּבְרֵי חֲכָמִים בְּנַחַת נִשְׁמָעִים
מִזַּעֲקַת מוֹשֵׁל בַּכְּסִילִים: טוֹבָה חָכְמָה מִכְּלֵי
קְרָב וְחוֹטֶא אֶחָד יְאַבֵּד טוֹבָה הַרְבֵּה: זְבוּבֵי מָוֶת
יַבְאִישׁ יַבִּיעַ שֶׁמֶן רוֹקֵחַ יָקָר מֵחָכְמָה מִכָּבוֹד
סִכְלוּת מְעָט: לֵב חָכָם לִימִינוֹ וְלֵב כְּסִיל
לִשְׂמֹאלוֹ: וְגַם־בַּדֶּרֶךְ °כשהסכל הֹלֵךְ לִבּוֹ חָסֵר ‎°כְּשֶׁסָּכָל ק׳
וְאָמַר לַכֹּל סָכָל הוּא: אִם־רוּחַ הַמּוֹשֵׁל תַּעֲלֶה
עָלֶיךָ מְקוֹמְךָ אַל־תַּנַּח כִּי מַרְפֵּא יַנִּיחַ חֲטָאִים
גְּדוֹלִים: יֵשׁ רָעָה רָאִיתִי תַּחַת הַשָּׁמֶשׁ כִּשְׁגָגָה
שֶׁיֹּצָא מִלִּפְנֵי הַשַּׁלִּיט: נִתַּן הַסֶּכֶל בַּמְּרוֹמִים
רַבִּים וַעֲשִׁירִים בַּשֵּׁפֶל יֵשֵׁבוּ: רָאִיתִי עֲבָדִים עַל־
סוּסִים וְשָׂרִים הֹלְכִים כַּעֲבָדִים עַל־הָאָרֶץ: חֹפֵר
גּוּמָּץ בּוֹ יִפּוֹל וּפֹרֵץ גָּדֵר יִשְּׁכֶנּוּ נָחָשׁ: מַסִּיעַ
אֲבָנִים יֵעָצֵב בָּהֶם בּוֹקֵעַ עֵצִים יִסָּכֶן בָּם: אִם־

nor does bread come to the wise, riches to the intelligent, nor favor to the learned; but time and death will happen to them all. ¹² For man does not even know his hour: like fish caught in a fatal net, like birds seized in a snare, so are men caught in the moment of disaster when it falls upon them suddenly.

¹³ This, too, have I observed about wisdom beneath the sun, and it affected me profoundly: ¹⁴ There was a small town with only a few inhabitants; and a mighty king came upon it and surrounded it, and built great siege works over it. ¹⁵ Present in the city was a poor wise man who by his wisdom saved the town. Yet no one remembered that poor man. ¹⁶ So I said: Wisdom is better than might, although a poor man's wisdom is despised and his words go unheeded.

¹⁷ The gentle words of the wise are heard above the shouts of a king over fools, ¹⁸ and wisdom is better than weapons, but a single rogue can ruin a great deal of good.

¹ **D**ead flies putrefy the perfumer's oil; a little folly outweighs wisdom and honor.

² A wise man tends to his right; while a fool's mind tends to his left. ³ Even on the road as the fool walks, he lacks sense, and proclaims to all that he is a fool.

⁴ If the anger of a ruler flares up against you, do not leave your place, for deference appeases great offenses.

⁵ There is an evil which I have observed in the world as if it were an error proceeding from the ruler: ⁶ Folly is placed on lofty heights, while rich men sit in low places. ⁷ I have seen slaves on horses and nobles walking on foot like slaves.

⁸ He who digs a pit will fall into it, and he who breaks down a wall will be bitten by a snake. ⁹ He who moves about stones will be hurt by them; he who splits logs will be endangered by them.

14-16. An allegory: Although the wisdom of a poor man is despised and deprecated and he himself is ignored, in an emergency the wise can accomplish more than the mighty — as illustrated by this story where one's simple wisdom, not enhanced by esteem, saved the whole town from the might of the king (Rashi; Ibn Ezra).

18. In the ethical perspective, man must view himself as being the deciding factor in the world's righteousness or guilt. Thus if Israel were equally divided between righteousness and guilt, one rogue alone could tip the scales and condemn the whole world (Kiddushin 40b).

10/2. There follows a series of one-sentence proverbs: To his right. One's wisdom is always prepared to lead him in the correct path for his benefit (Rashi); and his intellect is always at hand when he needs it (Metzudas David).

8. He who plots against his fellow man will himself fall into the trap (Rashi).

קֵהֶה הַבַּרְזֶל וְהוּא לֹא־פָנִים קִלְקַל וַחֲיָלִים יְגַבֵּר

יא וְיִתְרוֹן הַכְשֵׁיר חׇכְמָה: אִם־יִשֹּׁךְ הַנָּחָשׁ בְּלוֹא־

יב לָחַשׁ וְאֵין יִתְרוֹן לְבַעַל הַלָּשׁוֹן: דִּבְרֵי פִי־חָכָם

יג חֵן וְשִׂפְתוֹת כְּסִיל תְּבַלְּעֶנּוּ: תְּחִלַּת דִּבְרֵי־פִיהוּ

יד סִכְלוּת וְאַחֲרִית פִּיהוּ הוֹלֵלוּת רָעָה: וְהַסָּכָל

יַרְבֶּה דְבָרִים לֹא־יֵדַע הָאָדָם מַה־שֶּׁיִּהְיֶה וַאֲשֶׁר

טו יִהְיֶה מֵאַחֲרָיו מִי יַגִּיד לוֹ: עֲמַל הַכְּסִילִים תְּיַגְּעֶנּוּ

טז אֲשֶׁר לֹא־יָדַע לָלֶכֶת אֶל־עִיר: אִי־לָךְ אֶרֶץ

יז שֶׁמַּלְכֵּךְ נָעַר וְשָׂרַיִךְ בַּבֹּקֶר יֹאכֵלוּ: אַשְׁרֵיךְ אֶרֶץ

שֶׁמַּלְכֵּךְ בֶּן־חוֹרִים וְשָׂרַיִךְ בָּעֵת יֹאכֵלוּ בִּגְבוּרָה

יח וְלֹא בַשְּׁתִי: בַּעֲצַלְתַּיִם יִמַּךְ הַמְּקָרֶה וּבְשִׁפְלוּת

יט יָדַיִם יִדְלֹף הַבָּיִת: לִשְׂחוֹק עֹשִׂים לֶחֶם וְיַיִן

כ יְשַׂמַּח חַיִּים וְהַכֶּסֶף יַעֲנֶה אֶת־הַכֹּל: גַּם בְּמַדָּעֲךָ

מֶלֶךְ אַל־תְּקַלֵּל וּבְחַדְרֵי מִשְׁכָּבְךָ אַל־תְּקַלֵּל

עָשִׁיר כִּי עוֹף הַשָּׁמַיִם יוֹלִיךְ אֶת־הַקּוֹל וּבַעַל

יא א הַכְּנָפַיִם יַגֵּיד דָּבָר: שַׁלַּח לַחְמְךָ עַל־פְּנֵי הַמָּיִם ‪°‬ ‪°‬בְּכָנָפַיִם ק׳

ב כִּי־בְרֹב הַיָּמִים תִּמְצָאֶנּוּ: תֶּן־חֵלֶק לְשִׁבְעָה וְגַם

לִשְׁמוֹנָה כִּי לֹא תֵדַע מַה־יִּהְיֶה רָעָה עַל־הָאָרֶץ:

ג אִם־יִמָּלְאוּ הֶעָבִים גֶּשֶׁם עַל־הָאָרֶץ יָרִיקוּ וְאִם־

יִפּוֹל עֵץ בַּדָּרוֹם וְאִם בַּצָּפוֹן מְקוֹם שֶׁיִּפּוֹל הָעֵץ

ד שָׁם יְהוּא: שֹׁמֵר רוּחַ לֹא יִזְרָע וְרֹאֶה בֶעָבִים לֹא

ה יִקְצוֹר: כַּאֲשֶׁר אֵינְךָ יוֹדֵעַ מַה־דֶּרֶךְ הָרוּחַ

כַּעֲצָמִים בְּבֶטֶן הַמְּלֵאָה כָּכָה לֹא תֵדַע אֶת־

ו מַעֲשֵׂה הָאֱלֹהִים אֲשֶׁר יַעֲשֶׂה אֶת־הַכֹּל: בַּבֹּקֶר

זְרַע אֶת־זַרְעֶךָ וְלָעֶרֶב אַל־תַּנַּח יָדֶךָ כִּי אֵינְךָ

יוֹדֵעַ אֵי זֶה יִכְשָׁר הֲזֶה אוֹ־זֶה וְאִם־שְׁנֵיהֶם כְּאֶחָד

¹⁰ If an axe is blunt and one has not honed the edge, nevertheless it strengthens the warriors. Wisdom is a more powerful skill.

11. There is no advantage to wisdom if, while his fellow men sin, the wise man maintains his silence and does not teach them Torah *(Rashi).*

¹¹ If the snake bites because it was not charmed, then there is no advantage to the charmer's art. ¹² The words of a wise man win favor, but a fool's lips devour him. ¹³ His talk begins as foolishness and ends as evil madness.

14. Not only does the fool speak nonsense, as mentioned in the previous verse, but he *constantly* chatters, discussing all subjects, even those of which man is ignorant, such as the events of the future.

¹⁴ The fool prates on and on, but man does not know what will be; and who can tell him what will happen after him? ¹⁵ The toil of fools exhaust them, as one who does not know the way to town.

16. The prime concern of these ministers is not the welfare of the state but their own satiety. They indulge in revelry when they should attend to the duties of state *(Ibn Latif).*

¹⁶ Woe to you, O land, whose king acts as an adolescent, and whose ministers dine in the morning. ¹⁷ Happy are you, O land, whose king is a man of dignity, and whose ministers dine at the proper time — in strength and not in drunkenness.

17. They eat to live rather than live to eat *(Ibn Yachya).*

¹⁸ Through slothfulness the ceiling sags, and through idleness of the hands the house leaks.

19. Money is needed by all and makes everything possible. In the previous verse slothfulness is deprecated; here man is encouraged toward industry, because lazy people do not earn the money required for living *(Rashi; Metzudas David).*

¹⁹ A feast is made for laughter, and wine gladdens life, but money answers everything. ²⁰ Even in your thoughts do not curse a king, and in your bed-chamber do not curse the rich, for a bird of the skies may carry the sound, and some winged creature may betray the matter.

11/1. Charity should be given even to strangers who will never be seen again. The generosity will not go unrewarded; the favor will be repaid.

¹ **S**end your bread upon the waters, for after many days you will find it. ² Distribute portions to seven, or even to eight, for you never know what calamity will strike the land.

³ If the clouds are filled they will pour down rain on the earth; if a tree falls down in the south or the north, wherever the tree falls, there it remains.

4. One must perform the tasks required of him and have faith that God will bless his works.

One who forever waits for ideal conditions will never get his work done *(Ibn Latif).*

⁴ One who watches the wind will never sow, and one who keeps his eyes on the clouds will never reap. ⁵ Just as you do not know the way of the wind, nor the nature of the embryo in a pregnant stomach, so can you never know the work of God who makes everything. ⁶ In the morning sow your seed and in the evening do not be idle, for you cannot know which will succeed: this or that, or whether both are equally good.

6. Some explain the verse metaphorically: *morning,* i.e., youth; *evening,* i.e., old age.

ז טוֹבִֽים: וּמָת֥וֹק הָא֑וֹר וְט֥וֹב לַֽעֵינַ֖יִם לִרְא֥וֹת אֶת־
ח הַשָּֽׁמֶשׁ: כִּ֣י אִם־שָׁנִ֥ים הַרְבֵּ֛ה יִֽחְיֶ֥ה הָֽאָדָ֖ם בְּכֻלָּ֣ם
יִשְׂמָ֑ח וְיִזְכֹּר֙ אֶת־יְמֵ֣י הַחֹ֔שֶׁךְ כִּֽי־הַרְבֵּ֥ה יִֽהְי֖וּ כָּל־
ט שֶׁבָּ֣א הָֽבֶל: שְׂמַ֧ח בָּח֣וּר בְּיַלְדוּתֶ֗יךָ וִֽיטִֽיבְךָ֤ לִבְּךָ֙
בִּימֵ֣י בְחֽוּרוֹתֶ֔יךָ וְהַלֵּךְ֙ בְּדַרְכֵ֣י לִבְּךָ֔ °וּבְמַרְאֵ֖ה ק'
עֵינֶ֑יךָ וְדַ֕ע כִּ֧י עַל־כָּל־אֵ֛לֶּה יְבִֽיאֲךָ֥ הָֽאֱלֹהִ֖ים
י בַּמִּשְׁפָּֽט: וְהָסֵ֥ר כַּ֨עַס֙ מִלִּבֶּ֔ךָ וְהַֽעֲבֵ֥ר רָעָ֖ה
א מִבְּשָׂרֶ֑ךָ כִּֽי־הַיַּלְד֥וּת וְהַֽשַּׁחֲר֖וּת הָֽבֶל: וּזְכֹר֙ אֶת־
בּֽוֹרְאֶ֔יךָ בִּימֵ֖י בְּחֽוּרֹתֶ֑יךָ עַ֣ד אֲשֶׁ֤ר לֹֽא־יָבֹ֨אוּ֙ יְמֵ֣י
הָֽרָעָ֔ה וְהִגִּ֣יעוּ שָׁנִ֔ים אֲשֶׁ֣ר תֹּאמַ֔ר אֵֽין־לִ֥י בָהֶ֖ם
ב חֵֽפֶץ: עַ֣ד אֲשֶׁ֤ר לֹֽא־תֶחְשַׁךְ֙ הַשֶּׁ֣מֶשׁ וְהָא֔וֹר
וְהַיָּרֵ֖חַ וְהַכּֽוֹכָבִ֑ים וְשָׁ֥בוּ הֶֽעָבִ֖ים אַחַ֥ר הַגָּֽשֶׁם:
ג בַּיּ֗וֹם שֶׁיָּזֻ֨עוּ֙ שֹֽׁמְרֵ֣י הַבַּ֔יִת וְהִֽתְעַוְּת֖וּ אַנְשֵׁ֣י הֶחָ֑יִל
וּבָֽטְל֤וּ הַטֹּֽחֲנוֹת֙ כִּ֣י מִעֵ֔טוּ וְחָֽשְׁכ֥וּ הָֽרֹא֖וֹת
ד בָּֽאֲרֻבּֽוֹת: וְסֻגְּר֤וּ דְלָתַ֨יִם֙ בַּשּׁ֔וּק בִּשְׁפַ֖ל ק֣וֹל
הַֽטַּֽחֲנָ֑ה וְיָקוּם֙ לְק֣וֹל הַצִּפּ֔וֹר וְיִשַּׁ֖חוּ כָּל־בְּנ֥וֹת
ה הַשִּֽׁיר: גַּ֣ם מִגָּבֹ֤הַּ יִרָ֨אוּ֙ וְחַתְחַתִּ֣ים בַּדֶּ֔רֶךְ וְיָנֵ֤אץ
הַשָּׁקֵד֙ וְיִסְתַּבֵּ֣ל הֶֽחָגָ֔ב וְתָפֵ֖ר הָֽאֲבִיּוֹנָ֑ה כִּֽי־הֹלֵ֤ךְ
הָֽאָדָם֙ אֶל־בֵּ֣ית עֽוֹלָמ֔וֹ וְסָֽבְב֥וּ בַשּׁ֖וּק הַסֹּֽפְדִֽים:
ו עַ֣ד אֲשֶׁ֤ר לֹֽא־°יֵֽרָחֵק֙ חֶ֣בֶל הַכֶּ֔סֶף וְתָרֻ֖ץ גֻּלַּ֣ת °יֵרָתֵק ק'
הַזָּהָ֑ב וְתִשָּׁ֤בֶר כַּד֙ עַל־הַמַּבּ֔וּעַ וְנָרֹ֥ץ הַגַּלְגַּ֖ל אֶל־
ז הַבּֽוֹר: וְיָשֹׁ֧ב הֶֽעָפָ֛ר עַל־הָאָ֖רֶץ כְּשֶֽׁהָיָ֑ה וְהָר֣וּחַ
ח תָּשׁ֔וּב אֶל־הָֽאֱלֹהִ֖ים אֲשֶׁ֣ר נְתָנָֽהּ: הֲבֵ֧ל הֲבָלִ֛ים
ט אָמַ֥ר הַקּֽוֹהֶ֖לֶת הַכֹּ֥ל הָֽבֶל: וְיֹתֵ֕ר שֶֽׁהָיָ֥ה קֹהֶ֖לֶת
חָכָ֑ם ע֗וֹד לִמַּד־דַּ֨עַת֙ אֶת־הָעָ֔ם וְאִזֵּ֣ן וְחִקֵּ֔ר תִּקֵּ֖ן
י מְשָׁלִ֥ים הַרְבֵּֽה: בִּקֵּ֣שׁ קֹהֶ֔לֶת לִמְצֹ֖א דִּבְרֵי־חֵ֑פֶץ

8. One must keep in mind the transitory nature of this world and strive to improve his ways, for *the days of darkness* — an allusion to death and the judgment of the wicked — *will be many.* Those days are eternal, not like the short duration of life in this world *(Rashi).*

9. This is similar to a man admonishing his son: 'Go on, persist in your iniquities. But realize that you will be punished in one blow for all your misdeeds!' *(Rashi).*

12/1. This verse is closely related to the preceding one. Solomon continues that man should spend his vigorous youth in the service of his Creator.

2. The following verses poetically conjure up an image of the fading of life as old age approaches. The allegory refers to the waning powers of the organs of the body.

6. The body — near death — is likened to the malfunctioning machinery of a well: rope, wheel and pitcher. The cord (spine) snaps; the skull shatters; the stomach breaks; and the body is smashed.

8. EPILOGUE

Having discoursed on the life and trials of man, and described the vicissitudes which man experiences *under the sun* until death, Koheles reiterates the recurring refrain of his conclusions: *All is futile* *(Rashbam; Kehillas Yaakov).*

⁷ Sweet is the light, and it is good for the eyes to behold the sun! ⁸ Even if a man lives many years, let him rejoice in all of them, but let him remember that the days of darkness will be many. All that comes is futility. ⁹ Rejoice young man, in your childhood let your heart cheer you in the days of your youth; follow the path of your heart and the sight of your eyes — but be aware that for all these things God will call you to account. ¹⁰ Rather, banish anger from your heart and remove evil from your flesh — for childhood and youth are futile.

¹ **S**o remember your Creator in the days of your youth, before the evil days come, and those years arrive of which you will say, 'I have no pleasure in them,' ² before the sun, the light, the moon and the stars grow dark, and the clouds return after the rain; ³ in the day when the guards of the house will tremble, and the powerful men will stoop, and the grinders are idle because they are few, and the gazers through windows are dimmed; ⁴ when the doors in the street are shut; when the sound of the grinding is low; when one rises up at the voice of the bird, and all the daughters of song grow dim; ⁵ when they even fear a height and terror in the road; and the almond tree blossoms and the grasshopper becomes a burden and the desire fails — so man goes to his eternal home, while the mourners go about the streets.

⁶ Before the silver cord snaps, and the golden bowl is shattered, and the pitcher is broken at the fountain, and the wheel is smashed at the pit. ⁷ Thus the dust returns to the ground as it was, and the spirit returns to God Who gave it. ⁸ Futility of futilies — said Koheles — all is futile!

⁹ And besides being wise, Koheles also imparted knowledge to the people; he listened, and sought out; and arranged many proverbs.

¹⁰ Koheles sought to find words of delight, and

יא וְכָתוּב יֹשֶׁר דִּבְרֵי אֱמֶת: דִּבְרֵי חֲכָמִים כַּדָּרְבֹנוֹת
וּכְמַשְׂמְרוֹת נְטוּעִים בַּעֲלֵי אֲסֻפּוֹת נִתְּנוּ מֵרֹעֶה
יב אֶחָד: וְיֹתֵר מֵהֵמָּה בְּנִי הִזָּהֵר עֲשׂוֹת סְפָרִים
יג הַרְבֵּה אֵין קֵץ וְלַהַג הַרְבֵּה יְגִעַת בָּשָׂר: **ס**וֹף
דָּבָר הַכֹּל נִשְׁמָע אֶת־הָאֱלֹהִים יְרָא וְאֶת־
יד מִצְוֹתָיו שְׁמוֹר כִּי־זֶה כָּל־הָאָדָם: כִּי אֶת־כָּל־
מַעֲשֶׂה הָאֱלֹהִים יָבֵא בְמִשְׁפָּט עַל כָּל־נֶעְלָם
אִם־טוֹב וְאִם־רָע:

The following verse is recited aloud by the congregation,
then repeated by the reader:

סוֹף דָּבָר הַכֹּל נִשְׁמָע, אֶת הָאֱלֹהִים יְרָא
וְאֶת מִצְוֹתָיו שְׁמוֹר, כִּי זֶה כָּל הָאָדָם:

words of truth recorded properly. ¹¹ The words of the wise are like goads, and like nails well driven are the sayings of the masters of collections, coming from one Shepherd.

¹² Beyond these, my son, beware: the making of many books is without limit, and much study is weariness of the flesh.

¹³ The sum of the matter, when all has been considered: Fear God and keep His commandments, for that is man's whole duty. ¹⁴ For God will judge every deed — even everything hidden — whether good or evil.

The following verse is recited aloud by the congregation, then repeated by the reader:

The sum of the matter, when all has been considered: Fear God and keep His commandments, for that is man's whole duty.

12. King Solomon cautions: 'Not everything that man thinks must he say; not everything he says must he write, but most important, not everything that he writes must he publish' (Rav Yisrael Salanter).

13. Koheles concludes, 'Although I have expounded many esoteric and difficult concepts, nevertheless, דָּבָר סוֹף, the summation of the Book, הַכֹּל נִשְׁמָע, is obvious to all, and unquestionable: Fear God with your every limb and organ, for this is all of man (Derech Chaim). It was for this that all men were created (Rashi). And 'the entire world was created only for such a man' (Shabbos 30b).

This volume is part of
THE ARTSCROLL SERIES®
an ongoing project of
translations, commentaries and expositions
on Scripture, Mishnah, Talmud, liturgy,
history, the classic Rabbinic writings,
biographies, and thought.

For a brochure of current publications
visit your local Hebrew bookseller
or contact the publisher:

Mesorah Publications, ltd

4401 Second Avenue
Brooklyn, New York 11232
(718) 921-9000

MW00526803